GUIDE to the coast of NEW SOUTH WALES

Reader's Digest Guide to the coast of New South Wales was edited and designed by Reader's Digest Services Pty Limited, Sydney

Contributing editor: Robert Pullan

Contributors
Elizabeth Denley, PhD, Hopkins Marine Station, California
Robert Duffield
Jenny Flute
Edgar Frankel, PhD, Lecturer in Sedimentology, Department of Geology
    and Mineralogy, University of Queensland
Carol Frith, BSc(Hons), Coastal Studies Unit, University of Sydney
Pat Hutchings, PhD, Curator of Marine Invertebrates, The Australian Museum, Sydney
Brian Lees, BA(Hons), Coastal Studies Unit, University of Sydney
Dick Lewers
Dr Ian Mackie, Honorary Education Officer, The Surf Life Saving Association of Australia
Gia Metherell
Jo Moss, BSc
David Pollard, PhD, Senior Research Scientist, New South Wales State Fisheries
Jeff Toghill
Lyle Vail, Technical Officer, The Australian Museum, Sydney
Alan Yuille, BArch

Aerial Photography
Qasco Pty Limited, Sydney
Additional aerial photography by Stereometric
Services, Melbourne

Illustrators
Sheila Hadley
David Horne
Sue Oakes
Margaret Senior
Robyn Single

Maps by Reader's Digest

First edition
Published by Reader's Digest Services Pty Limited (Inc. in NSW)
26-32 Waterloo Street, Surry Hills NSW 2010
Part of the material in this book first appeared in Reader's Digest
Guide to the Australian Coast, first published by Reader's Digest in 1983.

© 1986 Reader's Digest Services Pty Ltd
© 1986 Reader's Digest Association Far East Limited
Philippines copyright 1986 Reader's Digest Association Far East Limited

National Library of Australia cataloguing-in-publication data:
Reader's Digest Guide to the coast of New South Wales.
  Includes index
  ISBN 0 86438 009 7
  1. Coasts – New South Wales – Guide-books.
  2. New South Wales – Description and travel – 1976
  – Guide-books. I. Reader's Digest Services
  II. Title: Guide to the coast of New South Wales.
919.44'0463

Typeset by Adtype Photocomposition, Sydney
Printed and bound by Dai Nippon Printing Co. Ltd., Hong Kong

Reader's Digest

GUIDE to the coast of
NEW SOUTH WALES

Contents

Introduction

ALTHOUGH New South Wales, with a population approaching five and a half million, is Australia's most lived-in state, its generous coastline readily affords everyone a place in the sun. Even in Sydney, where more than half the people live, the shore includes a surprising number of secluded sandy pockets accessible to anyone prepared to seek them out on foot or by boat. Those who enjoy being in with the crowd can always join the throng at Bondi Beach, where on a hot summer's day the number of swimmers, surfers and sun-bathers can reach as high as 50 000.

The coast of New South Wales is host to every type of water-based recreation, added to which are such features as its lion's share of historical landmarks, its ever-increasing extent of national parks and its role as home to the Royal Australian Navy.

The grand sweep of this shoreline—from its northern border adjacent to Queensland's Gold Coast to lonely Cape Howe in the south—accommodates holidaymakers from inside the state and out. The beaches and waters of New South Wales play host to more overseas visitors than those of any other state.

Here, as elsewhere around Australia's coast, all water sports are enormously popular. Almost all Australians can swim; they surf in their hundreds of thousands and boat in their millions. But by far the most dominant water activity is fishing. An estimated 30 per cent of all Australians go fishing, and this proportion rises to 60 per cent among boys aged between 13 and 17. New South Wales fishermen alone spend more than 20 million days a year fishing for fun.

Guide to the Coast of New South Wales is for all those who visit the seashore—whatever their special interests. The core of the book, Discovering the Coast, is a guide for travellers and coast users. Scores of aerial photographs, many of them joined together into a unique series of panoramas, show the most attractive and easily accessible parts of the coast in unsurpassed detail. The photographs are supported by a thorough and up-to-date description of the places depicted and their attractions. We have divided coastal New South Wales into three regions, each of which is introduced with notes on its general nature and climate, and a map.

Three additional parts of the book provide important information for those who visit the coast. Part one—Understanding the Coast—describes the range of plants and animals that live around the shore. The aim is to help visitors identify some of the things they see, and also to understand how plants and animals interact with one another in a range of habitats. Drawings of birds, shells, and marine creatures, make identification of common species easy.

Part two—The Ocean and the Weather—will be particularly useful for swimmers, surfers and boat owners. A basic understanding of winds, tides, waves and currents will help readers to avoid some of the dangers of nearshore waters, and also to make the best use of conditions they encounter.

Part three—Advice for Holidaymakers—is addressed to particular groups of coast users. There is information for fishermen, boat owners, swimmers and surfers as well as general advice on first aid, access and hazards.

Two indexes, one listing all the places mentioned in the book and the other the subjects, make it easy to find any information quickly.

THE EDITORS

PART 1

Understanding the coast

Nature's ingenuity meets no sterner test than on the seashore. Life forms have to contend with changeable environments—neither wholly marine nor wholly terrestrial—and on much of the coast they must withstand the violent assault of waves.

In the face of such adversity, shore zones could be assumed to be biologically impoverished.

On the contrary, they are the special domains of a diverse range of animals and plants, intriguing in their ways of adaptation and often astonishing in their profusion.

Many of the most interesting creatures go unnoticed. And such is their degree of specialisation that they are restricted to particular habitats.

The curious need to know not only what to look for, but also where to look.

A grasp of geological and geographical factors brings a fuller appreciation of the richness of coastal life.

With it comes awareness of how delicately this life is balanced—and of the dangers posed by unwise human pressure.

A group of sea lions basking among seaweed on a Kangaroo Island beach

What makes a coast Natural forms that change with time

A coast is a battlefront—a line where land, sea and air meet that changes from second to second, season to season, decade to decade and millennium to millennium. Short term changes, over a range of metres, occur as waves break and move sediments on or off shore and as tide-waves cause the local sea level to rise and fall. In the longer term erosion and accretion change the coastline, sometimes on a scale of kilometres a century. Over tens of thousands of years sea levels rise and fall by hundreds of metres as ice ages come and go. Coasts are always changing—they can never be regarded as permanent. It is only because the large scale changes seem to occur so slowly, in terms of human lifetimes, that people come to regard the shoreline as fixed.

Ancient coastlines can be found scores of kilometres inland. Others are far out to sea. The earliest fluctuations were associated with the evolution of land masses over hundreds of millions of years: their emergence and erosion, their repeated submergences and reappearances, the transformation of their material under pressure, their distortion by twisting, folding and fracturing, and their disruption by volcanic activity. The coast near Mount Gambier in South Australia has risen in the last few thousand years, while the Murray River mouth region has subsided; Melbourne's shores on Port Phillip Bay surround an area of recent sinking. Nevertheless the Australian land mass is now relatively stable. Unlike New Zealand or New Guinea, it is far from any point where the earth's mobile crustal plates collide. So throughout the time of human occupation, the most striking shifts of the Australian coastline have been caused by changes in the sea level.

The planet's total store of moisture has probably remained much the same since its crust solidified. But the distribution of that moisture—in the oceans, on or under the land, in the atmosphere or locked in ice—has varied vastly. Even a small change in temperature affects the density of water, causing it to expand or contract signifi-

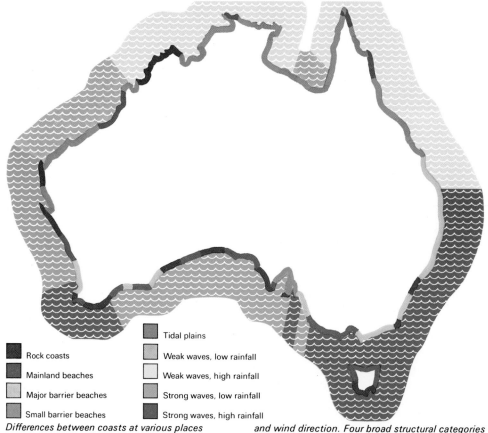

Rock coasts

Mainland beaches

Major barrier beaches

Small barrier beaches

Tidal plains

Weak waves, low rainfall

Weak waves, high rainfall

Strong waves, low rainfall

Strong waves, high rainfall

Differences between coasts at various places around the continent are the result of a combination of factors, such as rock type, the power of local waves, the width of the continental shelf, rainfall and wind direction. Four broad structural categories describe the physical appearance of any particular coast, and four climatic categories encompass the important forces that helped to shape the shoreline

cantly. A fall of just 1°C in the overall average temperature of the oceans would lower sea levels by about 2 metres. And that is only a minor effect of climatic change. Prolonged reduction of average atmospheric temperatures actually robs the oceans of water. Evaporated moisture, instead of returning in the usual cycle of conden-

sation, precipitation and run-off, stays frozen on the land. During the most recent ice age, which had its maximum effect between 50 000 and 10 000 years ago, so much moisture accumulated in icecaps that the sea level receded more than 100 metres. Its ascent when melting set in was an uneven process over thousands of years,

The evolution of Botany Bay

ANCIENT estuaries all around the coast were 'drowned' when the sea returned to its present level after the last ice age. It was a gradual process, with marine sand being pushed up to form barriers in places where there was a large enough supply of sand, and then driven ashore to form beach ridges and dunes, and also into estuaries. Here is a geologist's reconstruction of what happened in Botany Bay, Sydney.

Vegetated land

Cliffs, rock platforms

Mobile sand

Water

Vegetated sand

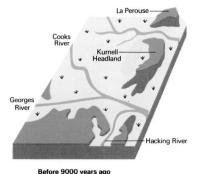

Before 9000 years ago
With the sea more than 20 metres below today's level, Botany Bay was a swampy plain, interrupted by occasional rocky outcrops. Many of the sediments were left over from the last period of high sea levels

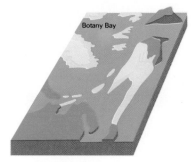

9000-7000 years ago
Seas rising to 9 metres below their present level moved a sand barrier onshore to enclose a shallow estuary: longshore drift swept sand north past the headland and around into the newly formed bay

interrupted by spells of renewed glaciation.

Sea levels regarded as normal today were attained about 6000 years ago. There are signs, however, that the oceans came even higher during some more recent periods. At no time may constancy be taken for granted.

Scientists may classify coasts of various kinds in a dozen or more categories, related mainly to their origins. In terms of natural life and the human use of Australia's shores, climatic conditions are more important and only four broad structural distinctions are needed: rock, mainland beach, barrier beach and tidal plain. **Rock coasts,** all cliffed to some degree, occur largely in the south and the north-west. If beaches occur at all, they are pockets of minor significance. **Mainland beach coasts** (the term applies also to Tasmania and other major islands) may have some rocky sections, accompanied by shore platforms, but extensive open beaches are predominant. On **barrier beach coasts,** beaches have formed offshore in the vicinity of rocky promontories, enclosing or nearly enclosing lagoons and estuaries between themselves and the old shore. Where wave action is consistently powerful the barrier is the dominant feature, containing a massive accumulation of sand. Otherwise it is the lagoon or estuary margins that give the coast its character. Major barriers are commonest on the east coast between the Tropic of Capricorn and Bass Strait, and in eastern South Australia and south of Perth. Small barriers are mostly found on the tropical Queensland and Northern Territory coasts. **Tidal plain coasts** are usually marked by the growth of salt-marsh plants or mangroves, and sometimes in the tropical zone by fringing coral. They are extensive between North-West Cape and Port Hedland, and occur elsewhere in gulfs.

On a coastline as extensive as Australia's, location and climate play significant roles in determining what kind of structure evolves. Deep ocean waves are generally bigger and more powerful in the southern latitudes, and day-to-day local winds are usually stronger. The offshore slope of the sea floor is also steeper towards

Measuring Australia's shores

THE MORE precisely a coast is measured, the longer it becomes. Tracing a simplified outline of Australia, for example, makes the mainland coast seem to be about 15 000 km long. Measurements from detailed sectional maps would produce a total twice as great. And taking the argument to absurdity, it is estimated that if the slightest twists and turns of the coast were charted millimetre by millimetre, the length would be more than 130 000 km. Precision is a matter of what is practical. Geographers have a choice of measuring methods, and a choice of rules as to what should be included—literally, where to draw the line.

Australia's officially recognised measurement was made by government cartographers in 1973. High-water lines were chosen, so mangrove flats and coral reefs were excluded. Open estuaries were cut off where they appeared to take the shape of rivers. On maps of 1:250 000 scale, points about 500 metres apart were plotted. Then it became a theoretical exercise: the straight-line distances between those points were computed and totalled. By that method, the shores of the mainland, Tasmania and the continental shelf islands were taken to be about 36 735 km long.

In 1980, a CSIRO geographer, Dr Robert Galloway, directed a manual measurement of greater precision. Maps of the same scale were used, but this time the entire line of coasts was followed with fine wire. A mid-tide level was taken; mangroves were included but coral reefs were still left out. Islands less than 12 hectares in area were ignored, as were straits less than 1 km wide. Estuaries were cut off where they narrowed to less than 1 km. The total length of the mainland and Tasmanian coasts came to about 30 270 km. Coastline lengths of islands, computed from their areas after one-sixth of them had been measured in detail, came to a further 16 800 km. So by Dr Galloway's method the total is 47 070 km—rather more than the circumference of the earth.

the south and the continental shelf is narrower, permitting more wave energy to be transmitted ashore. This north-south difference in wave energy levels is accentuated by the shape of the continent: its bulges at each side mean that the sections running south from North-West Cape and Fraser Island tend to confront the normal approach of waves, while the receding northern sections do not. Much of the Queensland east coast is further shielded from the full impact of waves by the Great Barrier Reef system.

Another major geographical distinction, in this case roughly between east and west, is created by unevenness of rainfall. Where there is a substantial run-off of rain, at least seasonally, material washed from inland formations contributes to the building of beaches, river mouth bars and nearshore barriers. It also hastens the infilling of enclosed waters, producing new land. But its long-term effects are not so constructive. Sand from inland rocks is rich in silica, which keeps it loose. Water soaks through easily, leaching out minerals that are redeposited on the grain surfaces of underlying material as a skin—this red skin gives silica sand its typical colour, as silica sand without such a skin is white. The layers of heavy 'black sand' sought by mining companies are a result of the different densities of mineral sand and silica sand, and the sorting effect of waves and swash. The sorting effect is similar to that used by prospectors in separating gold from gravel in a pan. Meanwhile the loose, light material above, whether in beaches or dunes, remains prone to destruction by high winds and storm waves.

On arid coasts, however, the major chemical component of beach material is often calcium. Where winds drive the sand inland, piling it up in dune ridges out of the reach of sea water, it is eventually calcified and forms a solid mass of new rock. Many of today's limestone cliffs, islands, offshore stacks and reefs originated as high dune ridges, formed when the sea level was lower and the climate of their hinterland was arid. In the scale of coastal evolution, eons long, such a transformation is merely a passing phase.

7000-4000 years ago

Seas reaching today's levels pushed barrier sand shoreward to form beach ridges along Bate Bay. Wind-waves transported sand from the bed of Botany Bay north and west to the shores of the bay

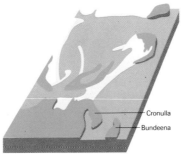

4000-1000 years ago

With the sea close to its present level, there were two phases of parabolic dune emplacement and stabilisation by plants; a long period of coastal stability seems to have followed

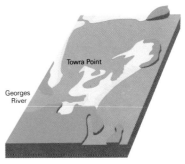

Last 1000 years

The tidal delta of the Georges River took shape, forming Towra Point from a complex of levees, spits and bars; renewed erosion of the barrier beach fed a dune sheet that continues to move today

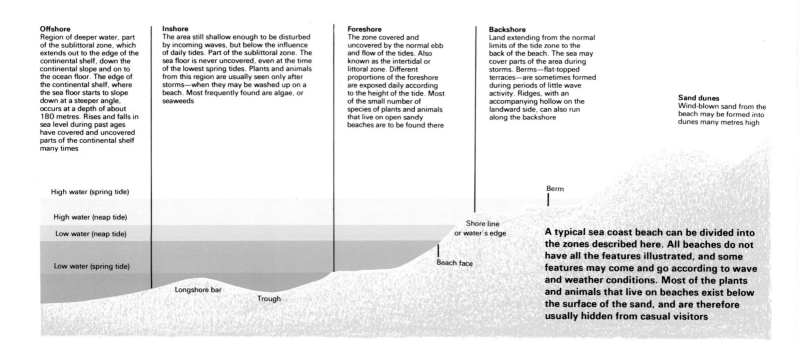

Offshore
Region of deeper water, part of the sublittoral zone, which extends out to the edge of the continental shelf, down the continental slope and on to the ocean floor. The edge of the continental shelf, where the sea floor starts to slope down at a steeper angle, occurs at a depth of about 180 metres. Rises and falls in sea level during past ages have covered and uncovered parts of the continental shelf many times

Inshore
The area still shallow enough to be disturbed by incoming waves, but below the influence of daily tides. Part of the sublittoral zone. The sea floor is never uncovered, even at the time of the lowest spring tides. Plants and animals from this region are usually seen only after storms—when they may be washed up on a beach. Most frequently found are algae, or seaweeds

Foreshore
The zone covered and uncovered by the normal ebb and flow of the tides. Also known as the intertidal or littoral zone. Different proportions of the foreshore are exposed daily according to the height of the tide. Most of the small number of species of plants and animals that live on open sandy beaches are to be found there

Backshore
Land extending from the normal limits of the tide zone to the back of the beach. The sea may cover parts of the area during storms. Berms—flat-topped terraces—are sometimes formed during periods of little wave activity. Ridges, with an accompanying hollow on the landward side, can also run along the backshore

Sand dunes
Wind-blown sand from the beach may be formed into dunes many metres high

High water (spring tide)

High water (neap tide)

Low water (neap tide)

Low water (spring tide)

Longshore bar

Trough

Shore line or water's edge

Beach face

Berm

A typical sea coast beach can be divided into the zones described here. All beaches do not have all the features illustrated, and some features may come and go according to wave and weather conditions. Most of the plants and animals that live on beaches exist below the surface of the sand, and are therefore usually hidden from casual visitors

Sandy shores Beaches and the life they support

What lives on and under beaches, between the high and low tide limits, depends on how the beaches are composed. Beaches of coarse sand usually slope more sharply than those of fine sand, and are more exposed to wave action. They support the lowest number of organisms. Protected beaches with fine sand have many more creatures—provided that the sand is of the right consistency for them to burrow. Plenty of water must be held between the particles. Few animals will be found in the sort of sand that whitens around an area that is trodden. Such sand gives up its moisture too readily under pressure: deeper down, it is too tightly packed to allow

much movement. Some fine sands, however, react to pressure in the opposite way. They become softer and easier to penetrate, and remain moist below the surface.

Sands behave differently because they are made differently—from rocks of varying structure and mineral content. That affects the size, smoothness and slipperiness of particles, as well as the colour of beaches. By no means all beach sand comes from coastal rock in the immediate vicinity. Much may be carried from inland by rivers, by rain run-off or by wind. In some places sand from other coasts is pushed onshore from the sea floor by waves. Tropical mainland

beaches are often composed mostly of coral fragments from reefs. And sands nearly always contain worn-down shell from a multitude of marine organisms, in concentrations that vary locally. On Australia's most frequented non-tropical coasts, however, the mixture is usually dominated by silica in the form of quartz. Its glassy quality keeps the sand loose. Bigger particles and heavier minerals slip down easily, leaving the sands near the surface fine and light. They are prone to erosion and other damage, but in protected conditions they support a fairly large range of animals. Plants in the tide zone are almost non-existent, except for microscopic algae. Bigger seaweeds may inhabit the nearshore if they find purchase on pebbles or heavy shell fragments, and stable backshore and foredune areas are frequently vegetated by banksias, casuarinas and acacias among spinifex grasses and a few flowering plants.

Tiny organisms abound in the spaces between particles of subsurface sand, but special laboratory procedures are required to isolate and study them. In Australia almost nothing is known about such creatures. Only animals more than 3 mm long have been the subject of detailed study, and that has been concentrated on New South Wales beaches. The most obvious of beach-dwellers are ghost crabs, *Ocypode*, distinguished by their paleness and long eye-stalks. Their burrows are well above high water but they forage in the tide zone at night, scampering ahead of human intruders. Also common high on the shore are various species of isopods—little crustaceans that are sometimes called sea-slaters or marine lice. Nearer the water are their

When sand turns back into rock

SAND collecting at great depths in the ocean is converted by pressure into sandstone rock. On arid coasts, dunes rich in calcium solidify as limestone if left undisturbed. Both processes are very slow. But beach sands sometimes cement themselves together as if of their own accord, and with surprising speed. Recent artefacts such as coins and war relics are found in shelves of Australian beach rock.

Scientists are unable to agree on the binding agent in beach rock. Some believe it is calcium carbonate, precipitated during the repeated risings and fallings of the water table under the sand. Others think it is salts deposited when sea water evaporates. Micro-organisms deep in the sand and warm temperatures may aid the process.

The rock is tough enough to resist erosion, so that sheets of it are sometimes left jutting out as the only evidence of a vanished beach.

Beach rock with aircraft wreckage from 1945

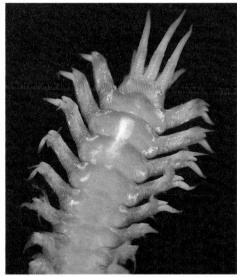

Giant beach worms can exceed 2 metres in length. Fishermen use the worms for bait and lure them from their holes with rotten fish. Once the worm's head (below) emerges it can be grasped and the worm pulled from the sand

relatives the amphipods, often known as sand-hoppers or sea-fleas. Sand bubbler crabs, *Scopimera*, are prominent in the intertidal zone. They burrow to the water table, leaving blobs of sand in radiating lines on the surface. Battalions of little pink-and-blue soldier crabs, *Mictyris longicarpus*, frequently emerge from sandy tidal flats, but seldom from beaches where waves break. Of bivalve molluscs buried in the sand, by far the most common is the pipi, *Plebidonax deltoides*. Wedge pipis, cockles and dog cockles are found in deeper water. Smaller bivalves are the principal prey of the giant beach-worm, *Onuphis teres*, which grows to more than 2 metres in length. It is prolific, but seldom seen unless a lure of smelly fish is trailed in the backwash of waves. A smaller worm, *Diopatra dentata*, is best known by the tube that it builds to live in, consisting of shell fragments, small stones and other debris embedded in a fibrous substance. The worm can move freely in and out, so if a tube is pulled from the sand there is rarely an animal inside it.

Small holes seen in a beach surface behind a retreating wave are often assumed to be signs of animals below. If the wave was unusually strong, a few holes or depressions may have been left by pipis or crabs which were uncovered by it and had to burrow deeper. But most holes are formed by the escape of air bubbles, trapped among sediments washed onto the beach. Another false indicator of animal movement is a sharply etched, branched mark at the flattened 'toe' of a sloping beach. Such patterns, called rill marks, are made by runnels of water escaping from higher sand after the tide has ebbed. Other marks, more regularly formed, are clearly the result of water action. Swash marks—sand ridges about 1 mm high, overlapping like curved roof tiles—indicate the farthest points reached by waves. Sand ripples—ridges and troughs in roughly parallel rows—are formed by the churning action of waves running up a beach. If wave motion alone was responsible, the ridges are evenly curved. But if a current was present as well, each ridge is steeper on the side towards which the current was running.

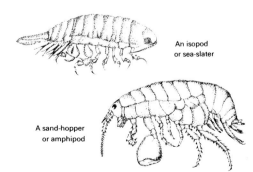

An isopod or sea-slater

A sand-hopper or amphipod

Amphipods and isopods are common on beaches

What the colour of a beach reveals

ALL BEACH sands are mixtures. They include shell and other marine material as well as grains from various types of rock. Nearly all Australian beaches are essentially light-coloured, being dominated either by silica from quartz and feldspar rock or by calcium carbonate of marine origin. Other minerals can produce different hues—some by coating the sands. Colour can be an indicator of many of the principal materials:

Sparkling white	Quartz grains coated with extra silica deposit
Dull white (non-tropical)	Worn quartz on rainy coasts; limestone on arid coasts
Dull white (tropical)	Coral, perhaps with pumice
Creamy/pinkish white	More than 90 per cent quartz
Yellow/gold/light brown	Impure quartz, feldspar, coloured shell
Darker brown	Compounds of iron, etc., coating sand grains
Silver/gold sheen when wet	Surface mica
Grey	Higher concentrations of volcanic or darker sedimentary rock—e.g., basalt or shale
Dark olive	Iron-magnesium-silica compound (eastern Torres Strait)
Black	Basalt dominant; surface iron ore
Dark flecks on pale beach	Fragments of compound granitic rock
Red flecks on tropical beach	'Organ pipe' coral debris
Brown/black lower band	Rutile, ilmenite, iron
Red/brown lower band	Garnet, rutile
Brown/black beach streaks	Organic acid staining
Red/brown/green dune layers	Oxides, etc., of iron or other minerals coating quartz (Queensland 'coloured sands')
Brown/black 'coffee rock'	Sand coated and cemented by iron or manganese compounds

Elusive inhabitants of sandy beaches

The most obvious things on sandy beaches are usually dead plants and animals washed up by the waves. But there are also many things that live in the sand, although they are often difficult to find because they spend most of their lives below the surface, or are too small to see. Many migrate vertically underneath the sand—such as the tiny, shrimp-like amphipods and isopods—while others migrate up and down the beach, towards and away from the water. Very little plant life is found on beaches because there is nothing for the plants to hold on to. There is a greater variety of creatures to be found in fine sand than there is in coarse sand— not so much because of the size of the particles, but rather because fine sand is found where the beach is not being churned up. In particularly calm areas there are lugworms—burrowing worms that leave a coiled cast. Giant beach worms, some longer than 2 metres, abound in some places, but nearly all the bubbling that you see and hear at the water's edge is caused not by worms but by air.

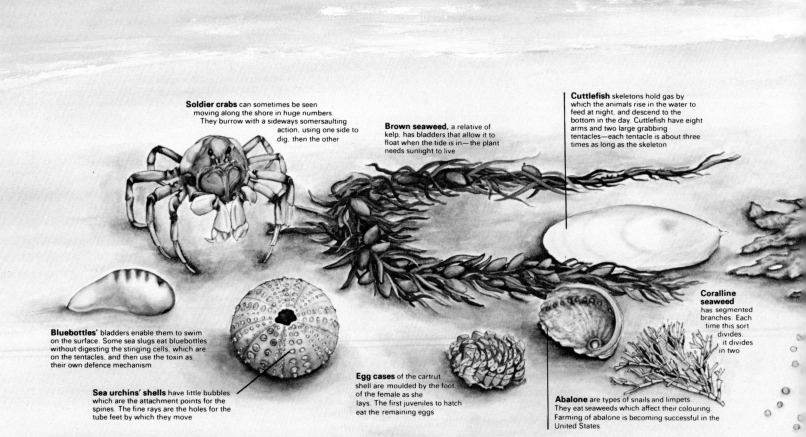

Soldier crabs can sometimes be seen moving along the shore in huge numbers. They burrow with a sideways somersaulting action, using one side to dig, then the other

Brown seaweed, a relative of kelp, has bladders that allow it to float when the tide is in—the plant needs sunlight to live

Cuttlefish skeletons hold gas by which the animals rise in the water to feed at night, and descend to the bottom in the day. Cuttlefish have eight arms and two large grabbing tentacles—each tentacle is about three times as long as the skeleton

Coralline seaweed has segmented branches. Each time this sort divides, it divides in two

Bluebottles' bladders enable them to swim on the surface. Some sea slugs eat bluebottles without digesting the stinging cells, which are on the tentacles, and then use the toxin as their own defence mechanism

Sea urchins' shells have little bubbles which are the attachment points for the spines. The fine rays are the holes for the tube feet by which they move

Egg cases of the cartrut shell are moulded by the foot of the female as she lays. The first juveniles to hatch eat the remaining eggs

Abalone are types of snails and limpets. They eat seaweeds which affect their colouring. Farming of abalone is becoming successful in the United States

Coastal vegetation of this kind, including she-oaks (casuarinas) and banksias, grows best in estuaries and sheltered bays where there is some relief from salt spray and the pruning action of the wind. Since these areas are dry, the plant communities are particularly subject to fire

Sedges have narrow leaves and stiff stems to reduce moisture loss

Hairy spinifex has long runners which grow on bare sand so that it makes an excellent dune stabiliser. The male and female parts of this grass are on separate plants

Crabs often have elaborate mating rituals. It is invariably the male that has one colourful claw which it waves in a sort of dance

Pipis, of which this is an empty half-shell, are often killed by a whelk that drills into their shell with an action like a diamond cutting glass. You can often see the hole with its neatly chamfered edge

Kelp, a seaweed, has a holdfast to attach it to rock or the sea floor. Many creatures live in and around and on the holdfast—particularly worms, and sometimes mussels

Pigface or noonflower has an unusual method of photosynthesis, allowing it in particularly dry periods to absorb carbon dioxide at night and reduce moisture loss

Bubbler crabs roll the sand they excavate into tiny balls. They use the hole as a burrow during low tide, and come out at night to feed on algae during high tide

Sponges are very primitive animals. They feed off the planktonic animals and bacteria that enter the passages of the sponge. The part we use is their skeleton

Goose barnacles are ocean-dwellers, settling on anything that floats—bottles, lumps of oil, the bottom of ships. In medieval times they were thought to be the young of migrating geese

Common Australian sea shells

The tightly packed shelves and display boards in seaside museums exhibit the shells of only some of over 10 000 species of molluscs so far discovered in Australia. An estimated 80 000 species exist in the world, and new ones are constantly being found. Some large, brightly coloured and intricately patterned shells are much sought after by collectors and command high prices because of their rarity. The shells illustrated here are those commonly seen on beaches or in rock pools by casual visitors to the coast. Do not collect shells containing live animals. Sizes of average specimens are given.

Orange cockle
Acrosterigma reeveanum
Length 60 mm

Combed auger
Hastula strigilata
Length 30 mm

Orange jingle shell
Anomia descripta
Diameter 55 mm

Bubble shell
Bulla quoyii
Length 50 mm

Common southern bean cowrie
Trivia merces
Length 10 mm

Venus shell
Katelysia rhytiphora
Width 45 mm

Arrowed sand snail
Tanea sagittata
Diameter 10 mm

Banded or silver kelp shell
Bankivia fasciata
Length 15 mm

Leafy chama
Chama pulchella
Diameter 40 mm

Erroneous cowrie
Cypraea errones
Length 30 mm

Pretty trough shell
Mactra eximia
Width 60 mm

Dog whelk
Nassarius pyrrhus
Length 15 mm

Melon or baler shell
Melo amphora
Length 70-220 mm

Doughboy scallop
Mimachlamys asperrimus
Width 65 mm

Sand snail
Natica gualtieriana
Length 30 mm

Southern olive shell
Oliva australis
Length 30 mm

Olive shell
Oliva oliva
Length 30 mm

Orange sand snail
Polinices tumidus
Length 35 mm

Dove shell
Pyrene scripta
Length 10 mm

Angas's murex
Pterynotus angasi
Length 20 mm

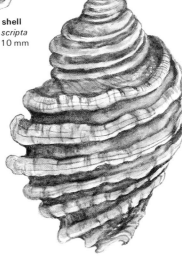

Dog winkle
Thais orbita
Length 70 mm

Pipi
Plebidonax deltoides
Width 60 mm

Pheasant shell
Phasianella australis
Length 55 mm

Creeper shell
Rhinoclavis sinensis
Length 50 mm

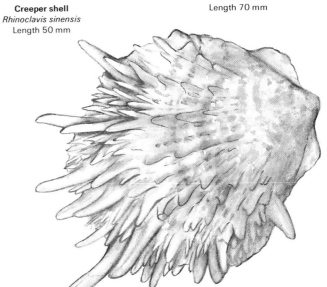

Long-spined thorny oyster
Spondylus wrightianus
Width 80 mm

Turban shell
Turbo undulata
Length 65 mm

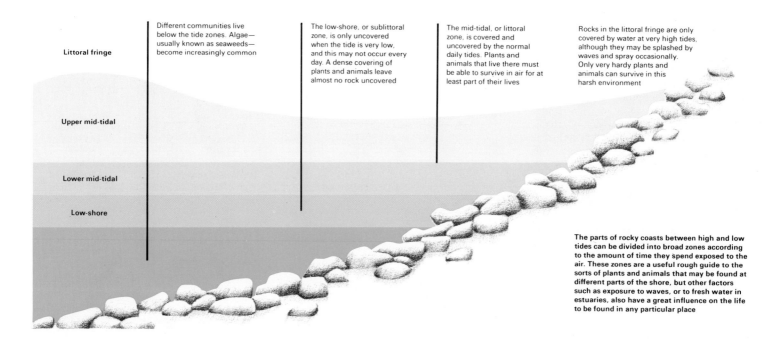

Littoral fringe

Different communities live below the tide zones. Algae—usually known as seaweeds—become increasingly common

The low-shore, or sublittoral zone, is only uncovered when the tide is very low, and this may not occur every day. A dense covering of plants and animals leave almost no rock uncovered

The mid-tidal, or littoral zone, is covered and uncovered by the normal daily tides. Plants and animals that live there must be able to survive in air for at least part of their lives

Rocks in the littoral fringe are only covered by water at very high tides, although they may be splashed by waves and spray occasionally. Only very hardy plants and animals can survive in this harsh environment

Upper mid-tidal

Lower mid-tidal

Low-shore

The parts of rocky coasts between high and low tides can be divided into broad zones according to the amount of time they spend exposed to the air. These zones are a useful rough guide to the sorts of plants and animals that may be found at different parts of the shore, but other factors such as exposure to waves, or to fresh water in estuaries, also have a great influence on the life to be found in any particular place

Rocky shores Where marine life takes a hold on the land

Shore platforms of rock, accommodating a rich diversity of marine animals and plants, are common in eastern and south-eastern Australia. They are formed by waves and rain eating at outcrops at and above the intertidal level. So they occur where wave energy is high and where the rock is only moderately durable. The sandstones of New South Wales, exposed to strong ocean swells and high rainfall, are ideal. Nearly every headland has its platform, to the delight of amateur fishermen. Platforms differ widely in character, however. Some are submerged at all but the lowest tides, while others are formed at or above the mean high tide level, and exposed to the air nearly all the time. Most are more or less flat but many have a slope, usually because a tilted block of more resistant rock has been uncovered. Some platforms have smooth surfaces; others are deeply fissured, pitted with pools, studded with pinnacles, raised with tiered benches, or strewn with boulders.

All those local differences have some bearing on the distribution of marine life. The degree of protection from heavy breakers is also important. So is the range between low and high tides: where it is greatest, marine communities are spread over the widest area. On many coasts the rock platforms are made up of discernible bands of height inhabited by different species. Many are fixed to the rock—for example, barnacles, oysters, tubeworms, sea-squirts, sponges and seaweeds. Some can move, but spend most of their time in one spot—anemones and mussels, for instance. Even the most mobile animals, such as gastropod shellfish, crabs and starfish, have habitual feeding areas. People who have learnt to distinguish a dozen or so dominant species of

animals, and a few seaweeds and grasses, can identify tide zones on different platforms. And they can tell where the tide is at a glance.

Many areas in the highest tide zone, the littoral fringe, are under water for only a tiny part of the tidal cycle. Some receive only the twice-monthly spring tides and a varying amount of spray. Marine organisms living here have to be hardy, and adaptable not only to fluctuating air temperatures but also to drastic changes in salinity—from salt water at high tide to fresh water if it rains while the tide is out. Littorinid snails of several species cope well with such conditions. The most common, throughout Australia

except in northern Queensland, is the periwinkle, *Littorina unifasciata*.

The mid-tidal area is often called the barnacle zone. At its higher levels barnacles are common except in Western Australia and so are gastropods such as sea snails and limpets. New South Wales has the six-plated grey barnacle, *Chthamalus antennatus*, and the small honeycomb barnacle, *Chamaesipho columna*. A limpet, *Notoacmea petterdi*, is widespread on vertical surfaces, and other gastropods occurring in some upper mid-tidal areas include a bigger limpet, *Cellana tramoserica*, and the black snail, *Nerita atramentosa*. Lower in the mid-tidal area,

Tools of the waves

CIRCULAR pools with smooth, vertical walls, often seen on wave-washed shore platforms, seem too perfectly formed to be natural. But at the bottom will be found at least one stray stone. It is these stones, of harder material than the platform rock, that make the pools. Lodging at first in shallow depressions, they are repeatedly spun about in swirling water. They become the tools of the waves, scouring the platform until they have drilled it to such a depth—sometimes more than 1 metre—that they are out of reach of disturbance by water movements and no longer move.

Pools still being scoured hold little marine life, though small fish are occasionally trapped in them. But when the drilling stones cease to move, the pools are soon colonised by seaweeds, anemones, gastropods and sometimes starfish—content to live in a sheltered environment.

A circular pool on a Sydney rock platform

barnacles continue in company with mussels, gastropods and sometimes oysters. On the most protected NSW shores, gastropods such as the mulberry whelk, *Morula*, limpets and three common grazing snails are dominant along with starfish, chitons, often called coat-of-mail shells because of their eight armour-like plates, and anemones. In slightly less protected areas, dense beds of honeycomb barnacles are often found with the limpet *Cellana* grazing over them. Plants are seldom obvious. An encrusting alga on many Sydney shores blends with the colour of sandstone and is only noticeable at close quarters. Pools often contain the brown seaweed *Hormosira banksii*, commonly called Neptune's beads, along with gastropods, anemones, starfish and sometimes the hairy mussel, *Trichomya hirsuta*. Areas exposed to stronger waves are usually dominated by one or both species of surf barnacles, *Catomerus polymerus* and the pink *Tesseropora rosea*. In South Australia, Victoria and Tasmania, mussels occupy a lot of space in many mid-tidal areas, while in parts of northern Queensland oysters are much more common.

Moving into low-shore areas, the covering of plants and animals becomes so dense that often no bare rock can be seen. Organisms may be exposed to the air only at low tide, or in some places not at all. Algae, particularly brown seaweeds, increase markedly. A fixed tube-worm, *Galeolaria caespitosa*, is found just above the seaweed or on patches among it. In Victoria, NSW and southern Queensland the sea-squirt or cunjevoi is so prolific on some platforms that the low-shore area is often referred to as the cunjevoi zone. Many other organisms live where they can find room among the dominant groups. Along with some that are more characteristic of higher shore levels, such as barnacles and whelks, are found turban shells, starfish, sea-urchins, sponges, octopuses and crabs.

Marine life distribution is consistent in its general patterns, but from time to time and place to place there can be significant changes. The most obvious causes of such changes are storm damage, human interference and water pollution. Shore communities are variable anyway, because of breeding and feeding behaviour. Most species spend a juvenile stage at sea. Larvae or spores drift for days, weeks or months at the whim of ocean currents. Many may be eaten by predators, or die before reaching a platform. Those that survive the seaborne phase do not necessarily find the same area or even the same shore as their parent colonies, and new-found homes may be less suitable. Barnacle larvae, for example, can fix themselves only to bare rock or to the hard shells of older barnacles and other gastropods. If other species already cover the rock, there will be no barnacles. Among the adult animals, many species prey on others, compete with each other for food or space, or interfere with the settlement of the tiny larvae. Some are even more variable because they are short-lived and seasonal, or because their young do not settle every year. The distribution of species on a rocky shore is continually changing.

Getting to grips with the cunjevoi

CRUSTY yet spongy, like a vegetable outside yet meaty inside, the sea-squirt or cunjevoi is a puzzle even to the rock fishermen who cut it up for bait. Just for fun a leading marine biologist, the late William Dakin, wrote to the Sydney *Sun* in 1945 inviting theories about the nature of this organism. A Dr Archibald Grubb replied:

'My observations of and on cunjevoi have been frequent, long, and even lurid, and its facility in depriving me of hooks and sinkers has always suggested that it is an animal, and a very low and objectionable animal at that. And when you walk over it gingerly to recover your hook, it looks up malignantly and spits sea-water into your eye; and when, in rage, you slash off the top of its crust, withdraw the animal or vegetable and place it upon a hook, all the other lowest animals in the water rush to the feast—woorrahs, or old boots, fortescues, weedies, muddies, sweep, toebiters, crabs, onkterspronks, mugfrubs, etc, and so forth, and you lose the an. or veg. off the hook and get snagged on its contemporaries and lose half your line. Yes, if the cunjevoi isn't a lower form of animal life, the barnacle is a melon-plant, or I'm an onion.'

Dr Grubb was right. The cunjevoi is an animal. It belongs to the same division of the animal kingdom as some free-swimming, sac-bodied creatures, some beach worms and all the vertebrates.

Hundreds of cunjevoi form a lumpy brown covering over rocks exposed only at very low tide

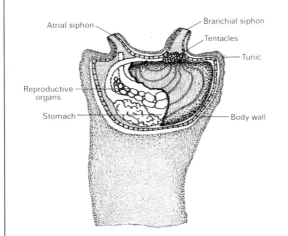

Atrial siphon
Branchial siphon
Tentacles
Tunic
Reproductive organs
Stomach
Body wall

The most commonly encountered cunjevoi on Australia's rocky shores, Pyura praeputialis, is only one of some 250 known species. Inside the animal's leathery outer coat is the tough, muscular tissue sought after by anglers as bait. The tissue forms a body wall to protect the branchial sac, the main food collecting and respiratory organ. Food-laden water is sucked down the branchial siphon, filtered by the tentacles and trapped in the sac. Waste water is released in a stream through the atrial siphon. The cunjevoi is hermaphroditic, with both male and female cells

Miniature worlds along rocky shores

Rocky shores, and the pools along them, accommodate myriad fascinating animals and plants. Explore them in the early morning at low tide, before the animals have sheltered from the heat and glare. Cause as little interference as possible—even apparently bare rocks may be covered with microscopic life. If you turn over any rocks, replace them exactly as they were, otherwise you will kill the plants and animals living on both sides.

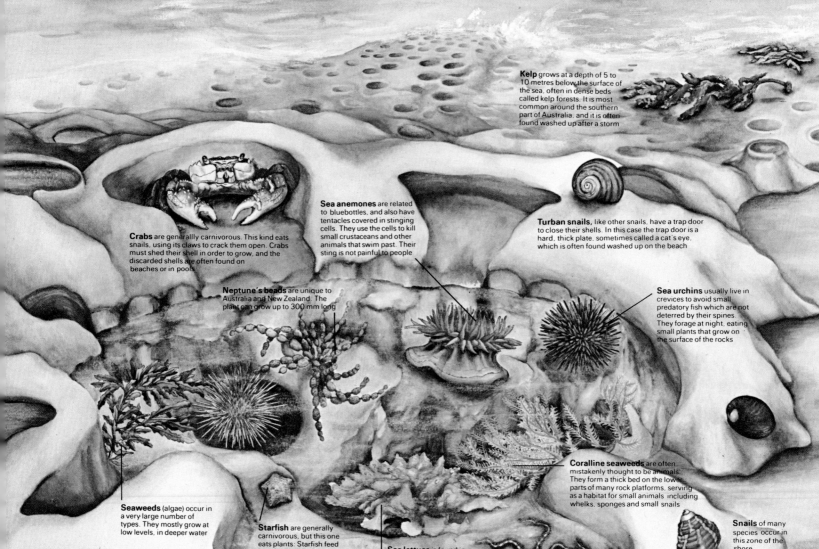

Kelp grows at a depth of 5 to 10 metres below the surface of the sea, often in dense beds called kelp forests. It is most common around the southern part of Australia, and it is often found washed up after a storm

Crabs are generally carnivorous. This kind eats snails, using its claws to crack them open. Crabs must shed their shell in order to grow, and the discarded shells are often found on beaches or in pools

Sea anemones are related to bluebottles, and also have tentacles covered in stinging cells. They use the cells to kill small crustaceans and other animals that swim past. Their sting is not painful to people

Turban snails, like other snails, have a trap door to close their shells. In this case the trap door is a hard, thick plate, sometimes called a cat's eye, which is often found washed up on the beach

Neptune's beads are unique to Australia and New Zealand. The plant can grow up to 300 mm long

Sea urchins usually live in crevices to avoid small predatory fish which are not deterred by their spines. They forage at night, eating small plants that grow on the surface of the rocks

Coralline seaweeds are often mistakenly thought to be animals. They form a thick bed on the lower parts of many rock platforms, serving as a habitat for small animals including whelks, sponges and small snails

Seaweeds (algae) occur in a very large number of types. They mostly grow at low levels, in deeper water

Starfish are generally carnivorous, but this one eats plants. Starfish feed by extruding their stomachs through their mouths and digesting what they find

Sea lettuce is found in most places around the coast. It has translucent, flat blades that are a source of food for many snails and fish

Snails of many species occur in this zone of the shore

Brittle stars are related to sea urchins. They prefer pools with a sandy bottom because they filter food from fine sediment

Do not take anything home. Even empty shells are used by creatures such as hermit crabs. Never reach into a crevice—there is the risk of encountering a blue-ringed octopus, a dangerous species of cone shell or a moray eel that could crush a finger badly.

Alga found at high levels usually occurs where it receives some rainwater. Lower down it is eaten by grazing animals

Mussels are nearly always found in clumps. They are filter feeders and pump seawater through their bodies, extracting all the minute animals from it

Lichens are a mixture of a fungus and an alga

Chiton or coat-of-mail shells live on algae. Some grow to 130 mm long

Barnacles are cemented to the rock and do not move. They often form dense clumps. There are very many species of these animals, which are related to shrimps

Mulberry whelks eat shelled animals, particularly barnacles, by softening the shell with a secretion and then drilling a hole in it with their proboscis. The process can take four days

Erosion holes in soft rocks often contain patches of salt formed when seawater has evaporated in the sun

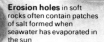

Hermit crabs have soft shells so they have to live in the shells of other, dead, animals. They try to dislodge other hermit crabs from larger shells as they grow

Limpets are usually slightly raised from the rock, but they clamp themselves down if threatened

Estuarine waters Fish habitats under human threat

Estuaries are principally the tidal parts of river mouths. Biologists also class some bay areas and lagoons as estuarine because they support similar marine life and fringing vegetation. Australia has few estuaries, considering the extent of its coastline. Where their shores were firm they made ideal Aboriginal campsites, offering fresh water close to an abundance of seafood and waterfowl. European explorers made for the same spots, not only for sustenance but also for protected anchorages. With colonisation the landing places became ports for access to the hinterlands, and many grew to be cities and sites of industry. Estuary beds have been raised for reclamations, or dredged to provide land-fill elsewhere. Other estuarine waters serve as fishing grounds and ever-busier holiday playgrounds—and some even as waste dumps.

These relatively rare waters are crucial to the existence of many fish, including some that are normally associated with deeper seas offshore. Snapper, for example, spend a juvenile stage in estuaries, where they may be known as cockney or red bream. In New South Wales, 31 of the 43 most important commercial species are caught in estuaries. Half of the total inshore and offshore catch, in tonnage and value, comprises species that depend on estuaries for at least a part of their lives. Including other seafoods such as prawns and oysters, the NSW fishing industry is about 70 per cent reliant on estuaries. The availability of smaller organisms for these fish to eat varies greatly in nature. Now it is increasingly threatened by human activities.

Seagrasses probably hold the key to marine animal life in estuaries. They are not important

as a direct source of food for commercial fish species, but they shield the youngest fish from predators and they generate the organic material on which a whole web of food supply is based. Dead or broken parts of eelgrass, *Zostera*, strapweed, *Posidonia*, or some other flowering plants and associated algae are grazed and further broken down by crustaceans and worms. The smaller particles are attacked by bacteria and fungi and eaten by other tiny organisms, which are in turn eaten. Reduced to its finest form—detritus—after repeated digestions and excretions, the organic matter readily yields up its mineral components to nourish more seagrass. Fringing mangroves and swamp plants contribute detritus in a similar way.

While the cycle continues, all marine animals have food—plant matter, micro-organisms, or

Protecting a complex environment

Careel Bay, north of Sydney, is a good example of a delicate estuarine environment threatened by residential and commercial development. The bay is rich in the number of species of plants and animals that live in and on its waters and surrounding mangrove forests, salt marshes and sandy beaches. Each of these areas plays a part in maintaining its neighbours, so the disturbance of one habitat could destroy others. Because the sheltered shores of estuaries offer so many possibilities for leisure activities, they will always be under threat until their importance in the life cycle of many creatures is properly understood and appreciated.

Grey mangroves, *Avicennia marina*, and river mangroves, *Aegicerus corniculatum*, grow here. Both need oxygen, which they obtain by their aerial roots or pneumatophores. The trees die if these are covered by even a shallow layer of silt or sand. Many species of crabs and snails live among the mangroves which are an important link in the food chain by which nutrients eventually enter estuarine waters. Mangroves also play an important part in stabilising mud so that surrounding water remains clear and seagrasses can grow

These brown areas are salt marsh. They are flooded with seawater only when the tide is particularly high, and they are an important part of the estuarine ecosystem, bridging the gap between mangroves and dry land, and producing much organic matter. Here there are sedges; the succulent, beaded glasswort, *Sarcocornia quinqueflora*; streaked arrowgrass, *Triglochin striata*; and she-oaks, *Casuarina*. The salt marsh is an important habitat for birds, and this one is the home of the bush stone curlew, *Burhinus magnirostris*, which is rare in urban areas. Salt marshes are often misused because they seem to have little value—people dump rubbish in them and children enjoy riding bikes around in the mud. Because they border dry land and housing developments, residents are tempted to increase the extent of uninundated land by filling adjoining soft areas

Proposals have been put forward to enlarge boating facilities on the southern shore of the bay and to dredge a deep-water access channel. Scientists fear that such a development would increase the amount of pollution and would also stir up sediments to cloud what is at present clear water

This strip of land beside the road was once covered by wetland salt marsh and mangroves. It was used for many years as a garbage tip, and the reclaimed land has now been turned into playing fields. Around Australia many similar areas have been reclaimed in this way. In some instances industrial waste was dumped, and there is a possibility that harmful chemicals may be leached from these tips into surrounding waters

Owners of waterfront houses sometimes pull out mangrove seedlings to keep their beaches clear

In this shallow water grow dense beds of seagrasses. Eelgrass, *Zostera*, grows on the flats uncovered at low tide, and strapweed, *Posidonia*, grows in the areas always submerged. Careel Bay favours seagrasses because it is well-flushed by tides and the water is quite clear, enabling light to filter through strongly. Fish and shellfish find this an ideal environment so the area is particularly rich in species and numbers. Unlike mangroves, with their ability to take oxygen directly from the air, seagrasses and the animals they shelter take oxygen from the water, so they are greatly affected by suspended sediment and pollution

Houses mean human waste. In unsewered suburbs septic tanks can leak or overflow, or effluent is released on purpose, into creeks and bays. Human waste is harmful because the bacteria that decompose it need a lot of oxygen, thus depriving the water of oxygen used by plants and animals

one another. But entire meadows of seagrass can be destroyed by massive movements of silt or sand, especially in floods or after storms. Even a milder disturbance making the water murky can stop their growth by cutting out sunlight. And human interference is not limited to the obvious effects of large-scale engineering. Seagrass beds are frequently damaged by water pollution, by high-speed boating over shallows, by bottom-trawling and by the dumping of junk.

Estuary beds are the world's most productive areas. Seagrasses alone generate as much as 4 kg of organic matter per square metre per year. The average is 2 kg in dry weight—equalled only by tropical forests. Temperate grasslands yield only 0.5 kg on average, and total land areas 0.75 kg. Ocean beds produce a mere 0.15 kg.

In addition, staggering quantities of animal tissue are produced in estuaries. Sampling of seagrass meadows in the United States indicated that every square kilometre harboured 90 million prawns, including larvae, and 36 000 million molluscs. And cultivated mussel beds in Lancashire, England, were found to produce 80 times more weight of flesh than cattle could gain by grazing on an equivalent area of pasture.

Sea water is heavier than fresh water, so an estuary fed by a big river—the Derwent passing through Hobart, for example—may be split into two levels with a wedge of sea water flowing upstream under river water flowing downstream. But Australia's generally low rainfall means that many estuaries are totally marine environments for most of the time. Their salt content is not much lower than the ocean's, except after heavy rain. Periods of reduced salinity are spasmodic and seldom long-lasting. In the far north, however, where rainfall is extremely seasonal, estuaries are virtually fresh for months during the 'Wet'. And over-saltiness, through evaporation, can occur in a lagoon when drought cuts its freshwater flow and waves build a sand bar blocking the entrance. That is common in the south-east and in parts of South Australia, and leads to the death of many animals and plants.

Most estuarine animals are sea creatures: their body fluids are in balance with sea water because the salt concentrations are similar. If floods overwhelm their habitat and drastically lower its salinity, they start absorbing extra water. For some species this is fatal. Fish can quickly retreat to more suitable waters. Molluscs and crustaceans have shells and regulatory mechanisms to delay water absorption. They may also be able to close their shells or burrow into the estuary bed—at the risk of starvation—until the crisis is over. The chief sufferers are soft-bodied animals such as worms. Some can stand a limited intake of water, slightly inflating their bodies, for a short time. But if low salinity continues, they die. After heavy floods, entire populations are wiped out. Other worms, especially those adapted to upstream areas, have organs that act like primitive kidneys and pump out water. But their young lack these organs, so reproduction has to be geared to periods of higher salinity.

Fish and other marine animals are renewable

Seagrass meadows, found in many bays and estuaries around the Australian coast, are among the most productive areas in the world

resources, provided that their habitats are preserved. But the estuarine plant life on which they depend can be destroyed forever by human actions, whether deliberate or unthinking. Not only are many uses of estuaries in conflict with nature—they are also often in conflict with one another. Port development, commercial fishing, sand mining, sewage disposal, oyster cultivation and recreation, for example, simply do not mix. Scientists are urging governments to consider all estuaries that are subject to human pressure and to allocate specific uses to each of them, taking into account their different physical characteristics, their type of vegetation, and their nearness to population centres. A major problem in planning their conservation, however, is the multiplicity of authorities in control of the wetland fringes (see overleaf).

The saving of Jervis Bay

SEAGRASS meadows in the sheltered northern reaches of Jervis Bay are probably the most extensive in NSW, reaching to depths of more than 10 metres. As well as being nurseries for commercially valuable fish and crustaceans, they are important feeding grounds for vast flocks of black swans. Yet in 1972 the shores behind were proposed as the site of a gigantic industrial complex. The north-western corner was earmarked for a steelworks bigger than Port Kembla's. To its east were to be engineering plants, metal refineries, a woodchip mill, a petro-chemical plant, an oil refinery and a power station. Separate port facilities for the steelworks, for bulk products, for general cargo and for oil products were to be strung along Callala Beach. Urban zones, at first on the coast to the north but later on the western shore of the bay, were to house 300 000 people. But evidence of the ecological impact was so damning that a government inquiry threw out the whole scheme, recommending that the bay shores be preserved for nature conservation and recreation.

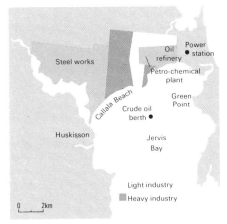

The plan of the 1972 development proposal gives some idea of the scope of the scheme

The shores of Jervis Bay remain unspoiled, despite attempts to establish heavy industry in the area

Wetland margins Where plants belong to both worlds

Mangrove swamps and salt marshes are customarily seen as nuisances. They are foul-smelling breeding grounds of mosquitoes and midges. They clog boating and fishing waters and impede land access to them. They collect floating rubbish. In the tropics, they harbour dangerous crocodiles. The eagerness of property developers to dredge out mangroves and wall the shoreline, or to refashion marshlands as canal estates, is understandable. But mangroves and marsh plants are vital, along with seagrasses, to estuary life. Where water, sunlight and nutrients are plentiful, each square metre of mangrove forest contributes an average 1 kg a year of organic matter to the food chain that supports most of the species sought-after by commercial fishermen.

The biological importance of mangroves was recognised only in the late 1960s, after pioneering research in southern Florida, USA. Only four species grow there, but Australia has more than 30, related to at least 15 different families of land-based trees. Mangroves were just as varied in South-east Asia, but their habitats are in heavily populated, underdeveloped tropical regions. Asian mangroves have been traditionally cut for firewood and for building jetties and fish traps. Now international companies in some places are mowing them down for woodchip production. They are being depleted so rapidly that by the

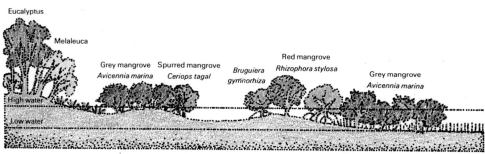

Different species of mangroves form distinct zones in tropical estuaries, partly as a result of the amount of time that the land spends under water. The landward zone is generally the richest in species

1990s Australia may have the world's last mature stands of highly diverse mangrove forest.

Mangroves are trees and shrubs with many different and unrelated characteristics. What they have in common is a unique tolerance of high concentrations of salt in their soil moisture. Some species discharge salt through glands on their leaves; others are able to restrict its entry through their roots. They have various ways of drawing air into oxygen-starved soil. All have adapted to daily flooding by sea water—in fact they rely on it. They use the tides to disperse their seeds, so that new areas can be colonised away from the shade of older trees.

Australia has the southernmost distribution of mangroves in the world. The common grey mangrove, *Avicennia marina*, is found in Corner Inlet, just north of Wilsons Promontory, and in other shallow, protected Victorian bays such as Western Port. Isolated *Avicennia* swamps also occur in the gulfs of South Australia and on the west coast, south of Perth. Mangroves are widespread in estuaries and sheltered bays on the east coast, with the number of species increasing northward. Two occur at Merimbula, NSW, and seven near Brisbane, while communities of more than 20 species are found in northern Queensland and north-western Australia. The breadth of swamps increases with the number of species, as does the height of plants. Southern mangroves are stunted and sparse; around Sydney they form open parklands and grow 10-20 metres tall; mangroves in the far north comprise broad,

Red mangroves, Rhyzophora stylosa, *with their tangled roots are the classic mangroves of tropical shores*

Fish that climb trees

MUDSKIPPERS, the oddest creatures in tropical mangrove swamps, are fish that prefer the open air and hot sun, as long as their skins are moist. They emerge from the water at low tide and walk over the mud on fins that are modified for use as limbs. Through stalked, swivelling eyes on top of their heads, these fish of the *Periophthalmus* genus watch for the small crabs and insects on which they feed. If alarmed they do not retreat into the water but skip across it to a safer mudbank. And if still hungry when the tide is rising, many species use their fins to elbow their way up mangrove trees. Queensland's commonest species grow to 100 mm in length, but others reach 250 mm.

A mudskipper, Periophthalmus koelreuteri

Altogether, over 30 species of mangroves live around the Australian coast, but all are only found north of 12°S. Only one species—the grey mangrove, Avicennia marina (far left)—grows in Victoria, South Australia and south-western Western Australia. Spurred mangroves, Ceriops tagal (left), and milky mangroves, Exoecaria agallocha (above), illustrate the diverse forms that these plants take

dense forest climbing to a height of 30 metres.

Because they grow in tidal mud, mangroves need extensive root systems to hold them in place. As well as subterranean systems, many species have branching aerial roots. The prop-roots of *Rhizophora* descend from higher on the trunk as the tree grows. *Bruguiera*, the tallest mangroves, send out low-level roots that travel horizontally and bend upwards before anchoring in the mud. Some other species have wide, flat aerial roots resembling planks wandering far from the tree. The tangle of roots put out by a community of mangroves traps fine silt carried down by any creeks draining into the swamp. Sediments brought in on the high tide also tend to settle out and remain among the mangroves. In this way the trees stabilise shorelines, and in the absence of floods or storm waves they can add to the land area.

Avicennia, Bruguiera and some other mangrove species send pegs into the air for metres around each tree. Called pneumatophores, these are root extensions with lip-like cracks through which the tree can draw oxygen while its lower levels are in poorly aerated mud. Other species have similar breathing openings in their aerial roots. Another peculiarity of many mangroves is that their seeds germinate before they leave the tree. In *Rhizophora* species, the seedling may protrude more than 300 mm from the fruit. When it falls into the water the fruit floats with the seedling shoot pointing down, ready to catch in shallows and quickly take root. *Avicennia* seeds, however, need long soaking in sea water before they will germinate.

Most land animals found in mangroves are casual visitors such as mice, canefield rats, flying foxes, snakes, goannas, crocodiles and many species of birds. Some come seasonally for protection while breeding, or because the trees are

flowering or fruiting. A diverse community of insects includes some species found only in mangroves. Fish and prawns come in with the tide to feed. Mud crabs breed among the mangroves, but spend most of their lives in deeper water.

The permanent marine population is dominated by worms, molluscs and crustaceans. Some—especially molluscs with shells that resist dehydration—live on the surface. Fiddler and semaphore crabs, needing constant access to water, live in burrows, but feed on the surface and sometimes in the trees. Oysters encrust the tree bases on the seaward margins, along with limpets, small shrimps and worms. Other worms inhabit tubes in the mud or in pockets of water under fallen logs. Small crabs and snails also live under dead wood, while other creatures bore into it and gradually break it down. The 'ship worm', *Teredo*—really a tiny bivalve mollusc—is the dominant borer, though louse-like isopods

such as the gribble may be locally common. Once such animals have made holes, other small creatures may move in.

Salt marshes, often found on the landward margins of mangrove swamps, present conditions so variable that few kinds of animals or plants can survive. Inundation by the sea normally occurs only during fortnightly spring tides. At other times, especially in dry summer weather, evaporation causes a build-up of salt concentrations. In the tropics and in arid regions there may by salt pans—areas where the soil is covered in salt crystals and devoid of vegetation. On the other hand fresh water may flood a salt marsh during heavy rain. Burrowing crabs and some small snails can cope with this range of conditions. Of the shrubby succulent plants that may grow, the dominant species is marsh samphire or glasswort, *Salicornia*. The shores of a marsh are often marked by a band of rushes and casuarinas.

How the law sees mangroves

LAWS protecting mangroves were passed in all mainland states in the 1970s, after the importance of the trees was recognised. But biologists are far from satisfied with the effectiveness of such measures. In NSW, for example, the Fisheries Act was amended in 1979 so that any cutting of mangroves without a permit could incur a $500 fine. But three years later the amendent was still not in force: there was no machinery for apprehending and prosecuting offenders.

The effects of proposed coastal developments on mangroves can now be taken into account if environmental impact assessments are called for. The authority controlling a particular area of wetlands, however, need not call for such a study unless it already believes that the impact is likely to be sig-

nificant. And that authority may have little ecological interest; its official concern could be port administration or shipping, or public works. Control of wetlands may be in the hands of as many as seven or eight different state government departments or statutory authorities, or it may be vested in local government councils.

Singling out certain mangrove areas for complete protection offers no permanent solution because they are changing environments. Through the gain or loss of soil, mangroves create their own fluctuations in sea levels and growth limits. And wildlife, especially migratory birdlife, is unpredictable. A mangrove swamp of no apparent interest in one season may become all-important breeding ground the following year.

Mangroves, an unattractive but vital nursery

Mangrove swamps have clearly zoned regions. In the waterfront mudflats exposed at low tide, the air-breathing roots of some mangrove species and sapling trees sprout through the oozing surface. Adult trees from over 30 kinds of mangroves found around the Australian coast form dense thickets of branches and ground and aerial roots further inland, but still on the tidal mudflats. As the swamp merges into firm land, mangroves intermingle with land plants.

Mud is trapped by the mangrove's tangled roots and, because the waters are unusually calm, algae, bacteria and fungi are held there. These organisms are what makes the swamps such smelly places, but they are also the basis of a food chain which supports a great diversity of molluscs, crustaceans and fish that are sought

Pulmonate slugs— like all slugs—are shell-less snails. They are air-breathers and feed on algae. The most common in mangrove swamps grow to about 70 mm long. They are very hard to see as they are usually covered in mud, but they can be traced by the trail they leave

Shipworms are misleadingly named—they are actually bivalves, relatives of oysters, mussels and cockles. They have a long siphon that they extend to the surface to breathe and eat. There are several species of shipworm; they used to be relished as food by Aborigines, but now they are only considered as pests, being responsible for much of the destruction of wooden pilings and other timber in water

Oysters occur in huge numbers around mangrove pneumatophores—many mangrove swamps in New South Wales are leased as nursery areas for the spats (young oysters). Sydney rock oysters change sex during their lifetime—they spawn as males but become females later. The females produce about

1 500 000 eggs every few weeks in the breeding season (mostly in summer); the eggs develop into larvae that can swim in a few hours. After two or three weeks they settle, and are collected from their first sites to be farmed in batteries. They take about three and a half years to grow to table size

Oysters are stationary, with one side of their shell cemented to a surface. They are filter feeders, using their gills—the gill forms a sieve and when taking in oxygen the creature also collects food particles

Snapping shrimps can often be heard in mangrove swamps, making a crack like glass breaking—it is not known why. Saltwater yabbies (which can be eaten but are generally used for bait) look somewhat similar, but snapping shrimps are quickly recognised by their single large-clawed leg—this has a peg on one finger which fits into a socket on the other. The feathered end sections are used as rudders

Hermit crabs are soft-bodied, with an abdomen that can be coiled to fit into their borrowed homes. As they grow they need to move into larger shells

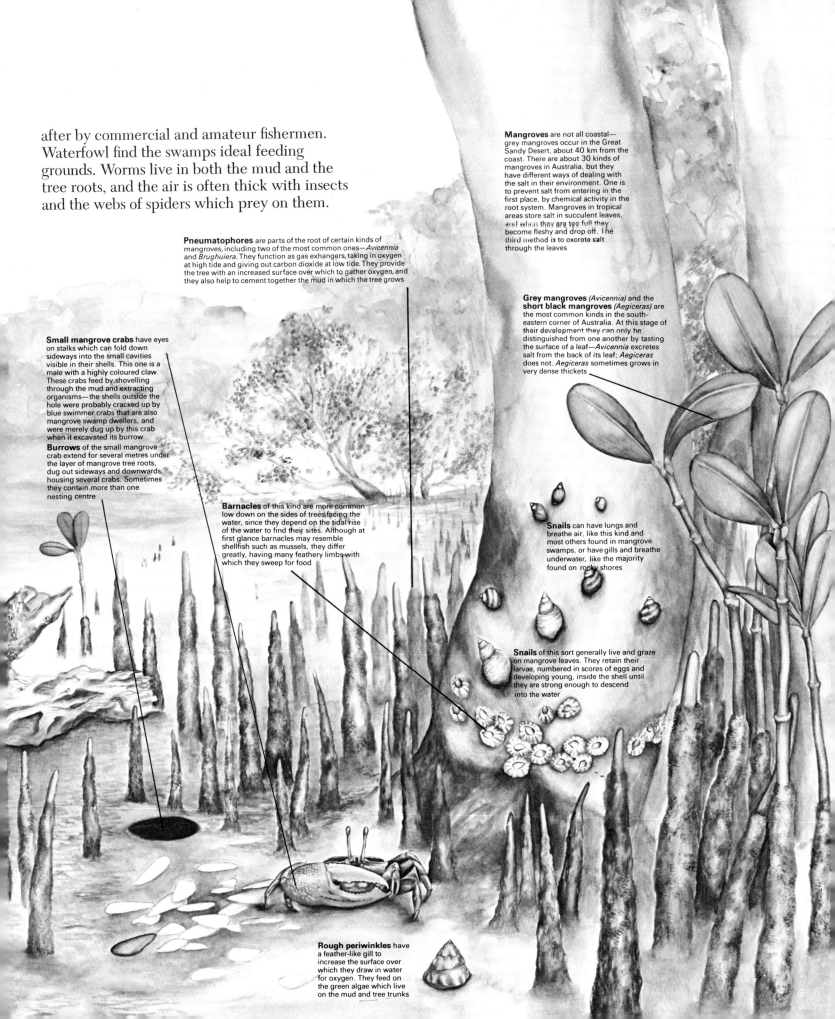

after by commercial and amateur fishermen. Waterfowl find the swamps ideal feeding grounds. Worms live in both the mud and the tree roots, and the air is often thick with insects and the webs of spiders which prey on them.

Mangroves are not all coastal—grey mangroves occur in the Great Sandy Desert, about 40 km from the coast. There are about 30 kinds of mangroves in Australia, but they have different ways of dealing with the salt in their environment. One is to prevent salt from entering in the first place, by chemical activity in the root system. Mangroves in tropical areas store salt in succulent leaves, and when they are too full they become fleshy and drop off. The third method is to excrete salt through the leaves

Pneumatophores are parts of the root of certain kinds of mangroves, including two of the most common ones—*Avicennia* and *Brughuiera*. They function as gas exhangers, taking in oxygen at high tide and giving out carbon dioxide at low tide. They provide the tree with an increased surface over which to gather oxygen, and they also help to cement together the mud in which the tree grows

Grey mangroves *(Avicennia)* and the **short black mangroves** *(Aegiceras)* are the most common kinds in the south-eastern corner of Australia. At this stage of their development they can only be distinguished from one another by tasting the surface of a leaf—*Avicennia* excretes salt from the back of its leaf; *Aegiceras* does not. *Aegiceras* sometimes grows in very dense thickets

Small mangrove crabs have eyes on stalks which can fold down sideways into the small cavities visible in their shells. This one is a male with a highly coloured claw. These crabs feed by shovelling through the mud and extracting organisms—the shells outside the hole were probably cracked up by blue swimmer crabs that are also mangrove swamp dwellers, and were merely dug up by this crab when it excavated its burrow

Burrows of the small mangrove crab extend for several metres under the layer of mangrove tree roots, dug out sideways and downwards, housing several crabs. Sometimes they contain more than one nesting centre

Barnacles of this kind are more common low down on the sides of trees facing the water, since they depend on the tidal rise of the water to find their sites. Although at first glance barnacles may resemble shellfish such as mussels, they differ greatly, having many feathery limbs with which they sweep for food

Snails can have lungs and breathe air, like this kind and most others found in mangrove swamps, or have gills and breathe underwater, like the majority found on rocky shores

Snails of this sort generally live and graze on mangrove leaves. They retain their larvae, numbered in scores of eggs and developing young, inside the shell until they are strong enough to descend into the water

Rough periwinkles have a feather-like gill to increase the surface over which they draw in water for oxygen. They feed on the green algae which live on the mud and tree trunks

Coral reefs
Marine builders reaching for the light

Coral reefs are complex associations of marine animals and plants, living on and in a framework built primarily of the skeletons of corals. When coral polyps die their cups of calcium carbonate fill with the skeletal debris of other creatures such as molluscs and sea-urchins, and with limy material from seaweed. The skeletons and their contents are bound by encrusting red algae and cemented by carbonic acid salts to form reef rock. It is porous, but rigid and tough enough to resist waves and provide a platform on which more corals can build.

Water warmth is the paramount factor in reef-building. Average minimum temperatures must not be less than 18°C. Reefs are largely confined to the tropics, but consistent warm currents foster their growth far to the south at Lord Howe Island, off NSW, and at the Houtman Abrolhos Islands, opposite Geraldton, WA. Great Barrier Reef formations could perhaps have extended much farther, well to the south-east of Fraser Island, but for the masses of shifting sand north of the island. Loose sediments smother corals, or prevent them from gaining a hold on the rock. And they cloud the water, cutting out sunlight—the other major factor in reef-building. Plant organisms that stimulate coral tissue growth and bind the coral together are so restricted by poor light that reef corals do not flourish below about 50 metres. Drilling has shown that reef structures go much deeper under the sea

Limpid water covers Wistari Reef—a reef flat near Heron Island, which can be seen on the horizon

than that—they are many hundreds of metres thick—but the lower levels were built when the sea itself was lower, during the last ice age, or even earlier when the continental shelf stood higher. Reefs as they are known today are veneers, no more than about 8000 years old, overlaying the earlier structures.

When a reef reaches sea level, exposing its top surface at low tide, upward growth stops. Corals reaching any higher would be starved of their plankton food and dehydrated. But sideways growth takes over, principally in the direction from which ocean swells normally come. Incoming waves have more plankton, and the sluggish waters on the sheltered side of a reef may be muddy. The further development of

reef surfaces, once they are at sea level, is largely a matter of wave and wind action.

A *barrier* reef in the strict sense is a long, almost continuous chain of ribbon reefs roughly parallel to a mainland shore, at a considerable distance from it. It screens the coast from ocean movement and creates an offshore lagoon. The Great Barrier Reef is not one in that sense, though it contains some barriers among its complex mixture of formations. Matthew Flinders named it simply because of the difficulties it presented for sailing ships. Scientists prefer to call the Great Barrier region a 'reef province'.

Platform reefs rise from the shallower parts of continental shelves in the shelter of barrier reefs. They are flat-topped and commonly oval in

The animals that start it all

Coral polyps, some with their tentacles extended

CORALS are closely related to sea anemones. They can reproduce sexually, in which case the young have a free-swimming larval stage. Once a coral polyp has developed its tentacle-fringed mouth and gut, to catch and digest its diet of floating plankton, it settles on a firm support and secretes a limestone base. Then it starts building up a skeleton. In soft corals this is a set of splinters or ridges embedded in the body, or a horny or chalky central rod. But in true corals the skeleton forms a stone casing around the polyp, which can draw itself inside for protection. Corals of many kinds may be found on submerged rocks in most parts of the world—sometimes solitary, sometimes in clusters. But only in warm waters will they be reef-builders.

Reef corals, whose vast communities could in theory have been founded by just one polyp of each species, reproduce asexually by budding. They keep on building upwards, then outwards, basing themselves on the skeletons of their dead predecessors. They are linked with membranes of living tissue overlapping their inorganic casings. Each species has its own colour and each is genetically programmed to follow a particular growth pattern. Some are branch-like, others form clumps, layers, fans and so on, giving a diverse reef its extraordinary variety of hues and shapes.

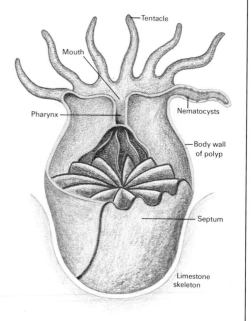

Cross-section through a polyp and its skeleton

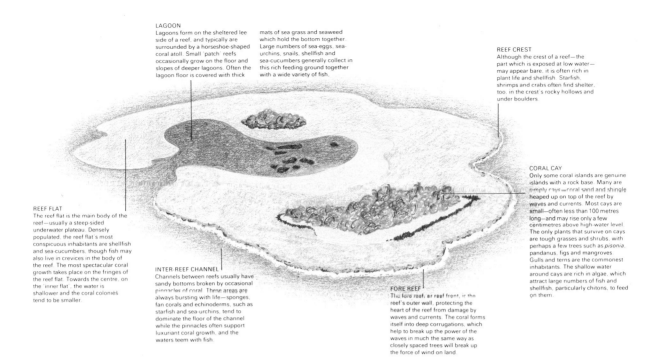

LAGOON
Lagoons form on the sheltered lee side of a reef, and typically are surrounded by a horseshoe-shaped coral atoll. Small 'patch' reefs occasionally grow on the floor and slopes of deeper lagoons. Often the lagoon floor is covered with thick mats of sea grass and seaweed which hold the bottom together. Large numbers of sea-eggs, sea-urchins, snails, shellfish and sea-cucumbers generally collect in this rich feeding ground together with a wide variety of fish.

REEF CREST
Although the crest of a reef—the part which is exposed at low water—may appear bare, it is often rich in plant life and shellfish. Starfish, shrimps and crabs often find shelter, too, in the crest's rocky hollows and under boulders.

CORAL CAY
Only some coral islands are genuine islands with a rock base. Many are simply cays—coral sand and shingle heaped up on top of the reef by waves and currents. Most cays are small—often less than 100 metres long—and may rise only a few centimetres above high-water level. The only plants that survive on cays are tough grasses and shrubs, with perhaps a few trees such as pisonia, pandanus, figs and mangroves. Gulls and terns are the commonest inhabitants. The shallow water around cays are rich in algae, which attract large numbers of fish and shellfish, particularly chitons, to feed on them.

REEF FLAT
The reef flat is the main body of the reef—usually a steep-sided underwater plateau. Densely populated, the reef flat's most conspicuous inhabitants are shellfish and sea-cucumbers, though fish may also live in crevices in the body of the reef. The most spectacular coral growth takes place on the fringes of the reef flat. Towards the centre, on the 'inner flat', the water is shallower and the coral colonies tend to be smaller.

INTER-REEF CHANNEL
Channels between reefs usually have sandy bottoms broken by occasional pinnacles of coral. These areas are always bursting with life—sponges, fan corals and echinoderms, such as starfish and sea-urchins, tend to dominate the floor of the channel while the pinnacles often support luxuriant coral growth, and the waters teem with fish.

FORE REEF
The fore reef, or reef front, is the reef's outer wall, protecting the heart of the reef from damage by waves and currents. The coral forms itself into deep corrugations, which help to break up the power of the waves in much the same way as closely spaced trees will break up the force of wind on land.

shape, with their longer axis aligned parallel to the prevailing wind direction. Smaller platform reefs may be called patch, shelf, bank, table or hummock reefs.

Fringing reefs grow outwards from continental or rocky island coasts. Because sedimentation and freshwater run-off are more pronounced on mainland shores, these reefs are more richly developed in the clear waters round islands.

An *atoll* is a ring of reefs, some surmounted by low cays of sand or shingle, enclosing a lagoon. Australia has none of the atolls common in the central Pacific—they usually occur in open oceanic waters, and are associated with volcanic activity. But some *lagoonal reefs* in Queensland waters, rising above the lagoon floors of bigger structures, may be ring-shaped.

All types of coral reefs have similar zones, running in bands that usually parallel their outer edges. Each zone is a distinct environment for characteristic forms of natural life. The *fore reef* extends from the lower limit of coral growth, up through the tide zone to the windward crest of the reef. The top edge often has closely spaced grooves running between ridges of coral. The grooves are pathways for tidal waves moving on to the reef, and for sediments to be removed. The *reef flat* extends to the back slope of the reef, or to a lagoon if there is one. The inner flats of some reefs may collect so much sediment that they are termed *sand flats*. Occasionally waves and currents push sand or shingle to a point towards the back of the reef where it forms a *cay*, permanently above the high-water mark. Cays, generally low-lying but up to 1 km long, are often colonised by vegetation and stabilised by the formation of beach rock around their rims. Green Island and Heron Island, well known to holiday-makers, are cays based on much more extensive reef platforms.

Subtidal fore reefs, with their profusion of

Enemies of coral

STARFISH are the leading predators of living corals, but few species do much harm. Since the 1960s, however, swarms of the huge, fast-breeding crown-of-thorns starfish, *Acanthaster planci*, have done immense damage to Great Barrier Reef structures. Adults may measure more than 500 mm across, and each may be capable of eating the polyps from a square metre of coral every week. In one survey at Green Island, off Cairns, nearly 6000 of them were found in 100 minutes. The crown-of-thorns seems to thrive on pollution that kills its own natural predators, such as the big triton shell-fish. That may be the reason for the present population explosion, although there appear to have been others in the past.

Some coral is killed accidentally during the attacks of big marauding fish on other species. The swallowing of smaller invertebrates by predators such as crabs and octopuses depletes the supply of skeletal material that goes into reef rock. Burrowers and borers, including sponges, molluscs, algae and bacteria, penetrate the rock at all levels. Algae-grazing fish, sea-urchins and molluscs further erode the rock in their quest for food. Browsing animals break down the sediment to extract nutrients.

A crown-of-thorns starfish eating polyps

living corals, seaweeds and colourful fish, can be adequately examined only by snorkelling or scuba diving. The outer reef flat, also with living corals as well as an abundance of sea-urchins, starfish and molluscs, can be viewed in a glass-bottom boat or on foot at the lowest tide. Walkers must exercise great caution, however, to avoid unintentional damage to reef life. The reef crest is usually swept clear by waves, and supports only an algal mat. But big blocks of reef rock, broken from the mass below and cast up in storms, are often found just inside the crest. Many small animals shelter beneath them.

Sandy inner zones of reef flats have occasional clumps of living corals interspersed with patches of dead coral supporting heavy algal growths. Sausage-like sea-cucumbers are the most obvious animal inhabitants, but the sands hide a variety of burrowing molluscs. Some reef flats have mangrove swamps, with features generally similar to those of coastal wetlands. Reef lagoons, if they have internal reefs of their own reaching to low-water level, may provide the best viewing of all with a variety of true corals and soft corals and a multitude of small mobile fauna. The sheets of fine sediment of lagoon floors are constantly reworked by molluscs, shrimps and worms.

Vegetated cays are commonly dominated by dense stands of *Pisonia grandis*—sometimes called 'the bird killing tree'. Its seeds have a sticky coating which can trap nesting sea birds. The central forest is surrounded by a bank of small salt-tolerant trees and shrubs, with grasses on the seaward side. Along with a wide variety of birds, the inner parts of cays are inhabited by reptiles—mainly lizards—and numerous insects. Ghost crabs are the most prominent occupants of cay beaches, although big turtles are nocturnal visitors during their breeding season. If beach rock has formed, it will be encrusted with limpets and 'coat-of-mail' chitons.

Builders and inhabitants of coral reefs

The Great Barrier Reef's massive coral ramparts and maze of island-fringing reefs stretch for 2000 km along the Queensland coast and support an amazing range of marine plants and animals. The reefs, and especially the 1400 species of fish that live around them, are best seen with the help of a mask and snorkel. But even walkers on the upper surface, when it is exposed or awash at low tide, can discover the great variety of coral shapes and the brilliant colours of the reef's other inhabitants, just some of which are illustrated here.

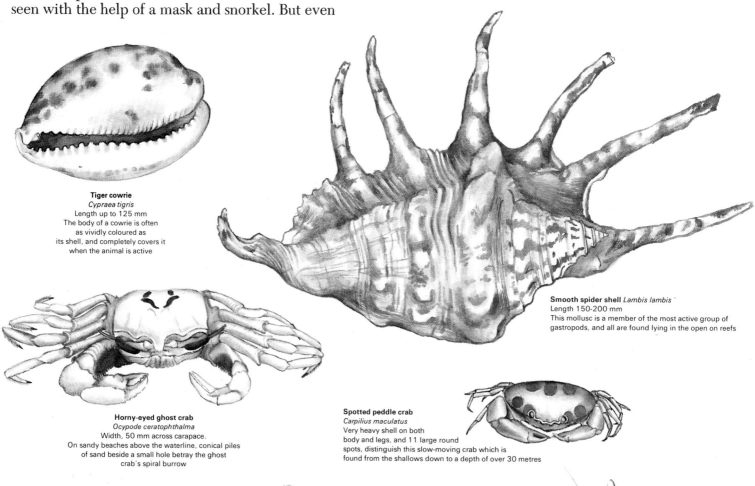

Tiger cowrie
Cypraea tigris
Length up to 125 mm
The body of a cowrie is often
as vividly coloured as
its shell, and completely covers it
when the animal is active

Smooth spider shell *Lambis lambis*
Length 150-200 mm
This mollusc is a member of the most active group of
gastropods, and all are found lying in the open on reefs

Horny-eyed ghost crab
Ocypode ceratophthalma
Width, 50 mm across carapace.
On sandy beaches above the waterline, conical piles
of sand beside a small hole betray the ghost
crab's spiral burrow

Spotted peddle crab
Carpilius maculatus
Very heavy shell on both
body and legs, and 11 large round
spots, distinguish this slow-moving crab which is
found from the shallows down to a depth of over 30 metres

Crenate swimming crab
Thalamita crenata
Width 100 mm across carapace
Five sharp spines behind the eyes on
each side clearly identify this crab.
It is caught in large numbers
for commercial markets

Double-lined sand crab
Matuta planipes
Width, 40 mm across carapace
This crab has wide, flattened claws,
well adapted for digging and swimming.
Matuta are common all around the continent

Leopard-spotted sea-cucumber
Bohadschia argus Length 250 mm
Sea cucumbers are animals, related to starfish
and sea urchins. They live among
coral debris on reef flats

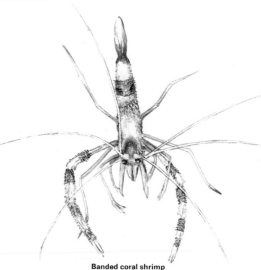

Banded coral shrimp
Stenopus hispidus
Length 50 mm. From crevices in coral, *Stenopus*
picks parasites and fungus growths from reef fish which
remain still while being cleaned

Staghorn coral *Acropora*
Forests of staghorn can
be up to 1.5 metres high and often cover
75 per cent of the reef area

Turban shell
Turbo perspeciosus
Length 50 mm
A hard, round plate on the
foot of the animal that inhabits
this shell allows it to withdraw
into complete protection

Orange-spotted mitre *Mitra mitra*
Length up to 150 mm
Also known as the giant mitre.
When alive, the shell of this
mollusc is covered with a thin skin
which partly hides the pattern

Cloth-of-gold cone shell
Conus textile
Length up to 100 mm. The timid *Conus* will
shrink into its shell at the least disturbance, but
it has a deadly venom, and a live one
should never be handled

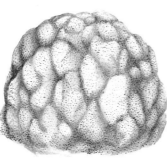

Round-head coral *Porites*
Some species of *Porites* form micro-atolls,
over 2 metres in diameter, which are
common on many reef flats

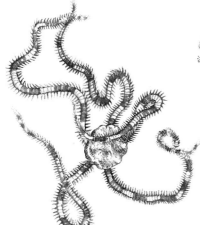

Brittle star
Ophiocoma scolopendrina
Diameter 200 mm
Brittle stars move much faster than starfish and have a more
clearly defined central disc. They inhabit rubble areas of
coral reefs and lie with only part of their bodies exposed

Soft coral *Xenia*
Soft corals do not make hard skeletons, and are
therefore not reef builders. When exposed at low tide
they look tough and leathery

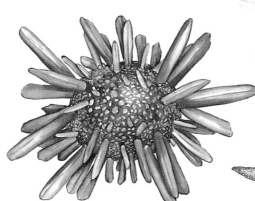

Slate-pencil urchin
Heterocentrotus mammillatus
Diameter 250 mm
The heavy, blunt spines of this sea
urchin may be up to 10 mm thick and
125 mm in length

Sea slug *Halgerda aurantiomaculata*
Length 40-50 mm
Colourful sea slugs carry their gills
on the outside of their bodies

Blue starfish *Linckia laevigata*
Diameter 250 mm
Great powers of regeneration allow
Linckia to grow a whole new disc and set
of arms on any severed arm

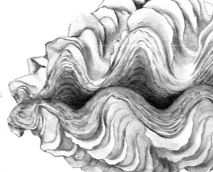

Giant clam *Tridacna*
Width up to 350 mm. A pair of shells from
the largest of all giant clams, *Tridacna gigas*,
exhibited at the Australian Museum
in Sydney, weighs over 220 kg

Honeycomb coral *Favites*
Colonies of honeycomb coral, up to 300 mm across,
grow on reef fronts and flats. Individual corallites
are about 15 mm wide

Birds of ocean and shore

Australia's extensive coastline is made up of many natural habitats—from rocky cliffs to tropical forests. Each habitat is the home of a great variety of birds. The 75 species illustrated on the following pages are the ones most commonly seen near the coast, although there are also occasional casual visitors and rarer species. The birds are all illustrated in their usual adult plumage, but there are sometimes slight differences between the sexes, and between adult and immature birds. The drawings are not all in proportion to one another, but an average length is given for each bird.

Sooty tern
Sterna fuscata
Length 460 mm,
wing-span 920 mm

Common tern
Sterna hirundo
Length 305-380 mm

Crested tern
Sterna bergii
Length 460 mm,
wing-span 1020 mm

Caspian tern
Hydroprogne caspia
Length 560 mm,
wing-span 1400 mm

Fairy tern
Sterna nereis
Length 215-265 mm,
wing-span 455-510 mm

Little tern
Sterna albifrons
Length 205-255 mm,
wing-span 445-495 mm

White-fronted tern
Sterna striata
Length 420 mm,
wing-span 760 mm

Roseate tern
Sterna dougallii
Length 360 mm,
wing-span 630 mm

Gull-billed tern
Gelochelidon nilotica
Length 355-430 mm

Pacific gull
Larus pacificus
Length 635 mm

Silver gull
Larus novaehollandiae
Length 400-425 mm

**Southern
black-backed gull**
Larus dominicanus
Length 570 mm

Sacred kingfisher
Halcyon sancta
Length 190-230 mm

Grey-tailed tattler
Tringa brevipes
Length 270 mm

Ruddy turnstone
Arenaria interpres
Length 230 mm

White-capped noddy
Anous minutus
Length 360 mm,
wing-span 650 mm

Mangrove kingfisher
Halcyon chloris
Length 250-280 mm

Banded stilt
Cladorhynchus leucocephalus
Length 380-410 mm

Common noddy
Anous stolidus
Length 400 mm,
wing-span 800 mm

Pied stilt
Himantopus himantopus
Length 385 mm

Beach stone curlew
Burhinus neglectus
Length 530-570 mm

Whimbrel
Numenius phaeopus
Length 400-460 mm

White-necked heron
Ardea pacifica
Length 910 mm

White-faced heron
Ardea novaehollandiae
Length 670 mm

Royal spoonbill
Platalea regia
Length 750 mm

White ibis
Threskiornis molucca
Length 700 mm

Little black cormorant
Phalacrocorax sulcirostris
Length 610 mm

Black cormorant
Phalacrocorax carbo
Length 800 mm

Mangrove heron
Butorides striatus
Length 480 mm

Pied cormorant
Phalacrocorax varius
Length 760 mm

Little pied cormorant
Phalacrocorax melanoleucos
Length 610 mm

Darter
Anhinga melanogaster
Length 900 mm

Black-faced cormorant
Phalacrocorax fuscescens
Length 650 mm

Wandering albatross
Diomedea exulans
Length up to 1350 mm,
wing-span to 3250 mm

Black-browed albatross
Diomedea melanophrys
Length 880 mm,
wing-span 2200 mm

Little egret
Egretta garzetta
Length 560 mm

Large egret
Egretta alba
Length 830 mm

Brown booby
Sula leucogaster
Length 740 mm

Sooty oystercatcher
Haematopus fuliginosus
Length 480 mm,
female usually larger
than male

Australian pelican
Pelecanus conspicillatus
Length 1600-1800 mm

Pied oystercatcher
Haematopus ostralegus
Length 480 mm,
female usually
larger than male

Swamp hen
Porphyrio porphyrio
Length 440-480 mm

Southern giant petrel
Macronectes giganteus
Length 900 mm, male
larger than female

Great skua
Stercorarius skua
Length up to 630 mm,
wing-span up to 900 mm.
Female larger than male

Australasian gannet
Morus serrator
Length 875 mm

Northern giant petrel
Macronectes halli
Length 900 mm,
male larger than female

Black swan
Cygnus atratus
Length 1200-1300 mm,
male larger than female

Bar-tailed godwit
Limosa lapponica
Length 380-430 mm,
female larger than male

Eastern curlew
Numenius madagascariensis
Length 650 mm

Reef heron
Egretta sacra
Length 600-750 mm

Black-tailed godwit
Limosa limosa
Length 380 mm,
female larger than male

Red-necked avocet
*Recurvirostra
novaehollandiae*
Length 440 mm

Greenshank
Tringa nebularia
Length 340-360 mm

Knot
Calidris canutus
Length 250 mm

**Sharp-tailed
sandpiper**
Calidris acuminata
Length 215 mm,
female smaller
than male

Curlew sandpiper
Calidris ferruginea
Length 210 mm

Large-billed dotterel
Charadrius leschenaultii
Length 225 mm

Hooded dotterel
Charadrius rubricollis
Length 205 mm

Terek sandpiper
Tringa terek
Length 240-290 mm

Mongolian dotterel
Charadrius mongolus
Length 200 mm

Double-banded dotterel
Charadrius bicinctus
Length 180 mm

Red-capped dotterel
Charadrius ruficapillus
Length 150 mm

Brahminy kite
Haliastur indus
Length 450-510 mm

White-breasted sea eagle
Haliaeetus leucogaster
Length of female 840 mm,
male 760 mm

Osprey
Pandion haliaetus
Length 500-630 mm

Grey plover
Pluvialis squatarola
Length 290 mm

Red-necked stint
Calidris ruficollis
Length 150 mm

Eastern golden plover
Pluvialis dominica
Length 250 mm

Black duck
Anas superciliosa
Length 470-610 mm,
male larger than female

Little penguin
Eudyptula minor
Length 330 mm
standing

Short-tailed shearwater
Puffinus tenuirostris
Length 400 mm

Fluttering shearwater
Puffinus gavia
Length 330 mm

Fairy prion
Pachyptila turtur
Length 230 mm

Flesh-footed shearwater
Puffinus carneipes
Length 450 mm

Wedge-tailed shearwater
Puffinus pacificus
Length 430 mm

PART 2

The ocean and the weather

The sea, even at its most placid, is the ruler of coasts. It draws its own boundaries. It determines the nature and extent of shoreline life.

Often its action moulds land margins and nearshore contours, prescribing what human activities a coast will support. Yet the sea is never its own master.

Global forces direct its movements, and atmospheric conditions dictate its moods. The ocean must do the bidding of winds.

And it can be made an agent of awesome destructiveness.

Science has achieved a broad understanding of weather systems and the sea's responses to them.

Vast current circulations can be charted and surface disturbances tracked.

But the complexity of coastal effects, in fair weather or foul, remains endlessly fascinating. Waves and shore formations, interacting, give each locality its own rules of water and sand movement.

Those rules can change—sometimes forever. People are learning, usually from costly errors, that coasts are dynamic environments.

They cannot conform with human notions of stability.

Winter winds whip spray from the crests of a choppy sea

Ocean currents   How warm water can flow on a cold coast

Gentle currents in the world's great oceans represent massive movements of water. They carry chilled polar seas towards the equator, and they shift warm water far from the tropics. Near a coast, they are more important than the local climate in determining water temperature and the range of marine life.

Major currents have their origins in the push of prevailing winds. The steadiest winds—from the east near the equator and from the west in high latitudes—are deflected by the earth's rotation so that they circulate. Currents follow the same pattern of circulation—counterclockwise in the Southern Hemisphere and clockwise in the Northern Hemisphere. Incidental winds may produce surface flows in other directions, but the basic pattern is constant.

Only northern Australia, shielded by islands, is not subject to currents flowing on an oceanic scale. The rest of the coast lies between the vast circulation systems of the South Indian, Southern and South Pacific Oceans.

Australia differs from all other continents in having no cold surface current on its west coast. A cold current does run consistently northward in the depths, but the central-west coast has two warm currents on the surface at different times of the year. Between October and April, anti-cyclones passing to the south push warm surface water up the coast from the Great Australian Bight at 1-2 km/h. From May to September, when anti-cyclones cross farther to the north, they push warm water from the Timor Sea to the Bight, usually at less than 1 km/h.

In the Southern Ocean the currents, forced by westerly winds, move generally eastward along the South Australian and Tasmanian coasts, but they are not constant. The water at any point may flow in any direction, usually at less than 1 km/h but often more rapidly in Bass Strait.

The East Australian current is really a series of eddies from a westward tropical flow which

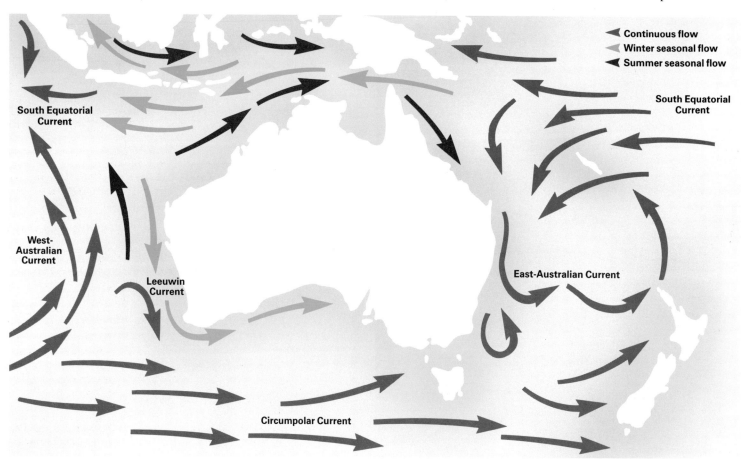

Continuous flow
Winter seasonal flow
Summer seasonal flow

South Equatorial Current

West-Australian Current

Leeuwin Current

South Equatorial Current

East-Australian Current

Circumpolar Current

Australia is bounded on three sides by large oceans; as a result much of the coast is affected by large, oceanic scale movements of water. In northern Australia, currents change direction in response to the annual monsoon winds.

Different fish for different water

FISH are called 'cold-blooded' but their body heat closely matches that of the surrounding water and varies with it. Each species has its own range of tolerance; at too high or too low a temperature, it may stop breeding or eating.

Fish and other creatures capable of moving can stay within their safe temperature range by travelling as seasons change. Many species, for example sharks and squid, migrate to warmer waters, and others simply change depth. Within the survival range of temperatures, fish have a narrower range at which they exhibit certain patterns of behaviour. Southern bluefin tuna, for example, feed alone in water below 16.7°C. Above 20° they move in schools but do not bite well. Only between these two temperatures are large quantities caught.

Under 16.7°C	16.7 to 20°C	Over 20°C

Exploring the currents from space

Buoys fitted with radio beacons have been set adrift off eastern Australia since the early 1970s. Their movements have been monitored by space satellites and charted by the Commonwealth Scientific and Industrial Research Organisation.

In 1979, as part of a much bigger international global atmosphere research programme, nearly 300 buoys carrying instrument packages were released in Southern Hemisphere oceans. Three satellites, Tiros-N and NOAA from the USA, and Argos from France, pick up transmissions. Their information, along with shipboard measurements, is expected to add much to the understanding of Australia's ocean currents, water temperatures and coastal weather. Other satellites, such as the US Seasat, continue and expand radar and microwave experiments that were begun with the Landsat and Skylab satellites. Seasat is presently testing an all-weather system of monitoring major currents, ice movements, sea conditions and fish productivity.

Satellite scanning of surface heat radiation can produce images, similar to photographs, known as thermal maps. Around the Australian coast they show the persistent but seasonally shifting fronts between bodies of water of different temperature, where fish congregate to feed.

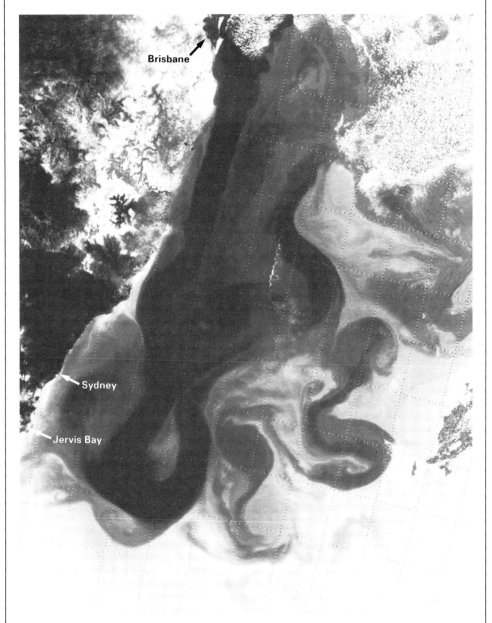

An infra-red satellite picture of the north Tasman and south Coral Seas in early December. Warm areas appear dark and cool areas light. The broad, warm East-Australian Current, flowing down the coast past Brisbane and Sydney and looping around off Jervis Bay, is very prominent

splits north-west towards Torres Strait and southward along the Great Barrier Reef. Inside the reef, circulation patterns are confused. The southward flow is strongest and most constant from outside the reef opposite Townsville, Qld, to Coffs Harbour, NSW. There it forms a belt 30-100 km wide and reaches speeds of 2-4 km/h in summer. Farther south the flow is less consistent and normal speeds are about 1.5 km/h in summer and 1 km/h in winter.

In northern Australia, currents are slow-moving and they change direction in response to the annual monsoon winds. Close to the north-west coast, the current flows predominantly north-east to east in winter, and north in summer. In Torres Strait the current flows eastward from December to March—when it is driven by the monsoons blowing from the north-west, and westward for the rest of the year.

The greatest temperature variation in Australian waters occurs off the mid-latitude Pacific coast, from central Queensland to central New South Wales. There the ocean currents shift most, and the origins of water masses change with the seasons. The temperature in a current can quite often vary as much as 3°C from that of the surrounding seas.

The surface of the sea also warms and cools with changes in air temperature, but not nearly as much as land surfaces. The sea is scarcely affected by day-and-night contrasts, and lags in its response to summer or winter extremes. It is usually warmest in February and coldest in August, with a year-round range in one place of only about 10°C.

Deeper in the ocean, temperatures vary little and the water is always cold. Shifts of current or strong winds blowing persistently from the shore can drive warm surface water out to sea, to be replaced by an upwelling of cold water. Upwelling from the continental shelf occurs within 15 km of the central east coast between July and December. It increases the concentration of dissolved nitrates and phosphates that nourish marine organisms. In extreme cases, the surface bloom of algae can be so profuse that the sea takes on a red tinge.

The richest concentrations of nutrients occur at the boundaries between bodies of water of different temperature. So fish—whether their diet is marine organisms or other species of fish—head for the margins of currents. They find them by aligning themselves to the flow of the current and adapting to its speed, or even by using visual markers such as the sun. Eggs and larvae drift passively with a current until they reach its edge.

Fishermen can sometimes spot a front of contrasting temperature as choppy water—caused by conflicting currents—or as a line of litter or scum. Often a change of colour can be seen. Another clue may be sea birds flocking to feed. But commercial fishing boats are increasingly equipped with instruments to detect changes in water temperature at a distance. Others follow courses plotted from thermal maps—aerial or satellite 'pictures' of the heat radiated from different bodies of water.

The tides Intricate rhythms of ocean advance and retreat

High tide comes twice a day to some parts of the Australian coast and only once to others. Even where two tides a day are usual, they may arrive at uneven intervals and reach markedly different levels. The height of the tide also differs widely on different parts of the coast. In the north-west the water level sometimes rises and falls by as much as 12 metres, changing the look of the coast beyond recognition in an hour or two. Yet along the coast south of Perth the tidal range is sometimes negligible.

The diversity of Australian tides is partly accounted for by the fact that each of the oceans and semi-enclosed seas around the continent has its own tidal system. Where systems meet, the tidal forces combine in some places and cancel each other out in others.

All the tidal systems have their origins in the gravitational pulls of the Moon and the Sun. The waters of the oceans are drawn towards the point of the Earth's surface nearest the Sun or the Moon so that they bulge outwards. This ocean bulging is slight, but if the world were a smooth sphere and covered to an even depth by water the bulges could be depicted as low waves, half as long as the world's circumference, moving continuously round the globe in company with the Moon and the Sun.

In practice, tides do not cross entire oceans but are trapped in ocean basins of irregular shape and depth, and they rock around one or more points in mid-ocean. Because the Earth is rotating beneath them, they take apparently curving courses, rebounding from coasts sideways so that they progress around the rims of ocean basins. They cannot match the speed at which the Moon orbits around the Earth. That is why the highest tides come just after new or full Moon.

Tidal waves rebounding from land masses run

Narrow range
Medium range
Wide range

The range of the tide—the difference between high water and low water—around the Australian coast varies from 600 mm in the south-west to more than 12 metres in the north-west of the continent

into one another. If they meet head-on and their wave motions match, they form 'standing waves' of constantly high water. Those waves are extremely long and low compared with the waves kicked up by winds at sea.

When a tidal wave travels in over a continental shelf, it shoals—slows and steepens—in much the same way as an ordinary wind-wave reaching a beach. The more extensive the shelf, the

steeper the tidal wave when it reaches the coast. But even after steepening, tidal waves are low in relation to the slope of most beaches. So they usually rebound without breaking.

If a tidal wave carries on into an estuary or a river mouth, it continues to shoal. In extreme cases it may oversteepen and break, picking up speed and moving up the river as a wall of surf called a tidal bore. Bores have been reported

---

How the oceans are pulled out of shape

THE MOON'S gravitational pull reduces the weight of anything on the part of the Earth's surface facing it by a mere 0.0000001 per cent, or 1 gram in 10 tonnes. The Sun, because it is so far away, exerts only about half that

pull. But each of these gravitational forces causes the oceans to bulge slightly towards it. The Earth's rotation produces a balancing force and on the opposite side of the planet the oceans bulge away from the direction of

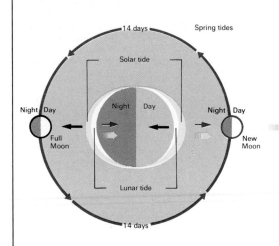

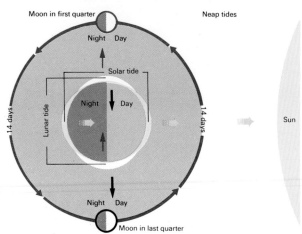

Tides are formed as ocean waters bulge towards the gravitational pulls of the Sun and the Moon. The Earth's rotation causes a balancing bulge on the opposite side. When Moon and Sun are in line their pulls combine to produce the greatest tidal bulge and spring tides result. The lowest tides, neap tides, occur when Moon and Sun are at right angles to each other

Two tides a day
Two different tides a day
One or two tides a day
One tide a day

There is wide variation in the type of tide around Australia. Little of the coast receives two equal tides daily. The part of the south-west that has only one tide a day is also a region of low tide range

Why tides bend

ANYTHING moving on the Earth or in its atmosphere, except along the Equator, is subject to a constant force, called Coriolus deflection, which pulls the moving body off a straight path. Caused by the earth's spinning, the pull is always to the left in the Southern Hemisphere and to the right in the Northern Hemisphere.

Friction is usually too great for the deflection to have any effect on movement over land. But if there is little or no friction, as with air and water movements, the moving body goes on a curving course. Free of any interference, it will travel in circles. If there were no coast, tides would swing in the direction of Coriolus deflection, as do all winds, except cyclones. Southern Hemisphere tides, continually bent leftward, would circulate anticlockwise, like bath water spiralling toward a plug hole. But interference by the coast is great. The tide rebounds from a shore and the leftward deflection sends it farther along the same coast, so that its progress is to the right of its original direction—clockwise in the Southern Hemisphere.

more than 80 km upstream in the Victoria River, 300 km south of Darwin.

Shoaling over a broad continental shelf causes a tide to rise quickly but ebb more slowly. It also increases the difference between high and low water levels. This tidal range is generally greatest on a broad continental shelf or in a wide-mouthed bay or gulf where the inner shores confine the rising tide and amplify it. In a wide bay with a narrow entrance, such as Port Phillip Bay in Victoria, the tidal range is reduced because the flow in and out is restricted.

Only one high tide a day reaches the shore on the Western Australian coast from Geraldton south, and in corners of the Gulf of Carpentaria. Many other parts of coastal Australia, including the stretch between Melbourne and Adelaide, receive a mixture of daily and twice-daily tides.

The times and levels of tides are predicted in the national tide tables, which are drawn up by the Royal Australian Navy's hydrographic office. They predict low and high water for each day of the year at 66 primary ports.

The tables also list variations for 352 secondary ports which have tidal characteristics related to a primary port. There are additional data from which to calculate levels at times between high and low water, and information on tidal currents.

The tide at any particular time and place may, however, be markedly different from the prediction in the tables. The calculations cannot allow for short-term local weather forces such as wind or atmospheric pressure.

---

the gravitational force. The oceans bulge most when the Sun, Moon and Earth are in line, at new Moon and full Moon. Then the gravitational effects of Sun and Moon are combined in the same direction. Soon afterwards, coasts receive spring tides—so called not because of the time of year but because of the way they jump up. The range between low and high water levels is up to 20 per cent greater than average.

When the Moon and Sun are at right-angles in relation to the Earth, at the first and third quarters of the Moon, each counteracts the other's effect. Ocean bulging is spread around the globe instead of being concentrated on two sides. The tides that result have a range of about 20 per cent less than average. They are called neap tides, from an Old English word which probably meant 'weak'.

The Moon exerts its strongest pull at any point every 24 hours 50.5 minutes, and its tidal effects on the open ocean occur twice in this period—when the point is nearest the Moon, and when the two are on opposite sides of the Earth.

Meanwhile, the Sun exerts its pull every 24 hours at any point, and its tidal effects at sea occur every 12 hours. Therefore after the Moon's and Sun's effects have

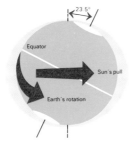

Tidal bulges of southern winter

The height of successive tides varies as the year progresses, because tidal bulges caused by the Sun's pull and the Earth's rotation change position on the Earth's surface. Like the seasons, the bulges move north and south, because the Earth's axis is tilted at 23.5° to its plane of orbit

coincided, at new and full Moon, there is a delay between solar and lunar influences, increasing by 25.25 minutes each time they occur.

The gap widens for seven days, with tides becoming correspondingly weaker, then starts to close again because the Moon's twice-daily effects catch up with those of the Sun. Tide heights go through a 14-day cycle of increase and decrease, twice every lunar month.

Heights of tides are further varied day by day because

the Moon's plane of orbit is tilted in relation to the Earth's axis of rotation, and because the Earth's axis is tilted in relation to the plane of its orbit around the Sun. A point on the Earth's surface passes through slightly different parts of the lunar and solar bulges in the oceans each time the Earth revolves. The Sun's maximum influence occurs when it is overhead at the Equator, so the highest tides of all come at the equinoxes, in late March and September.

Other slight variations in tide height occur because the Moon's orbit wavers, and because both it and the Earth's orbit are not circular but elliptical. The Moon repeats exactly the same orbit only every 18.6 years, although it swings in from farthest to its nearest point—a difference of 24 000 km—and out again every 27.55 days. The Sun is closest, exerting its greatest pull, in early January. Early in July it is about 5.5 million km farther away.

Friction is generated between the tides and the ocean beds and it is slowing the Earth's rotation by about a second every 120 000 years. Before land masses and oceans formed, the world probably rotated quickly so that days may have been less than 10 hours long and there may have been 1000 to the year.

Waves and their patterns
How the ocean carries wind energy to the coast

Ocean waves, arriving in never-ending procession, suggest to the eye that the sea is travelling with them. It seldom is. Apart from the slow movement of currents, the water beyond a coastal shelf virtually stays in the same place, rotating under the waves and rising and falling with them.

Some wave energy comes from tidal movement, and occasionally from disturbances such as coastal landslides or undersea earthquakes. But nearly all waves seen around the coast have been generated by winds transferring energy to the water surface.

The highest waves normally seen approaching a coast are driven by local storms. Sailors and weather forecasters call them 'seas'. Beneath them there is a smoother, more regular 'swell', born of faraway, long-ago gales. Their energy may have crossed an entire ocean.

Because winds seldom maintain exactly the same direction and strength for more than a few seconds, the waves they generate are confused and choppy at first. They have sharp individual peaks, and the intervals between successive peaks vary. Once waves move away from the influence of the wind, however, they settle into the regular patterns of ocean swell. They fan out about 35° on each side of the direction of the wind and take curving courses across the sea.

Eventually they form groups of long, low waves travelling at matching speeds. The group's width is that of the storm front generating the waves, and its length is determined by the location and duration of the storm.

Wave groups tend to generate long period waves. At the coast this long wave is often reflected seawards, and waves are higher or lower in relation to the shoreline depending on whether they arrive on the crest or in the trough of the long wave. Waves at the crest of groups are larger than those between groups, and the length of the group determines the number of waves between crests. The myth of the 7th or 9th wave being larger arises from local observation and may be correct for many days of the year—but it is only relevant to fully developed seas; developing seas are almost random.

Each wave in a swell pattern is evenly shaped. Smoothly curved crests are centred between troughs, with each crest as high above normal sea level as the following trough is below it. Water particles rotate under each wind-generated wave to a depth equal to about half the distance between successive crests. As the water shallows, the waves slow and bunch up. They steepen at the front and their crests mount to a peak.

Whether a wave breaks or not depends on its steepness in relation to the shore slope. Ocean swell waves and wind-driven local seas generally break if the slope is no steeper than 1:10. A gradual run-in gives them the distance needed to increase their height and angle of tilt. Where the sea meets a smooth cliff face, unstable local

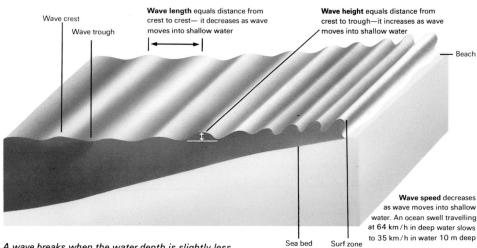

A wave breaks when the water depth is slightly less than its height. When waves enter shallow water successive crests catch up with one another, they slow down and grow taller until eventually they become unstable, topple over, and break

storm waves explode against it in showers of spray, but swell waves do not—unless they have already shoaled on a shelf at the cliff base.

The most consistent and easily observable result of wave action is beach drift. Waves rarely come in at right-angles to the shoreline: usually they carry sand, shingle and other debris obliquely up a beach. But when the water runs back, it takes the shortest way down. So successive waves shunt sand along in a series of zigzags.

More debris is drawn along, below the waterline, in a current set up by the thrust of the angled waves after they break. The combined effect is a gradual, massive shift of sediment. If, over the years, waves arrive predominantly from the

same direction, sand accumulates at one end of the beach, and may form a spit jutting out into the sea, or a tombolo linking the mainland shore with a nearby island.

Waves generally break when their height is slightly less than the depth of water under them, and isolated early breakers indicate a submerged reef. A line of breakers curving in towards both ends of a beach shows that the sea bed is raised in the middle; if the breaker line fans the other way, there is shallower water at the ends. Interrupted lines indicate variations in depth.

In general, the greater the distance over which waves are affected by a shallowing sea bed, the more they slow and bunch up and the higher they

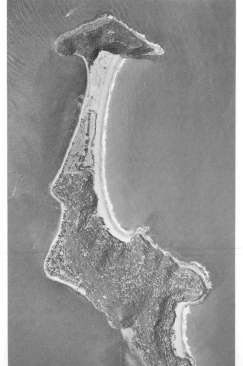

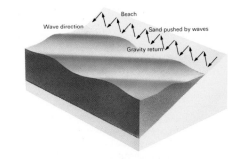

Incoming waves sweep water and sand up a beach at an oblique angle. Gravity pulls the same material down to the waterline again. In this fashion waves transport sand along beaches. This movement may be reversed when waves come from another direction, but over many years waves arriving from one principal direction can shift millions of tonnes of sand along an entire coast

Constant movement of sand in one direction can form a barrier that turns an inlet into a lagoon, or build a tombolo like that at Sydney's Palm Beach

How waves are bent

A WAVE slows only where the water particles rotating under it encounter friction with the sea floor. Elsewhere along the wave, in deeper water, its forward momentum is unchanged. So the wave bends around the point of interference—it is refracted. By the time all parts of a wave have reached shoaling depth, it may have been shaped into a curve almost matching that of the shoreline.

If a wave has no time to adapt fully and comes in at an angle, and if the beach is steep, it may rebound without breaking. Then it will be refracted further on its way out. It may even loop back, and in this fashion progress along the shore.

The refraction of waves around headlands into bays has a particularly noticeable effect on beaches. The bunching of waves just inside a headland concentrates their energy there. The surf is not high but the volume of water is. Farther up the bay, the waves are stretched—their energy and water volume are dispersed. The inequality creates a strong longshore flow, keeping sand out of the corner of the bay and depositing it in increasing amounts towards the other end.

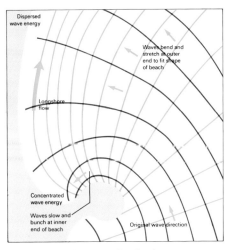

Above: A simplified headland refraction pattern, with red lines showing how wave energy is diverted to generate a longshore flow of water and sand. Left: Intricate refractions around a headland and islands at Batehaven, NSW

---

rise. Once this starts, all waves travel at the same speed over the same depth of water—regardless of their earlier velocity.

The tallest waves ordinarily seen on a coast, driven by gales in the immediate area, may break from heights of 20 metres or more. They may arrive twice as frequently as ocean swell waves, and be immensely destructive. But they travel no faster. And the harder a wind blows, the higher they mount. A wind averaging 37 km/h, blowing in a consistent direction for 10 hours, could be expected to produce waves about 2.44 metres high.

Even in violent and far-reaching gales, waves rarely exceed 25 metres on the deep ocean. If they are pushed to a height of more than one-seventh of their length, their surface tension is destroyed and they disintegrate in spray. There are exceptions, and the tallest ocean wave for which there is good evidence was observed from a US Navy tanker in the North Pacific in 1933, during a 125 km/h gale. It was judged to be 34 metres from trough to crest.

The length of a wave moving in a group does not have to be measured: it can be calculated from the time between the passage of one wave and the next. If a wave is followed 10 seconds later by another, it is about 157 metres long.

In ocean swell waves, the time interval can also be used to calculate velocity. So waves 10 seconds apart are travelling at about 16 metres per second, or 57 km/h. Wind-driven waves may hold together at more than 80 km/h, but do not normally exceed 60 km/h.

When any wave is crossing water of a depth less than half of the wave length, its speed is governed by water depth alone: a depth of 3 metres permits a speed of 20 km/h, but at six times the depth—18 metres—a wave cannot travel much more than twice as fast.

Mysterious patterns on the beach

No complete explanation for beach cusps has yet been found. They are probably the result of complex wave motions caused by the interaction of reflected and incoming waves. Cusp formations on surf beaches—such as these at Pearl Beach on the New South Wales central coast—are also often associated with the presence of rip currents. The effect is a scalloped waterline, with a series of crescent-shaped depressions regularly spaced along the beach face. The scooped-out areas may be only a few metres wide; or could reach for hundreds of metres.

Shock waves that cross the ocean

VIOLENT disturbances of ocean water occur with earthquakes and volcanic eruptions in or around an ocean basin. After such an event, waves hundreds of kilometres long and up to half an hour apart race from the shock zone at speeds approaching 800 km/h. Quite commonly but, in fact, wrongly called 'tidal waves', they are known to scientists as tsunami. The name comes from the Japanese words *tsu*, meaning port, and *nami*, meaning waves.

In mid-ocean, tsunami may be only a few centimetres high, and they are often so low away from the coast that their passing may not be noticed. But even over the deepest ocean they still slow and steepen—like all waves in shallowing water. They have time to build to terrifying heights—sometimes more than 30 metres—before running ashore for minutes on end with catastrophic effects. The highest recorded tsunami, which occurred off Alaska in 1964, measured 67 metres.

The coasts most menaced by tsunami are those facing and lying parallel to an earthquake fault line. The only area of Australia threatened this way is the east coast, which is aligned with major faults under the central South Pacific and on its eastern rim. But tsunami effects are largely buffered by the land mass of New Zealand and by the Great Barrier Reef.

Nearshore currents Powerful local water movements

No two parts of the coast are exactly the same. In places that look alike at first glance, shoreline features differ subtly—and swimming or boating conditions can vary drastically. In the interplay of waves and tides with the land and the sea bottom, each area has its own complex patterns.

The simplest local movement of water—and the one that most frequently surprises inexperienced swimmers—is the longshore current. This is the force that makes it difficult for a surf bather to stay between safety flags. It runs along any shore where waves break at an angle—and waves rarely come in exactly parallel to the beach.

When angled waves break they thrust water not only in a swash up the beach, but also in a persistent flow parallel to the shore. The current is spread right across the surf zone, but it is strongest about halfway between the breaker line and the beach. Its speed, which is related to the height and steepness of waves, may be as much as 1 metre a second. Longshore currents are not hazardous, however, unless they carry a swimmer into a deep channel or a rip.

Variations in the slope of the sea bed or the shape of a shore may cause unevenness in the height of a line of waves along a beach. When they break, the water level inside the surf zone is also uneven. That results in longshore currents of a different type: they run from high levels to low, and then they turn seawards to become feeders for rip currents.

Rips are strong, narrow currents running out through the surf zone to beyond the breakers. They flow at speeds up to 4 metres a second—a boon to board surfers seeking a free ride out, but a hazard for swimmers. People caught in rips exhaust themselves if they try to swim back to the shore against such a current. Confident swimmers are better off striking out sideways: rips are seldom more than 15 metres wide.

Weaker swimmers should conserve their energy and let a rip carry them out past the breakers. There, when the current slackens, it is easy to move to one side and make for a different point on the beach. Never rest for long on a sand bar—if the wave pattern changes even slightly the bar can collapse, with disastrous results.

Rip locations are not constant, however. They may come and go, or shift position, with changes in the direction of wave approach. And they do not always run straight out to sea: if the waves break at a considerable angle to the beach, rips are angled away in the opposite direction.

Tide movements are seldom of much significance in comparison with wave-induced currents near a mainland shore. In shallow estuaries and around islands and headlands, however, the effects of tidal currents are more pronounced, and sometimes startling.

Speeds of tidal currents fluctuate with the rise and fall of the tide, and there are usually two

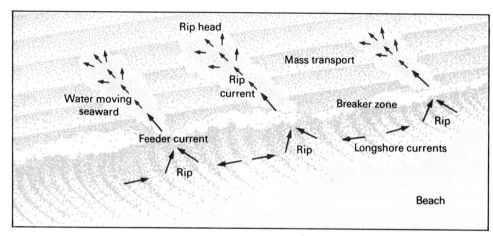

Rips are formed as the mass of water pushed up to a beach by breaking waves finds its path back to the sea in narrow, fast-flowing currents. Water runs down the beach, and sideways along the beach face, creating longshore currents which feed rips as they travel seaward through the surf zone, and between channels in any sand bars. The current dissipates beyond the breakers at the rip head

Twin, parallel rips push water seaward from Dee Why beach, north of Sydney. The two channels of deep, fast-moving water interrupt the lines of incoming waves. Plumes of sand, carried from the beach by the currents, spread out into the calm water beyond the breaker zone. Rips like these are usually less than 15 metres wide, and may be moving as fast as 4 metres per second

Channelled tidal races, such as this one at Walcott Inlet in the Kimberleys, WA, can reach 28 km/h

The empty threat of 'undertow'

STANDING in the shallows, you feel the seaward backwash of broken waves tugging at your feet. Just ahead of a sharply steepening wave, you may feel water being drawn backwards into it. And if a breaker dumps you, its churning motion pulls you down and away from the shore for a moment. But it is not undertow. No subsurface motion exists that can take people out to sea against the advance of waves on a beach. If the word undertow is used to describe a real danger, it is usually a mistaken reference to a localised rip, or to the existence of a channel with a strong ebb-tide current.

maximum and two minimum rates during each cycle. The currents reverse themselves so quickly that there is scarcely a moment when they are not running. In deep water their top speed is seldom more than about 1 km/h. Even in shallow water, as long as it is not confined, a tidal current rarely exceeds 7 km/h. But where tides are channelled, the currents can easily achieve twice that speed.

In areas of extreme tide range, such as north-western Australia, a channelled tidal race may reach 28 km/h. In the rocky estuaries of the Kimberleys district of Western Australia, water velocities on that scale produce tidal bores—steep-fronted, breaking waves that run far upriver. Dangerous bores, to be avoided by small boats, are usually noted in the official sailing directions for more frequented areas.

Fast tidal races also produce dangerous eddies and whirlpools. Vigorous eddies are encountered in Cambridge Gulf, the approach to the port of Wyndham, WA. There the tidal current reaches 17 km/h. Even in areas where the tide range is much less—in Sydney Harbour, for example—eddies frequently make boating tricky.

One area where tidal currents can be particularly surprising is around islands ringed by barrier reefs. However slowly the currents move in deep water at the edge of a reef, they may run over its shallow coral terraces at speeds as high as 7 km/h. When they are at their maximum speed, alternating eddies form and break away at the downstream margin of the reef.

Barrier reefs normally lie near mean sea level—the mid-tide height—and are uncovered at low tide. Often during high tide they are covered by less than 1 metre of water. For a major part of the tidal cycle, breakers carry water across the reef and keep the lagoon level above the sea level outside. So there may be a continuous flow of water out through channels in the reef, even when the tide is coming in.

Where a coral barrier is always above the water level, forming an atoll, there is no water inflow from breakers. Then the lagoon behaves like any bay with a restricted entrance: if the passage of a large lagoon is narrow, powerful tidal currents will flow through it.

Bars rebuild a beach

AFTER storm waves have left a beach, nearshore water circulation starts returning lost sand. Complex oscillations formed by rip currents and surface currents caused directly by winds blowing over the water, deposit sand in a series of half-loops, called crescentic bars, which are fully formed in about two days. They may remain static for weeks, but gradually they link up with beach cusps and the troughs between fill with sand. Eventually the bars are cut by channels. They decay, and all the sand is pushed on to the beach.

Crescentic bars about to decay and deposit their sand on to the beach at Redhead, near Newcastle, NSW

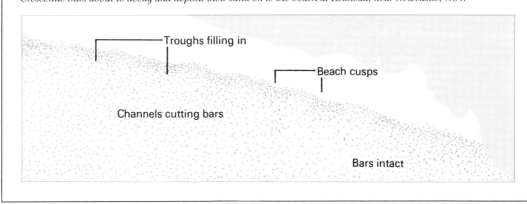

Troughs filling in

Beach cusps

Channels cutting bars

Bars intact

Middle Head

Harbour entrance

Georges Head

Bradleys Head

Sydney Cove

Wherever an estuary, bay or lagoon has its access to the open sea restricted by a narrow entrance channel, strong tidal currents can occur as the level within attempts to adjust to the level outside. This is most noticeable in the rocky estuaries of north-western Australia under extreme tidal ranges. But even in areas such as Sydney Harbour, where the tide range is much less, strong eddies can form, although they are much less dangerous. In this chart of the tidal pattern in Sydney Harbour at maximum ebb tide, eddies can be seen forming around Bradleys Head and Georges Head

Wind and weather patterns

The interaction of ocean and atmosphere

All weather stems from differences in air temperature and pressure. The earth's surface forms the bottom of an ocean of air, extending about 160 km above it. Although the gas molecules of the atmosphere are light, collectively they exert enormous pressure on the earth—about 10 tonnes per square metre at sea level. People are unaware of it because the pressure is not merely downwards: it is equal in all directions.

Air heated from the sun's radiation on the earth's surface expands and rises, carrying evaporated moisture if it is over an ocean. Expansion reduces its pressure, and this loss of pressure—not the height to which the air rises—causes it to cool and contract. Moisture condenses in clouds of water droplets. As contraction goes on the air sinks, and its increasing pressure raises its temperature again.

The sun's radiation promotes permanent convection systems which carry air from equatorial to subtropical regions at high level, and back to the equator at low level. This creates belts of sinking, high pressure air in both hemispheres, centred about latitude 30° but shifting with the seasonal track of the sun, and constant north-east or south-east 'trade' winds. There are further convection systems between the subtropical belt and the polar regions, causing strong airstreams from the west above latitude 40°.

Locally, however, the sun's effect is intermittent, especially over land. So the result is patchy: neighbouring bodies of air behave in contrasting ways. Sinking air creating a warm, calm, pressurised 'high' may be followed in a day or two by a cold, stormy, depressed 'low' of rising air. Moving pressure systems maintain their contrasts for days because of the time air takes to rise—to 15 000 metres above sea level—and sink again.

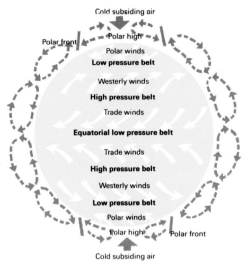

Surface winds and vertical convection systems create the basic pattern of global air movements

Prevailing winds are evidence of the movement of air of different origin, temperature and moisture in vast, consistent patterns. They play a big part in determining the basic climate of a coast. But its day-to-day weather is more noticeably affected by incidental, ever-changing winds created by a local unevenness of air pressure.

The air seeks to equalise pressure by flowing from a high to a low, but it cannot do so directly. The earth's rotation bends the airstream into an almost circular curve. Winds spiral gently out from a high until they are close to a low. Then they spiral in towards it much more rapidly.

At the same time, both the high and the low are moving. The distance between them may be changing, and each of them may also be changing in shape and intensity. So the direction and force of the winds they produce are highly variable in any one place. They can be forecast only by trying to predict exactly where the pressure systems will go and how they may by modified.

Winds around highs and lows spiral in opposite directions. In the Southern Hemisphere their motions are counter-clockwise around a high and clockwise around a low. High-pressure wind circulations are called anticyclones, and all low-pressure systems are technically cyclones. But those originating outside the tropics are normally termed depressions.

Subtropical anticyclones, separated by troughs of low pressure, move fairly regularly across Australia in a generally eastward direction. They are particularly well defined because they have formed from air sinking on to the flat surface of the Indian Ocean, and few mountains disturb them as they pass over the continent.

The anticyclone belt, shifting seasonally, is centred in late winter from around Geraldton, WA, to Cape Byron, NSW, and in late summer across northern Tasmania. On average, five individual highs occur every month, and each takes about five days to cross the continent. But at any particular time, a high may be almost stationary, or it may be travelling at more than 2000 km a day. The movement of one body of air is largely governed by the position of others.

Between highs and troughs there are frequently sharply defined boundaries—'cold

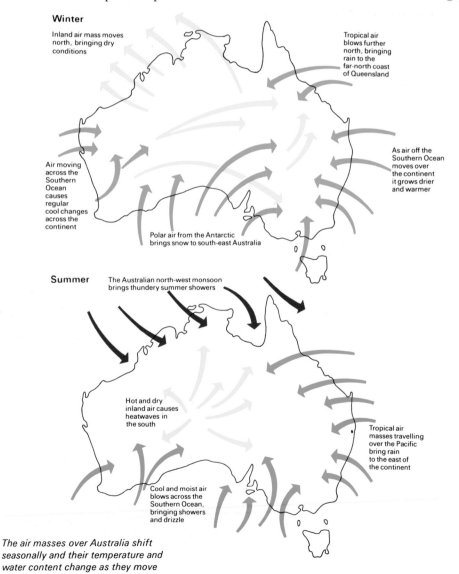

Winter

Inland air mass moves north, bringing dry conditions

Tropical air blows further north, bringing rain to the far-north coast of Queensland

Air moving across the Southern Ocean causes regular cool changes across the continent

As air off the Southern Ocean moves over the continent it grows drier and warmer

Polar air from the Antarctic brings snow to south-east Australia

Summer

The Australian north-west monsoon brings thundery summer showers

Hot and dry inland air causes heatwaves in the south

Tropical air masses travelling over the Pacific bring rain to the east of the continent

Cool and moist air blows across the Southern Ocean, bringing showers and drizzle

The air masses over Australia shift seasonally and their temperature and water content change as they move

fronts' marked in coastal regions by towering clouds, squalls, heavy rain and sometimes thunderstorms. Otherwise the weather in the anti-cyclone belt is dry and clear. Winds are light, and variable in direction.

South of the subtropical highs, and shifting seasonally in the same way, is an east-moving low-pressure system. Its major depressions are centred well towards Antarctica, but secondary lows and troughs bring disturbed winter weather to the south-western corner of Western Australia, to Victoria and Tasmania, and to New South Wales as far as its mid-north coast. Winter winds in these regions are mainly from the west, varying day by day from breezes to gales, and swinging from mild, drizzling north-westerlies to cold, showery south-westerlies.

North of the anticyclone belt, coastal regions are dominated except in summer by the strong, persistent flow of south-east 'trade' winds from the Pacific. Warm and moist when they cross the east coast, they are hot and parched by the time they reach the north-west. In Darwin they may blow at 50 km/h, and the accompanying dust haze may cut visibility to less than 2.5 km.

A third pressure belt rules summer conditions in northern Australia. The intertropical front—a 'weather equator' of rising air where the wind systems of the two hemispheres converge—starts to move south in October, carrying with it a string of highly unstable lows. The Asian northeast monsoon becomes the Australian northwest monsoon. From November to April, thundery showers saturate the far north. Winds are squally but light, except for stiff afternoon sea breezes—or unless a tropical cyclone develops.

Victoria and New South Wales, south of Port Macquarie, have Australia's most frequently changing coastal weather. Except in summer they lie just in the zone of disturbed westerlies, cold anticyclones and southern depressions. In summer a similar changeability comes from the troughs which separate warm anticyclones. Summer patterns may also be varied by the distant effects of tropical cyclones, bringing heavy rain and high seas.

Of all the coastal cities, Sydney is the most prone to sudden bouts of bad weather in summer. These spells come most commonly with south-easterlies after a cold front. Within about three hours, broken low cloud scuds in to the coast and showery squalls follow. Less commonly, a 'black nor-easter' with similar low cloud pattern may develop ahead of a trough.

A view from 1450 km above the South Pole shows the summer cloud patterns

Simple ways to measure the wind

SAILING ship crews judged surface wind force from the sea's appearance. In the Royal Navy, various observations were graded on the Beaufort scale—named after an admiral—as a quick indicator of how much sail a man-o'-war could safely carry. Early aviators revised and extended the scale to include land-based observations.

Signs at sea	Signs on land	Description	Beaufort number	Speed (km/h)
Surface like a mirror	Smoke rises vertically	Calm	0	0-1
Ripples look like scales	Smoke drifts	Light air	1	1-5
Wavelet crests look glassy and do not break	Leaves rustle, wind vanes move	Light breeze	2	6-10
Large but short wavelets; crests starting to break	Leaves and twigs move constantly, flags stand out	Gentle breeze	3	11-20
Small waves lengthening; some foam crests	Dust and loose paper are raised	Moderate breeze	4	21-30
Moderate waves obviously longer; many foam crests	Small trees sway	Fresh breeze	5	31-40
Large waves start to form; perhaps some spray	Power lines whistle	Strong breeze	6	41-50
Sea heaps up; foam starts to blow	Big trees sway	Moderate gale	7	51-60
Spindrift foam blown in well-defined streaks	Twigs break off; walking impeded	Fresh gale	8	61-75
Dense streaks of foam; sea starts to roll	Slight structural damage—roof tiles, etc.	Strong gale	9	76-87
Waves with long, overhanging crests; foam in sheets; heavy rolling	Trees uprooted	Whole gale	10	88-100
Waves high enough to hide medium-sized ships; all crests blown into froth; sea covered with foam patches	Widespread damage	Storm	11	101-120
Air filled with foam and spray, seriously impairing visibility; sea completely white	Severe damage—weaker structures demolished	Hurricane	12	over 120

Old sayings that foretell bad weather

BEFORE weather watchers could exchange information quickly and meteorology was developed as a science, farmers and fishing folk passed weather lore to new generations in little rhymes or sayings. Many have a scientific basis and apply in southern Australia—especially those which indicate rain:

'A red sun has water in his eye'

The probable cause of redness, apart from bushfire smoke, is water droplets screening out other light waves. Moist air is condensing, clouds will form and rain may follow.

'Red sky at night, Sailor's delight; Red sky in the morning, Sailor's warning'

At sunset, light reflecting from high clouds indicates that the western horizon—over which most weather approaches—is clear. The same occurrence at sunrise means the eastern horizon is clear but clouds are building up on the weather side.

'Take shelter when the sun (or moon) is in his (her) house'

The 'house' is the halo sometimes seen around the sun or moon. Invisible, high-altitude cirrostratus cloud is forming. Heavier cloud will build downwards and rain may follow.

'When the stars begin to huddle, The earth will soon become a puddle'

If cirrostratus cloud starts to form at night, it may blot out stars of lesser magnitude and blur the light from major ones. So familiar groups seem to move into clusters.

'Rainbow at morning, Shepherd's warning; Rainbow at night, Shepherd's delight'

Rainbows, the result of sunlight striking water droplets, are visible to people with the sun at their backs. So a rainbow in the morning means moisture in the west—the usual weather quarter. An evening rainbow is in the eastern sky and probably means the rain is going away.

'Sunshine and showers, Rain again tomorrow'

When rain is interspersed with sunny periods, especially near the coast, the moist airstream is unstable and cumulus clouds are being built up by surface heating. Such conditions often last for more than a day.

Thunderstorms, with high-piling cumulonimbus clouds, are the most common—and most consistently damaging—weather system over the Australian coastline

Storms and cyclones Threats to life, property and beaches

Coastal regions of Australia, so often the meeting ground of air masses of different moisture and temperature, are prone to some of the world's most violent weather. It can produce winds to rip apart houses, bolts of lightning that spark raging bushfires, hail to devastate crops, and rain torrents and floods that wash away buildings, livestock and roads. And it whips the ocean into storm surges and waves of enormous force, hastening the erosion of coasts and sometimes destroying beaches completely (*see* Beach Erosion, overleaf).

In terms of loss of life and property damage, the tropical cyclone is the most dangerous weather system on earth. But on average only five or six each summer have any marked effect on the Australian coast. Tornadoes rarely strike populated regions, and never attain the wind speeds that make them so terrifying in the United States. Gales and flooding from intense southern depressions affect only a limited area. In total

impact—high frequency, wide occurrence and damaging effect—Australia's worst weather system is the thunderstorm.

Thunderstorms begin as small clumps of fleecy cumulus cloud. Cumulus normally blows away or evaporates readily, but if there is a tall mass of unstable cold air above the warm, moist air that is forming the cumulus, and if something pushes from below—a mountain slope acting as a wedge, or a dense cold front moving in—a vigorous updraught starts. Cumulonimbus clouds pile higher, their moisture cooling and condensing beyond the point at which rain would normally be produced. Ice crystals form instead.

At the storm's mature stage, so much ice and water collect that the updraught can no longer support their weight. They sink, and forceful downdraughts start. These can produce surface winds of 110 km/h and more, with phenomenal rain and sometimes hail. Cold low-level air spreads for kilometres ahead of the storm.

Air turbulence and the freezing process break up water particles and regroup them so that some parts of the cloud system have a positive electrical charge and some are negative. Early in the storm's life, huge sparks flash from positive to negative zones. Their reflections are seen as 'sheet' lightning. When the storm is mature, directly visible 'fork' lightning flashes between the cloud and the gound. The electrical charge may be as much as 30 million volts. It heats the air along its path to about 10 000°C, causing instant expansion and pressure waves that are heard as thunder. The sound travels at about 0.3 km a second, and can sometimes be heard more than 40 km away.

In the storm's dying stages, rain gradually eases and the remaining ice crystals are blown out by high-level winds into a cloud of flat-topped, anvil shape. The usual duration of one system is about half an hour, but it may start a chain of storms lasting for hours.

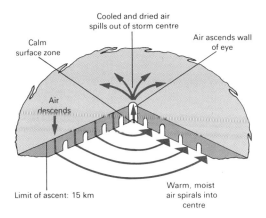

Starting over warm water, the great majority of cyclones stay at sea until they weaken over cold water. The 'eye' of a tropical cyclone is a column of rising air, surrounded by a fast-spinning wall of cloud and bands of other cloud spiralling towards it

(Diagram labels: Cooled and dried air spills out of storm centre; Air ascends wall of eye; Calm surface zone; Air descends; Limit of ascent: 15 km; Warm, moist air spirals into centre)

Destructive tropical cyclones—also called hurricanes or typhoons in some parts of the world—start when existing depressions move over unusually warm patches of water. The normal process of rising air and falling pressure is intensified, and the heat of evaporated moisture is converted into wind energy that pulls the surrounding air into a tight, fast spiral.

A tropical cyclone's violence comes not from freakishly low pressure—some ordinary depressions are just as low—but from its compactness. Variation from highest to lowest pressure may be crammed into a diameter of less than 150 km in the early stages, resulting in winds so strong that they smash measuring instruments: their speed must be assumed from the impact of flying debris. Cyclone Althea recorded gusts of 194 km/h at Townsville in 1971.

Dangerous cyclone development requires open sea with a surface temperature of at least 27°C, high humidity, unstable air, and rotational wind deflection caused by the earth's movement. Only in two belts, between about 5° and 20° each side of the equator, do all those conditions coincide. Near Australia, the likeliest areas are to the north-east and north-west. Some cyclones originate to the north, in the Timor and Arafura Seas, and a few in the Gulf of Carpentaria, but they rarely occur before December or after March in any of these areas, and the great majority remain at sea until their force weakens over bodies of cold water.

Tropical cyclones never form over land even when conditions are very unstable. Surface friction slows the very low level air flows and too little water vapour is available to create a sufficiently high humidity. Water vapour is essential because cyclones derive much of their energy from the heat given off as the vapour condenses.

As a tropical cyclone develops, a spiralling mass of dense cloud forms, reaching from about 300 metres above sea level to 15 000 metres. The cloud base may descend to the sea with the rain torrent that soon sheets down, driven by violent winds. Lightning is frequent at first.

In a fully developed system there is an 'eye' of light winds or complete calm, more or less in the middle. It is a rainless area of fairly clear skies, averaging about 35 km in diameter in Australian waters, caused by condensed air sinking from the top of the cloud column. By this time the whole system is moving across the ocean, usually at less than 30 km/h.

The changing courses of tropical cyclones are determined by the locations of other pressure systems, which are themselves moving. A cyclone travels towards its side of steepest pressure gradient—where the rise to normal pressure occurs in the shortest distance. The general direction is easily seen on a weather map from the crowding of isobars, or lines of pressure.

When a cyclone moves outside the warm waters of the tropics, its width increases and its winds slacken. If it moves over land—even if still in the tropics—it is also quickly stretched and weakened. Its force is usually spent on the coastal region. There the destruction may be massive—because of the effect on the sea.

Storm surges of 5 metres above normal tide level, topped by waves 7 metres tall, are commonly reported. How disastrous such a surge may be depends on whether it coincides with high tide. The biggest surge reported in Australia, at Barrow Point, N. Qld, in 1899, was said to have swamped a policeman on a ridge more than 13 metres above normal sea level.

A tornado is most likely to form at the base of a high cumulonimbus thunderstorm system. Its fierce rotation results from a twisting of the updraught that feeds such a storm. A narrow funnel, widening towards the cloud, creates a small zone of such low pressure that movable objects—including people—can be sucked up in the spiralling column of air.

Tornadoes are so localised and destructive that central pressures and wind speeds cannot be measured. Pressure may fall below 800 millibars—compared with an average of 980 in tropical cyclones and 1013 in normal air. Their track of destruction may be only a few metres wide, and they usually occur in sparsely populated inland areas. Seen out to sea, they are often called waterspouts.

Willy-willies are small, short-lived eddies that can spin sand, dust and light debris up to about 2 metres from the ground. They are mini-cyclones created when air already of low pressure passes over a particularly hot patch of ground. Some people call them 'dust devils'.

Tornadoes can occur on coasts and inland

Beach erosion

When shifting sands are not replaced

Sand movement is as natural as the weather. Beaches are fluid zones that respond to wave and wind action, sometimes losing material and sometimes gaining it. Sediments added during calm weather are taken offshore in storms, to be replaced during the next quiet spell. In Australia this normal cycle of cut-and-fill is accompanied on the east and west coasts by an overall northward transport of sand. The majority of strong waves strike those coasts at a more or less southerly angle. Sand pulled from a beach is carried by longshore currents and most often returned to the shore at a point farther north. The loss is made good by other sand from the south—as long as the supply is adequate. If it is not, long-term erosion sets in and the shoreline recedes.

The past century has been a period of widespread erosion and coastal recession. Reports have come from areas representing virtually all the eastern coast south of the Great Barrier Reef, and from much of the west coast. Erosion arouses the greatest public concern in settled districts, when properties or holiday amenities are menaced. Aggravated storm damage and slower recovery are noted where human works and behaviour interfere with beach structure and vegetation. But shoreline recession is occurring widely in remote areas and in protected coastal reserves and national parks. Clearly, the supply of replacement beach materials from the south is not sufficient at present to compensate for the

A satellite view of the New South Wales central coast taken from a height of 920 km above the Earth. The photograph stretches from Newcastle Bight and Port Stephens in the south to Port Macquarie and the Hastings River in the north. The hook-shaped beaches, narrow at the southern end and broad at the north, are formed by waves that arrive consistently from the south

heavy and continuing northward loss of sand.

Urgent problems created by erosion are problems only because people, in committing capital resources to the seashore, have misunderstood the nature of beaches. They may recede—or advance—for centuries. The wave movements to which they respond are themselves subject to variations in world climate patterns. Predominant wave directions can change. So can the sea level, depending on how much water is held in glaciers and polar icecaps. The position and extent of a beach signify only the net effect of physical forces at one particular time—not something that people can indicate on a map or a property title and expect to stay put forever. The human sense of equilibrium may be static, but nature's is dynamic.

The sea off eastern Australia has been near its present level for only about 6000 years. During the most intensive phase of the last ice age, about 20 000 years ago, it was more than 100 metres lower. Rivers carved valleys across the land that was exposed. The return of the sea 'drowned' those extended river systems and made deep inlets where there had been shallow estuaries. For that reason, many rivers no longer carry material eroded from inland rock—a major contributor to beach supply—all the way to the coast. Instead they deposit rock debris and sediments in the upper parts of estuaries, where the water first deepens.

On many parts of the coast, from Gippsland in eastern Victoria to southern Queensland, there are dual barrier-beach formations. They consist of sand mostly of marine origin, including a sub-

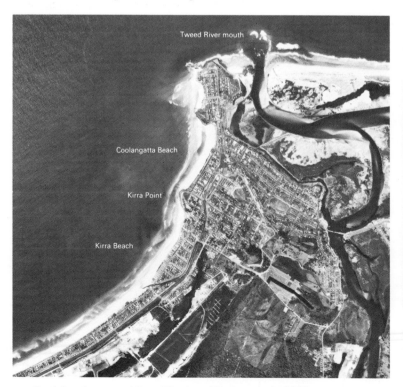

Sandy beaches around Tweed Heads and Coolangatta in 1962

Training walls impeding sand drift led to severe beach erosion by 1971

stantial input of material derived from the shells or skeletons of marine animals. Inner barriers were deposited about 125 000 years ago, when the sea was last near its present level. Modern barriers, established a little more than 6000 years ago, formed seaward of the ancient ones. Troughs of low-lying land were left in between. They became swamps and lagoons, typified by the Gippsland Lakes and the chains of waterways and wetlands on the NSW central coast. Such troughs act as traps for river-borne sediments that would otherwise have reached the coast. They also absorb wind-blown beach sand.

When the sea level was slightly lower than at present, Australia's eastern shores were probably one long barrier beach coast, with dunes stretching along the base of what are now the familiar cliff faces of central and southern New South Wales. As the sea level rose massive amounts of sand were lost when waves and tidal forces began to push barrier material into the deep inlets of newly drowned estuaries. The barrier system, with its easy northward flow of material, was broken at every such estuary—at Sydney's big sea inlets, for example. At the same time, rocky headlands began to interrupt the longshore drift pattern. More barrier material was pushed inshore between promontories, forming mainland beaches. Isolated longshore currents redistributed the material, scouring the southern ends of beaches and heaping sand to the north. Dunes and ramps of sand climbed cliff faces, spread over hilltops and spilled down the inland side. Sydney's eastern suburbs are founded on marine sand pushed up ramps that have long been stripped away.

Most of the conditions for large-scale beach depletion and shoreline recession are set by nature. There is nothing people can do about them. But the most active cause of further sand loss, contributed to by human activities, is the movement of destabilised dunes. Phases of dune migration seem to have been interspersed by periods of coastal stability for the past 4000 years. The changes were probably related to variations in the frequency of storms. If the cycle of storm-calm-storm cutting and filling is repeated too rapidly, plants may not have time to colonise regained sand and trap wind-blown sand at the back of the beach to rebuild foredunes. Without plant cover and foredune shelter, the inner dunes are mobile. Strong winds can drive them inland to swamp and kill any vegetation in their path. In that way formerly stable surfaces are also mobilised, and even more sand migrates. People destroying dune vegetation run the risk of triggering massive sand movements.

Man-made obstructions to normal longshore drift can cause dramatically sudden local erosion. A groyne built out from a beach, for example, traps sand on one side. But sand moving away from the other side cannot be replaced. The updrift beach, starved of materials, is progressively scoured by strong wave action. Such a situation has caused alarm on Queensland's lower Gold Coast since the 1960s. The region should not have much of a problem with erosion: its rivers supply plenty of sediments to the coast, and losses of sand into estuaries and inland-moving dunes are minor. But in 1964, to stabilise the Tweed River entrance for navigation, projecting training walls were built. The net quantity of sand supplied to beaches at Coolangatta and beyond decreased immediately. By 1967 they were unable to recover fully from storm effects. And the remedy, applied after severe storm damage in 1972, was worse than the ailment. A groyne built out to sea at Kirra Point trapped 300 000 cubic metres of sand on Coolangatta Beach within two years. But 500 000 cubic metres were lost from Kirra Beach, updrift of the groyne. The region's beaches, crucial to its tourist industry, are now maintained in their pre-1960s state by pumping enormous volumes of sand through a pipeline from the Tweed estuary, at heavy expense.

Dramatic changes to ocean beaches beside the mouth of the Tweed River, on the border between New South Wales and Queensland, demonstrate some of the problems caused by man-made alterations to the coast. In 1962 (far left) beaches to the north of the Tweed estuary had broad stretches of sand. In 1964 training walls were built at the mouth of the river to stabilise it for navigation. By 1971 (centre left) much of the sand had left Coolangatta Beach. A groyne built at Kirra Point in 1972, and another beside it (above), have solved Coolangatta's problem, but now the south end of Kirra Beach has all but disappeared

What can be done to save beaches

ANY approach to erosion that views the coastline as a fixed boundary is doomed to failure, or at best to be a never-ending drain on funds. But some steps can be taken to aid natural restoration fairly cheaply, and to reduce harmful human impact:

- Legal protection of foredune vegetation and the active encouragement of suitable plants on the upper parts of beaches, to reduce wind-blown sand losses.
- Measurement of a beach's sediment 'budget'—its income and outgoings of material—before positioning engineering works such as breakwaters and groynes.
- Zoning against future building in erosion-prone areas, to forestall community demands for costly and often fruitless protection measures.
- Educational emphasis on the dynamic nature of the shoreline, so that its changeability is respected and normal processes need no longer be regarded as disasters.

PART 3

Advice for holidaymakers

Seaside recreation is easy for most Australians. Ample beaches, coastal parks and inshore waters are seen not merely as holiday playgrounds but as enhancements of daily life. It is doubtful, however, whether many people take advantage of all their opportunities.

Leaving aside the limitations of expense and physical disability, there are benefits in exploring the fullest range of leisure activities. But the sea is an alien medium: it can be hostile, and so can its shores.

The drawbacks and dangers of inexperience cannot be lightly dismissed.

Information in the following pages is aimed at helping readers make more of the coast, without placing them in jeopardy.

It is presumed that they will also seek the best local advice before venturing into the unfamiliar.

They are urged to acquaint themselves fully with their rights of access and use, and to respect the rights of others.

And it is hoped that they will treat a fragile environment with all the care that a national treasure deserves.

Late afternoon sunlight turns the sea to the colour of liquid gold

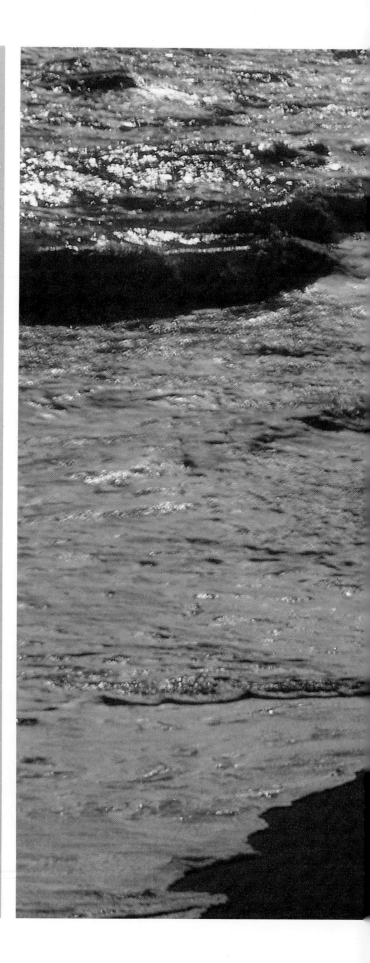

Who owns the coast? Answers to a complex question

The expanses of land around the Australian coast which have avoided the auctioneer's hammer and the developer's bulldozer remain unalienated public lands. They are necessary not only to preserve indigenous plants and animals, but also to provide valuable recreation space for an expanding human· population. Before governments were concerned with preserving the community's right of access to river banks, bay shores and ocean coasts, private ownership of waterfront property was not discouraged, and quite often only the narrow strip between low and high water marks remains public. Today, some coasts are not easily accessible because pasture lands back on to beachfronts, fences create barriers to public waterways, and industrial estates and port facilities create daunting obstructions.

Even the regulations governing public land form barriers of their own, with a maze of restrictions covering access, camping and caravanning, fire-lighting, vehicle entry and fishing. Consistent regulations face travellers all around the coast, but exceptions to the rule and temporary restrictions are frequent. When in doubt, always apply for information to regulating authorities, all of which have offices in the state capitals and branches in major towns. In some cases visitors may have to apply to a resident manager, ranger or forester for specific and seasonal restrictions.

Laws of trespass
It is generally not a crime simply to enter someone else's land whether it is privately owned or leased. The owner's only recourse is to sue for damages caused, though force in proportion to any danger or damage threatened may be used to eject a trespasser. Only if violence is threatened or appears to be threatened can injury to a trespasser be justified. Reasonable force may also be used to evict squatters, such as campers, who try to stay on a person's property without permission, and a caravan may be towed away if its owner refuses to leave. But no damage should be done to the trespasser's property. Laws relating to trespass on government installations such as port facilities, lighthouses, research stations and military reserves involve special offences and in some instances trespass on federal government property can incur a jail sentence of up to three months.

Crown land
Ocean beaches and the foreshores of tidal rivers and lakes are all part of Crown property. Like all unoccupied Crown land, they are generally accessible to the public, though entry may be restricted to paying users in places where commercial camping areas, boat ramps and other facilities have been established. Along popular city beaches, boating may be prohibited from nearshore waters during daylight hours to avoid danger to swimmers, but anglers are permitted inside the marker buoys after sunset. Beaching of boats is allowable in emergencies.

Where private property adjoins a tidal foreshore, public pedestrian access is preserved, although private ownership may extend to the high water mark. The point reached by water at a mean high tide can be accurately defined only by a surveyor, but can often be judged by the extent of land vegetation or marine growth on rocky foreshores.

Clubs or individuals may have permits or leases allowing jetties or club houses to be built over the foreshore for mooring and fishing. Permission to occupy this land must be obtained in the form of leases or licences which generally relate only to the structure itself. If public access to the foreshore is blocked, people have right of passage over the structure. In some regions, Port Phillip Bay for example, the public also has the right to embark and disembark from all private and public jetties. In many places there is a reserve 30 metres wide adjoining the mean high water mark. This may extend up to 150 metres or more inland and may be difficult to distinguish from the adjacent privately owned land. Where there is doubt about the status of foreshore land and the structures on it, a local government authority or lands department should be consulted.

Aboriginal lands
Most of the big sections of coast reserved for Aboriginal communities, or held freehold by them, are well out of populated areas. Some are only accessible by sea or air and there is little conflict with the routes taken by all but the best equipped and most adventurous travellers. Where the reserve lands are easy to get to, in areas of coastline attractive to tourists, they must be treated at all times as the property of their residents. The state offices of the Department of Aboriginal Affairs will direct people to the appropriate authority for the granting of entry permits, though few are issued for recreational purposes and the Aboriginal communities themselves review all applications. Transit permits are normally freely available and expeditions by scientific groups and wildlife clubs are given special consideration. Travellers to Cape York are provided with a camping ground within the Aboriginal township of Bamaga, but it is advisable to apply in writing to the community's council chairman giving comprehensive details of your proposed trips. On Bathurst Island the Tiwi people's community actively encourages visitors on scheduled air tours from Darwin and permission for entry is automatically included with tour bookings

Mining the rich 'black sands'

SAND mining leases are granted under the authority of state government mines departments, like any other mining right. Leases are held on extensive tracts of coastal Crown land, including some in national parks. Modern leases require mining companies to restore worked-over dunes as nearly as possible to their natural state. Since ecological objections aroused public protest in the 1970s, some leases have been terminated by agreement. In the case of Fraser Island (see page 331) the Federal Government halted mining by using its power to control exports. The unworked leases are still held, however. If profitable local markets could be found, a resumption of mining could be proposed and environmental arguments would start all over again.

Beach mining began in 1870, when gold was found in deposits of dark, heavy minerals at Ballina, NSW. 'Black sands' occurred then in surface outcrops called sniggers. Such easily found deposits were cleaned out by miners who extracted gold, tin and platinum. They dumped the major components—rutile (titanium dioxide), ilmenite (titanium iron oxide) and zircon (zirconium silicate). In roughly equal proportions, those three compounds comprise about 97 per cent of the heavy minerals that work their way to the bottom of Australian quartz sands. Their density is about twice that of quartz, and their grain size about half.

Soon after the turn of the century, titanium began to be sought after as the basis of white paint. Rutile and ilmenite were wanted as furnace linings, or as welding fluxes. Zircon became valuable as a lining material or a ceramics glaze. Rutile fetched high prices in the 1950s, with the use of titanium in jet engines.

Mining at Myall Lakes involved one of the largest dune systems in the Southern Hemisphere. The 110-metre high dunes were blown there only about 2000 years ago. It is hoped that replanted areas (right)—seen here after five years—will eventually return to their original condition (crest of dune, left)

Parks and reserves

Australia's first national park, Royal National Park near Sydney, was declared in 1879 with a Crown grant to the park's trustees exhorting them to use the land for the recreation of the inhabitants of the colony. Authority was given to establish lawns, ornamental gardens, a zoo, cricket pitch, racecourse and rifle range—which created a large bushland amusement park. The management of national parks has changed greatly over the past 100 years; interference with the natural environment to provide facilities for the community has been tempered by a greater appreciation of conservation requirements. Park administrations are now keenly aware that they hold the key to the survival of rare and vanishing wildlife species and the preservation of representative samples of all major habitats, as well as areas of geological and historic significance.

Many coastal reserves still principally aim to fulfil the recreational needs of the public—Victoria's Coastal Parks, Tasmania's State Recreation Areas and Coastal Reserves, State Recreation Areas in New South Wales and some of the Environmental Parks in Queensland. Such areas are normally narrow coastal strips with some land left in its natural state, but with picnic areas, walking tracks and camping grounds provided, and waterways where motorboating may be allowed. Some of the older national parks, such as the Royal in New South Wales, Victoria's Wilson's Promontory National Park, and Yanchep National Park in Western Australia, retain a legacy of facilities from days when their role was largely to cater for family holidays and recreational sportsmen. Newer national parks, with extensive areas of forest and heathland, are more firmly dedicated to the preservation of the natural environment—an important goal in Australia, where plants and animals are rapidly disappearing even in areas of little or no settlement.

Such conservation areas must be large enough to ensure that the environment is undisturbed by man's activities and that the ecological balance of plant and animal communities is maintained. Research has suggested that only areas of 20 250 hectares or more are likely to support the range of plants and animals that are representative of a particular Australian habitat. The largest proportion of all national park area is consequently left in its natural state. Vehicles are allowed only on existing tracks and roads provided for access to camp sites, picnic grounds and along scenic drives. Use of off-road vehicles, such as trail bikes, dune buggies and four-wheel drives, away from existing tracks, is expressly forbidden because of the threat to soil and vegetation.

Occasionally conservation requirements may lead to the closure of parts of a park. Overuse and damage by fire require long periods free of disturbance for plant regrowth and animal recolonisation. Areas of special conservation significance—the breeding site of a rare bird or the habitat of an endangered plant—may be permanently closed. Such areas include the wetlands of coastal lagoons and estuaries, which are a sanctuary for waterfowl during the interior's

A female noisy scrub bird and nest

Preserving endangered wildlife

As MORE and more of Australia's coastal fringe is developed for housing or industry, it becomes increasingly important that some areas of natural landscape are set aside to conserve the plants and animals that live there. Occasionally the demands of conservation may conflict with the wishes of holidaymakers. Access may have to be forbidden or restricted in areas where a delicate natural habitat may be destroyed or rare animals frightened away by the presence of people. In some cases, such as that of the noisy scrub bird in Western Australia, such action may be necessary to save a species from extinction.

In 1961 plans for a new township to be called Casuarina at Two Peoples Bay, just east of Albany, were abandoned after new sightings of a bird thought to be extinct since 1889. The 4639 hectares around the bay still carry the only known population of noisy scrub birds, *Atrichornis clamosus*, and were declared a nature reserve in 1966 to protect the species. Most of the population of about 72 breeding pairs and 20 non-breeding males lives in densely vegetated gullies in the Mount Gardner Peninsula, part of which has been declared a prohibited area to prevent interference with research programmes. No public entry is permitted into this part of the reserve and there are clearly marked signs on the access tracks. But about half the peninsula is a limited access area, and may be entered on foot by birdwatchers wishing to catch a glimpse of the shy and secretive bird. Its brown colouring and dark cross bars blend in with the vegetation and make it extremely difficult to see; it rarely flies, moving mainly in the thick, low scrub. But the loud song of the male bird is a strong and persistent reminder of its presence, and can be heard over a distance of nearly 1.5 km on calm days.

dry months, and many rugged and mostly inaccessible offshore islands where migratory birds and seal colonies breed for short seasons. Only people with genuine scientific interests are issued permits to enter these areas. Parks known as fauna sanctuaries, nature reserves, or conservation parks, unlike national parks, allow only limited public access, and camping is often prohibited or restricted to small areas and for short periods such as school holidays, when special consideration for camping permits is given to groups involved in educational wildlife projects.

Marine parks control activities below the waterline and aim to restrict spearfishing, specimen collecting and some surface fishing in favour of pastimes such as snorkelling and scuba diving. Australia's largest marine park, The Great Barrier Reef Marine Park, was empowered in 1976 to provide protection for the delicate coral formations by controlling tourist operations; some vulnerable areas have been made off-limits for boating and fishing.

Permits must generally be obtained for camping at organised camp sites in national parks and it may be necessary to make bookings well ahead, especially for holiday periods. For Wilson's Promontory National Park bookings for the busy Christmas season are open only during July, after which a ballot is held to allocate the camping and caravan sites. Even the traffic on walking trails in heavily used parks is strictly controlled.

State forests

In State Forests, multiple-use management ensures the country's timber industry a continuity of supply, while providing for recreation and education as well as the protection of wildlife habitats. The forests are most widespread in humid coastal regions; many adjoin national parks, where they act as conservation buffer zones. State Forests are normally open to the public and, with fire trails and former logger routes, are well served by tracks for vehicles. Many have recommended scenic drives, and developed areas for camping. Others permit hiking trips into remote regions where there are no facilities. Check with the local forestry office, where maps and information on the best routes to take, spots to see and locations of picnic grounds, as well as advice on logging and fire restrictions, may be readily obtained. Particular care in State Forests is recommended for drivers unused to rural roads which are often narrow and winding, offer poor visibility and are used by heavy trucks. Only firm gravel roads should be used during wet weather as many forest roads become slippery after even light rain.

Lighting campfires

Campfires are allowed in national parks, state forests and on Crown land for cooking and warmth, but should be kept small to conserve wood and, wherever possible, portable stoves should be used. Great care and attention should be given to the siting and extinguishing of fires and to the exact legal requirements in each state.

On days of total fire ban no fires are permitted in parks and forests. In campgrounds and picnic areas fires may be lit only in the fireplaces provided, or as directed by signs. Where there are no properly constructed fireplaces, fires should be contained in a trench at least 500 mm deep. All flammable material on the ground or overhanging the fire within a distance of 3 metres must be removed before the fire is lit. The fire must not be left unattended and must be completely extinguished, preferably with water, before leaving. Trenches must be filled in.

Water safety   Surviving in the surf and still water

It is safer to swim at a beach patrolled by members of the surf lifesaving association or professional lifeguards than it is to take a bath, according to statistics published on accidental drownings in Australia. More and more people, however, are venturing to unpatrolled and remote areas, where the surf may be better but the statistics are worse. In the decade of the 1970s there were no drownings on patrolled beaches, while an average of eight a year occurred at unsupervised surfing spots.

Groups who venture to isolated beaches must remember that they have the responsibility for their own safety. It is important to understand the sea, the surf and the formation of beaches, and to be able to recognize any danger signs that may be present. Anyone using the sea must also know their own swimming ability and level of fitness. Reasonable pool-swimmers may perform poorly in the surf, where there are no edges, the bottom is irregular, the water continually moving and the depth forever changing.

Swells erode the sandy face of a beach and carry a great deal of it seawards to deposit it as offshore bars or sandbanks. A sandbank absorbs the force of incoming waves so that the eroding action of storms is lessened. But even when a sandbank is present, turbulent waves are constantly moving masses of water towards the shore, all of which must return seawards. Much returns in the rip currents which form channels through the sandbanks. Where curved beaches end at rocky outcrops—either natural or man-made—corner rips sweep the water along its face. Most people have heard of rips, but will be unable to avoid their dangers unless they can recognise them.

Before entering the water always spend some time watching a beach and its near-shore waters to try and spot any rips. If you plan to surf at an unpatrolled spot, find an elevated place at the back of the beach, or on a headland, and study the water until the pattern of banks and rips becomes clear. Rips can usually be seen from the beach, but they may be obscured by heavy seas, onshore winds and high tide. At such times you cannot be confident of your safety in the water.

The waves and water over a rip are obviously different from those over adjoining sand banks. A headland view of a rip at the centre of Maroubra Beach, NSW (top) clearly shows a band of foam and churned-up sand moving seawards in the current. Foam towards the furthest line of breakers indicates the point at which the rip has reached its head and begun to dissipate after passing through a channel in the sand bank. Choppy water interrupts the pattern of the surf over the same rip seen from the beach (centre). Waves break irregularly over the channel, do not roll and are often out of line with those in surrounding water. On other beaches the colours of rips may be darker because the water is deeper. At times they may look clear and undisturbed, and thus attractive to swimmers. Do not fight against a rip, but allow it to carry you out until it weakens. Strong swimmers can move diagonally out of a rip, but weaker swimmers should swim parallel to the beach and then back to shore. Children must not leave their surfboards if carried out on a rip, but stay with them till help arrives as their support may be vital

A corner rip at Avoca Beach, NSW, sweeps a deep channel of darker water along the face of a man-made rock pool. Large waves break regularly to the left of the rip which appears deceptively calm

In a medium to heavy surf, rips can alter rapidly, creating very hazardous conditions. In a small surf, rips are fairly stable and predictable, but even so they should not be trusted.

If you are caught in a rip, calmly swim or scull sideways towards a sandbank. If possible, signal for help by raising one arm. There is little point in shouting for help because it causes fatigue and cannot be heard above the noise of waves. While waiting for help, lie face up in the water and float with your head partly submerged. A relaxed horizontal position aids flotation and the body's natural buoyancy will keep your face above water with a minimum of effort. Treading water—moving the legs as if walking upstairs and pressing outwards and down with the arms—gives a better view, but it is tiring.

On unpatrolled or deserted beaches, where there is no help available, you must be able to swim out of rips by yourself. Conserve strength as much as possible and do not fight against the current. As the rip reaches its head, on the seaward side of its path through the sandbar, the current will dissipate. Swim parallel to the shore for about 30 metres before turning back towards the beach. At low tide sandbars close to the edge of a rip may only be covered by shallow water and if you are in difficulty you can use them to rest on while making your way back to the beach.

The breast stroke is less fatiguing for the return swim than the crawl, and it will still enable you to maintain a reasonable speed. Use side stroke and back stroke for relief. Turn your head away from the wind and breathe in a regular rhythm. If possible swim out of a rip in the same direction as the longshore current is flowing. This is the current which is commonly noticed moving along a beach. It carries swimmers away from their point of entry and may sweep them into a rip or deep channel. When returning to the beach be careful not to swim back into a rip. Not all rips run at right angles to land. If waves strike the shorelines at an angle, the rip, too, will be angled away from the beach.

Children who are carried out of their depth by rips often jump off their surf craft and try to swim against the current. This is exactly the opposite to what should be done. Instead they should stay with their craft, paddle to calm water—even if it is beyond the breakers—raise an arm and wait for help. In such circumstances a surf mat is as important as a life jacket. A flexible strap attaching a surf craft to an ankle or wrist is a valuable additional safety device.

While the hazards of ocean swimming are usually obvious, rivers, bays and lagoons conceal their dangers beneath still waters. Most fatal drowning accidents occur in sheltered waterways—often in peaceful conditions. The misuse of power boats in swimming areas and the consumption of alcohol before swimming, particularly from houseboats, are major causes of accidents. The currents of fast-flowing rivers discourage most swimmers simply because they look dangerous. But slower streams and enclosed waters are often just as hazardous. The main problem is usually visibility. You risk severe spinal injuries if you dive into cloudy water without first checking its depth.

The beds of lagoons and rivers are often soft and weed-covered—oozing mud and tangled weeds can trap swimmers just as securely as heavy branches. Panic and quick, jerky movements may only tighten the grip of weeds. If trapped, gently unravel the weed with as little agitation of the water as possible.

Muscle cramp can disable a swimmer in deep water or rough surf and can cause drowning.

Cresting or spilling waves are ideal for body surfers and board-riders. The waves break from the top with foaming crests which tumble down their faces

Plunging waves or dumpers break dangerously by curling over into a tube before thumping down into shallow water. They should be left to experienced surfers

Surging waves often run ashore without breaking, and they can suddenly swamp children playing around rocks, or break on them near the water's edge unexpectedly

Three types of waves—spilling, plunging and surging—are commonly seen on ocean shores. Never underestimate the power of waves which can often appear small when seen from the shore. Dive under waves when surfing—trying to keep your head above water wastes energy

These painful spasms usually occur in the legs, and are more likely to happen to people in cold water and after strenuous exercise. Eating always impairs physical performance because greater quantities of blood are diverted to the digestive system, leaving less for other muscles that need it during physical exertion. Light refreshments or snacks, rather than a full picnic meal, are better for a day at the beach. If attacked by cramp either float on your back or scull gently with your hands in a breast stroke motion and signal for help. Relieve the pain of cramp in the thigh by straightening your knee and raising your leg to stretch the muscle. For cramp in the lower leg, straighten your knee and draw you toes upwards towards your shin. Apply a cold-compress or ice-pack wherever possible, and in hot conditions drink a tumbler of water containing half a teaspoon of salt to aid recovery.

Water safety signs
A new set of standard symbols is being introduced on Australian beaches to replace the multitude of different symbols and word signs used by local authorities. When the symbol is shown in blue it indicates that the nominated sport or activity is permitted and that the area is considered safe. When the symbol is shown in a red circle with a diagonal line through it, the sport is prohibited because conditions are unsafe or there may be danger to other people. On patrolled beaches swimmers must remain in the supervised area which is marked by red and yellow flags. Leave the water when the shark flag is shown or its accompanying siren is heard

Swimming

Fishing

Water skiing

Surf craft riding

Scuba diving

Shark alarm flag

Patrolled swimming area

Fishing for leisure/1 Where and when to find the fish

Fishing is by far the most popular water sport in Australia. An estimated 30 per cent of Australians are recreational anglers. A survey held in NSW in 1977 revealed that 26 per cent of the population had fished in the sea at least once within the year. Sixty per cent of New South Wales boys between the ages of 13 and 17 fished for leisure, and altogether New South Wales fishermen spent 20 million days a year fishing for fun. Wherever there is reasonable access to the bays, beaches and rock platforms around the Australian coast, someone can usually be found waiting optimistically for a bite. However, two basic problems confront the amateur angler—where to find the fish, and what tackle to use.

The most popular recreational fishing areas are the thousands of estuaries and bays around the coast, where lines are cast from the shore, jetties, wharves, rock retaining walls and boats. From boats the best fishing is in the main channels of rivers, streams and inlets. Spots near weeds, rocks and mangroves attract fish, as they are major feeding areas. Around wharves and jetties the supporting piles may be heavily encrusted with mussels, sea squirts, weeds and the other marine life that fish feed on. The species commonly caught within these partly enclosed waters are flathead, bream, tailor, mulloway, whiting, luderick, garfish, leatherjacket, and flounder, all of which make excellent eating.

Surf fishermen will catch most of the species above, but success among the waves requires an ability to recognise the water conditions each fish is likely to favour. Patches of dark water usually indicate the deep channels, where tailor and Australian salmon search for food along the edges. Mulloway travel the rips and gutters of a beach where they can feed on unwary tailor and whiting, and they may also move along the water's edge seeking out one of their favourite foods—beach worms. Flathead and whiting partly bury themselves in the sandy bottom of shallower zones, covered by the froth and foam of breaking waves, and often within a few metres of the shore. Bream spend most of their time foraging for crustacea, molluscs and worms dislodged by pounding waves, particularly among submerged rocks at the corners of beaches.

Rock fishermen can hope to catch snapper, rock cod and bream, while the more experienced and adventurous will attempt to catch tuna, kingfish, mulloway, and even marlin. Rock fishing can be hazardous, and great care should be taken to make sure the area is safe before stepping on to an exposed rock platform or ledge. Spend some time watching the sea's behaviour to see if the platform is a safe one. Even an apparently placid sea can produce freak waves which will submerge areas that were previously merely splashed by spray. Boots fitted with spiked metal strips give a better foothold on slippery rocks than rubber-soled shoes. Wet granite is extremely dangerous, no matter what footwear is worn. If a wave sweeps across the rocks, stand on one leg to present less surface area to the water, and so reduce the chance of being knocked over. If washed into the sea, do not remove shoes or boots as they will be needed to get a purchase on the rocks when clambering ashore. In smooth waters it may be safe to allow a rising swell to wash you back on to the rocks. But in rough seas swim away from shore to avoid being pushed under the waves, or dashed against the rocks.

Most fishermen choose a rod and reel rather than the simple handline wound on to a cork or bottle. Whether a rod or handline is used, choose tackle that suits the kind of fishing being carried out. No outfit is suitable for all conditions.

Surf and rock fishermen usually use hollow glass-fibre rods, 3.4 to 3.8 metres long. Any of the three basic reel types—threadline, overhead revolving spool, and sidecast—can be used, provided that the spool has a minimum line capacity of at least 250 metres of nylon line with a breaking strength of 10 kg. The position of the reel on the rod should suit the reel type—low for the sidecast, medium for the threadline, and high for the overhead. Estuary fishermen find shorter rods ranging from 2 to 3 metres best. Reel size, too, can be smaller—use any of the basic types with a spool capacity of 250 metres of 5 to 7 kg nylon. The most popular reel is the threadline because it is easy to use.

There are few poisonous fish in Australian waters. Nevertheless, if you cannot identify a fish, or find advice on its edibility, it is safer to throw it back. In tropical areas a type of poisoning known as ciguatera can kill people who eat the flesh of some reef species (see page 67). In southern waters the spiky toad fish, also known as the puffer, should never be eaten as its flesh is highly toxic and can cause a rapid death.

Some fish have venomous spines which can cause violent pain if they penetrate the skin. Catfish, bullrouts, fortescues and stonefish are common species that may be encountered. Do not even handle these fish. Release them by cutting the line just above the hook, which will event-

Choosing the best rig

It is important to find the best rig—a combination of hooks, swivels, sinkers and traces—to attract, play and land each species of fish. Fish behave differently as conditions change, so one rig will always be better than others in any set of circumstances. All the rigs shown have been successful, but they should only be used as a starting point for more experiments.

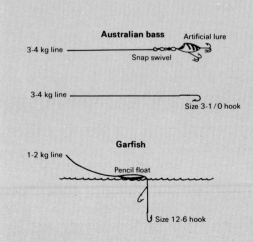

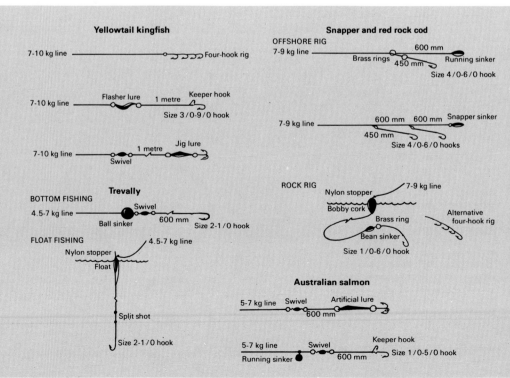

ually rust and drop out without harming the fish.

The 22 fish species most commonly caught in Australian coastal waters must each be fished for differently. Behaviour patterns differ widely, so a knowledge of where and when fish are likely to be feeding, and what the most tempting bait is will all increase the chances of success. The best arrangement of tackle may differ with location, so experiments are recommended. The size and placement of swivel, rings, hooks and other tackle shown in the illustrations below have all proved successful.

Dusky flathead Mud flathead, Estuary flathead, River flathead, Black flathead *Platycephalus fuscus*
Sandy bottoms, sparsely patched with weed beds, are the favourite haunt of flathead. These fish move slowly across the bottom searching for food, or lie partly buried waiting for small food fish to swim by. Boat owners can drift with the current and allow the bait to drag along the bottom. Flathead frequently lie on the edges of sandbars waiting for fish that retreat to deeper water as the tide recedes. Small, live poddy mullet and yellowtail, yabbies and prawns are excellent baits, as are fillets of fresh mullet, and whole garfish or blue pilchards. Any artificial lure that resembles a small baitfish, either in shape or action, will attract flathead. Their large mouths will easily accept big hooks, sizes 5/0 to 7/0 are popular. Do not use a wire trace, and the breaking strength of the line need be no higher than 7 kg.

Silver bream Yellowfin bream, Sea bream, Black bream, Surf bream *Acanthopagrus australis*
The delicate flavour of its flesh makes the bream a keenly sought species. They are very timid fish, and are more active after dark, when they should be fished for on a rising tide. Bream roam the shoreline, especially where there are oyster and mussel covered rocks, and they are often taken alongside bridge and wharf pylons. The edges of sandbars and weed beds are other worthwhile hunting grounds. Baits are many, but the best are blood worms, live saltwater yabbies and prawns, fresh mullet or garfish fillets, mullet gut and dough. Small hooks are best—sizes 2, 1, 1/0 or 3/0—and the breaking strength of the line should not exceed 7 kg.

Tailor Skipjack, Tailer, Chopper, Bluefish *Pomatomus saltatrix*
Recognised as one of the most voracious fish in the sea, tailor roam constantly at all depths in search of food. They have no specific habitats, but their presence is often betrayed by gulls and terns as they fight over scraps of torn fish, chopped to pieces by a passing school. Tailor will readily take pilchards and sea garfish, and are easy to catch with silver spoon or minnow-type lures. They invariably attack the tail of the bait, intending to disable their prey and make it easier to devour in a subsequent attack. The sharp, constantly chopping teeth can easily sever a nylon line, and a wire-trace between the main line and the hook is essential when single hooks are used, but not necessary when using a lure or ganged hook. Tow a lure, or bait, 10 to 12 metres behind a slow-moving boat. If fishing from a stationary platform, keep the bait moving by slowly winding it back in. Hook size depends upon the bait. With blue pilchards or garfish baits, gang three or more size 3/0 to 5/0 hooks by passing the point of one through the eye of another. A 5/0 hook is not too big for fillet baits. Use a 7 kg breaking strength line.

Mulloway Jewfish, Silver jew, Soapie (when small), School jew, Kingfish (Vic.), Butterfish (SA), River kingfish (WA) *Argyrosomus hololepidotus*
A prize mulloway can weigh over 50 kg. In estuaries these fish can travel beyond tidal influence, and many are captured several kilometres from the sea. They favour the deeper water of holes and the stream centre, feeding on small luderick, whiting, squid, mullet, tailor, octopus, prawns, and yabbies. Blue pilchards, garfish, and fillets of fresh fish can also be used as bait. One of the best times to fish is at night when the tide is rising or slack. Large hooks, up to size 9/0, and lines of 15 kg breaking strength are necessary for big mulloway.

Sand whiting Bluenose whiting, Summer whiting, Silver whiting *Sillago ciliata*
Small in size but tough fighters, whiting are much sought after. Their habitats are similar to those of flathead, but they are often found in much shallower water. Whiting will seldom take a fish bait, preferring worms, yabbies, or cockles. Light lines of up to 3 kg breaking strength and small hooks, sizes 6 to 1, are best. Keep the bait moving by winding the line in, casting out again, and repeating the process. Morning and evening are good fishing times. A tide rising over sandflats will flush out worms and small crustacea which attract these fish.

Luderick Blackfish, Nigger, Darkie, Black bream, Sweep *Girella tricuspidata*
Luderick will test any angler's skill. They feed mainly on green weed, sea lettuce and the minute marine organisms that cling to them, but they also occasionally take live yabbies and worms. Luderick are found close to shore near weed beds, reefs, rock retaining walls, and wharf or bridge pylons. The fish have very small mouths and dainty feeding habits so a size 8 or 12 hook must be used. Plait the hook with wisps of green weed and suspend it beneath a slim boat at a depth determined by trial and error. Fish on a rising to full tide. When a fish has been caught, cut its throat immediately to bleed it, or the flesh will deteriorate.

River garfish *Hyporhamphus regularis*
Eastern sea garfish Beakie *Hyporhamphus australis*
The flesh of these small fish is good to eat and well worth the trouble of removing tiny bones. They are usually found over weed beds or around jetties and wharves, and take small pieces of fish, worms, prawns, squid, bread crust or dough. Use a small hook, around size 12, and suspend it about 300 mm under a slim, lightweight float. Flashing silver or gold tinsel attract the fish to small artificial flies. To remove the bones prior to cooking, lay the cleaned fish gut down on a board and roll a milk bottle along the backbone. Turn the fish over and gently work the backbone and attached bones free of the flesh. Sea garfish make excellent bait for tailor.

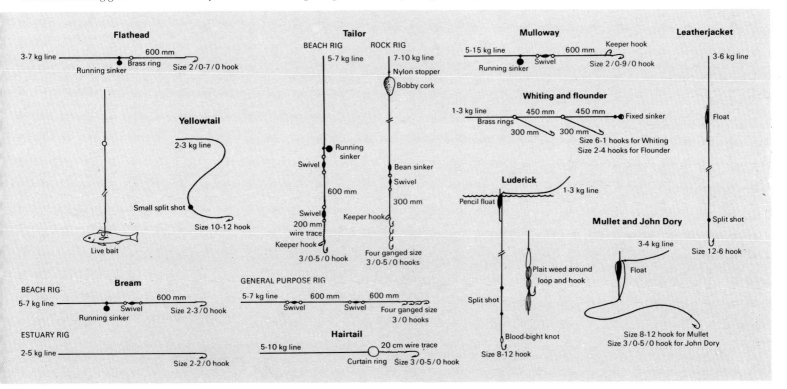

Fishing for leisure/2 Practical advice on bait and tackle

Chinaman leatherjack Yellow leatherjacket *Nelusetta ayraudi*
Scribbled leatherjacket Fantail leatherjacket, Fan-bellied leatherjacket *Alutera scripta*
Well-known scavengers, leatherjacket are found near jetties and wharves, around boat moorings, and in large weed beds. They will respond to any flesh bait, as well as to bread and cheese. They have a small mouth and incisor-like teeth so use a small hook with a long shank to prevent the fish from biting through the line. Float fishing is the most efficient method—suspend a baited hook, size 12-6, just above the sea floor. The flesh of a leatherjacket is tender and delicious. It makes an ideal food for invalids and children because the large bones are easy to see and remove.

Large-toothed flounder *Pseudorhombus arsius*
Considered a delicacy wherever it is served, flounder is principally a bottom dweller which feeds on worms, small crustacea and shellfish. Best baits are live yabbies and prawns used on size 2 to 4 hooks. The fish are poor fighters, and are often found to be hooked only when the line is reeled in to check the bait.

McCulloch's yellowtail Yellowtail, Yakka, Scad *Trachurus mccullochi*
Small yellowtail are abundant in most estuaries around the Australian coast and they are a popular bait fish.

They can be found around wharves and jetties, among moored boats, in weed beds, and close to underwater reefs in sheltered waters. The fish rarely exceed 200 mm in length, and they have a small mouth so a size 10 or 12 hook is adequate. Handlines are recommended. Best baits are small pieces of squid—which are tough and stay on the hook longer—peeled prawns, and worms. Yellowtail also respond well to small white lures hung in clusters from short leaders attached to the main line. As many as five or six fish can be caught at the one time by jigging the lures up and down. Mashed potato used as a berley will attract and hold yellowtail in the immediate fishing area, but it should be used sparingly—a teaspoon every 10 to 15 minutes—or they may stop biting. The fish may be kept alive in a tank, provided the water is changed regularly and adequate aeration is provided. Small battery-operated aerators can be used, but a constant flow of fresh seawater through the holding tank is more successful. Parents should not be concerned if their children, having caught a number of small yellowtail, want to cook and eat them. The flesh is delicious, although the bones must be removed carefully under adult supervision.

Silver trevally White trevally *Pseudocaranx dentex Pseudocaranx wrighti Caranx nobilis Usacaranx nobilis*
Silver trevally are a popular sporting fish because they are tough, determined opponents that never give in. They are caught in estuaries, off beaches and rocks, and

from the open sea near wrecks and reefs. Trevally are good table fish, but they must be bled immediately upon capture. To do this, simply cut the fish's throat. When fishing from a boat use a short 2 to 2.5 metre rod, and a reel holding about 200 metres of 4.5 kg breaking strain line. Fish weighing up to 2 kg can be caught with this equipment, but stronger line must be used for bigger fish. Rock fishermen should use long, light rods with reels carrying 6 to 7 kg breaking strain line. Good baits are fresh prawns, live saltwater yabbies, worms, and fillets of mullet, pilchard and garfish. Saltwater flies, metal spinners, or small lead-head jigs with a hair body are successful lures. Use a hook between sizes 2 and 1/0. Trevally have soft mouths and should be played gently to prevent the hook pulling out. Do not overcook the fish or the flesh will be dry.

Australian snapper Schnapper, Cockney bream-Red bream-Squire, as size increases *Chrysophrys auratus*
Young snapper are called cockney bream until they reach a weight of about 750 g. Adult snapper, with a fully developed snout bulge and bump on top of the head, can weigh up to 20 kg. Most large snapper are caught around coastal rocks and near offshore reefs, although the occasional stray can be caught from an ocean beach. Rock fishermen should use a medium to fast taper rod up to 4 metres long, a reel holding 7 to 9 kg breaking strain nylon line and hooks of sizes 4/0 to 6/0. Good baits for snapper are skinned octopus leg,

Gathering and preparing fresh bait

WHERE IT is difficult to buy bait, or to store it for long periods, anglers can successfully make their own or gather it around the shoreline. This not only saves money, but also provides the freshest bait possible. Stale bait is only useful as an ingredient in a berley—a mixture of various foods thrown on to the water to attract fish and hold them in the immediate fishing area. Mixtures of minced fish-flesh, bran, soaked wheat, minced prawns, stale bread, crushed shellfish, and a small quantity of tuna oil will produce a good, general-purpose berley.

Dough is one of the most popular baits for bream. Prepare it from flour and water and add a dash of tuna oil and a little cotton wool. The oil gives the dough a putty-like consistency, helps to keep it moist, and attracts fish, while cotton-wool keeps the dough on the hook. Use only sufficient to fill the bend of the hook.

Green weed and sea lettuce attract fish that live on marine algae. Sea lettuce grows abundantly on ocean rocks constantly washed by waves and can also be gathered in estuaries from submerged wharf pylons and rocks. It is normally plaited around the hook shank leaving a short piece hanging below the bend.

Pinkish-white saltwater yabbies are found in estuaries, where they live in burrows beneath sand and mud flats. They are caught with a specially made cylindrical pump. Place the mouth of the pump over a finger-sized yabby hole

and push it into the sand with one hand, while pulling the plunger with the other. This sucks sand, water, and yabby into the pump body. The contents are then ejected into a floating sieve, or on to the sand surface if the tide is out, from where the yabby can be collected.

Cunjevoi, or sea squirts as they are commonly known, are marine animals which grow on ocean rocks in the intertidal zone (see page 17). The animal's rough, leathery covering conceals a soft red flesh that is highly prized as bait. To reach the flesh, cut the cunjevoi from the rock with a knife and pull out the tough muscular tissue inside. The softer parts are difficult to keep on the hook, but can be toughened and preserved by salting down.

Beach worms grow to over 2 metres long and live in the sands of ocean beaches (see page 11). An hour either side of low tide is the best time to search for them. Wave a piece of fish flesh, attached to a cord, or in a stocking, in the water as a wave recedes. The worm's head will emerge from the sand as it searches for the bait, and it can be lured further from the sand using a smaller piece of bait held near its head. Quickly grip the worm behind the head with your thumb and forefinger and pull it firmly and steadily from the sand. Practice is needed to perfect the technique, as the worms are very quick at retreating.

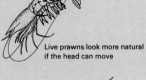
Live prawns look more natural if the head can move

Feed a small crab on to the hook to give it a natural position in the water

Secure the head and tail of dead prawns or yabbies

Break large crabs into small pieces so they can be used as bait

Allow the ends of worm sections to move on the hook

Bait live fish through the mouth, or in fleshy parts, to avoid damage to the spine

Allow the fronds of baited sea lettuce to move freely

Arrange a strip of fish flesh on the hook so that the end is left free

Make sure enough of the hook on ganged-rigs is left to penetrate the catch

squid, pilchard, garfish and slimy mackerel, live yellowtail, fresh prawns, crabs, and fillets of fresh mullet, bonito and striped tuna. Wherever possible do not use a sinker. A floating bait such as a blue pilchard on a series of ganged hooks, slowly reeled in, is most likely to attract snapper. If possible use a berley of chopped fish-flesh, crabs, prawns and squid mixed with stale bread and a dash of tuna oil. When rock fishing use a long-handled gaff to land the fish and reduce the risk of being washed into the water.

Red rock cod Cardinal scorpionfish, Red scorpion cod, Fire cod, Prickly heat *Scorpaena cardinalis*
Mottled reds, browns, and yellows decorate the red rock cod and camouflage it for life among rocks and seaweed. These fish are poor fighters but they can offer considerable resistance by opening their large mouths, expanding their pectoral and ventral fins and curling their tails to one side. The pressure of water against the fish's body has been known to snap light lines. The rock fishing rig for snapper will attract and hold the cod, but they will take almost any flesh-baited rig with hooks ranging from size 1/0 up to size 6/0, and even larger. The cod's mouth is so big that it has earned the nicknames swallow-all and mouth almighty. Venomous spines on the cod's fins can inflict a painful wound, so it should be handled with care, even when dead. The flesh is delicious, especially if lightly cooked and eaten cold.

Australian salmon Salmon trout *Arripis trutta*
These powerful fish grow to about 8 kg, but they are not a popular food fish because the flesh has a strong flavour. Juveniles are often caught in estuaries and bays and are called, colloquially, salmon trout or bay trout. Adults live in the open ocean and are popular sportfish with surf fishermen who find them one of the toughest adversaries. Use a 3 to 4 metre surf rod, a reel carrying at least 200 metres of 5 to 7 kg breaking strain nylon line and hooks of size 1/0 to 5/0. A sinker weighing 70 to 84 g will enable a long cast to be made. When fishing from a boat offshore use a 2.1 m rod and a line with a breaking strain of up to 6 kg. Best baits are sea garfish and blue pilchards, attached whole on ganged hooks, or small fillets used on single size 3/0 to 5/0 hooks. Chrome-plated hexagonal or round, sliced lures will also tempt Australian salmon. When fighting the fish it will be necessary to wind the line in quickly, so use a reel with a gear ratio around 6 to 1. Schools of migrating salmon encountered offshore will bite on a blue plastic squid lure, saltwater flies and feather jigs, cast from or towed behind a boat.

Sea mullet Bully mullet, Mangrove mullet, Hargut mullet, Poddy mullet, River mullet, Bullnose mullet *Mugil cephalus*
Mullet are one of the most common fish in the sea, but also one of the hardest to catch. They can be found in most estuaries and bays around Australia, and usually roam close to the shore or along the edges of sandbars where the juveniles, known as poddy mullet, fall prey to flathead, tailor, and mulloway. The gut of an adult mullet is a good bait for bream, and fillets of fresh sea mullet are a popular bait for most carnivorous fish. The mullet's basic diet is algae, but they can be caught using small pieces of prawn, fish flesh, and worms. Dough is an easy bait to prepare and is eagerly taken by mullet, especially if a berley of bread crumbs is used as well. Fly fishing, using small white or pink flies, is also successful. Use a size 8 to 12 hook suspended 200 to 300 mm below a float on a line of 3 to 4 kg breaking strength. A short spinning rod and reel are adequate. Mullet are determined fighters and skill is required to land them. The flesh has an excellent flavour, but when preparing it for the table make sure the black stomach lining is removed, because it can affect the taste.

Basic fishing knots

WELL-TIED knots distribute strain on a line through the knot, and avoid weak spots that might break under pressure. To obtain the utmost strength make sure the correct number of turns are completed, and that turns do not cross over one another, or slip out of place as the knot is being closed.

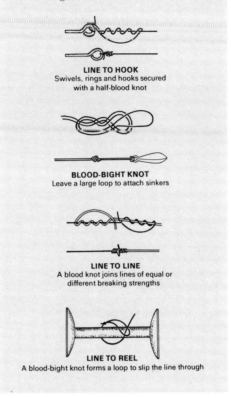

LINE TO HOOK
Swivels, rings and hooks secured with a half-blood knot

BLOOD-BIGHT KNOT
Leave a large loop to attach sinkers

LINE TO LINE
A blood knot joins lines of equal or different breaking strengths

LINE TO REEL
A blood-bight knot forms a loop to slip the line through

Yellowtail kingfish Kingfish, Kingie, Amberjack, Southern yellowtail *Seriola lalandi*
Strong, vigorous sporting fish, yellowtail kingfish can grow to 65 kg, but the average size encountered by most fishermen is about 5 kg. They can be caught with a fish bait, or with a lure towed behind a boat. Yellowtail are a good live bait, and small kingfish are sometimes used to catch the large record breakers. Strong size 5/0 to 9/0 hooks are needed to hold a large fish when live bait is used, and it pays to use a length of heavier line between the hook and main line when fishing over reefs. Kingfish have a habit of diving for the bottom where the line may be snagged and broken. Kingfish may also be caught with a jigged lure—a lure repeatedly dropped to the bottom and rapidly retrieved with a jerking pull. Metal jigs vary in weight and shape, but most are thin and long, with an average weight of 200 g. Colour does not seem to be important. Schools of kingfish roaming surface waters will readily attack red and white feather jigs or a pink plastic squid lure towed at speeds from 5 to 30 km/h. When one kingfish is hooked, the rest of the school generally follows and a large surface popper lure, cast to the surfacing school, should result in a strike. Kingfish can sometimes be caught with live bait cast into deep water from rocks along the ocean front.

Australian hairtail Ribbonfish *Trichiurus coxii*
Despite its forbidding appearance, hairtail is an excellent table fish which requires little preparation for cooking, as it has no scales. The undershot jaws of the fish's angular head are studded with razor sharp teeth and care must be taken to avoid a nasty cut. When a fish is landed, hold the line with a finger through the curtain ring near the end of the rig, grip the fish firmly behind the head and place it in a strong bag to prevent accidents. Hairtail are usually found in the deep water of bays and estuaries. When fishing from a boat use a stout handline of up to 10 kg breaking strength, and size 3/0 to 5/0 hooks. Rod and reel fishermen will find this an exciting fish to catch as it does not give in easily. Best baits are live yellowtail, prawns, gang-hooked garfish and blue pilchards. A steady supply of minced fish berley will attract and hold a school in the fishing area. The best depth for fishing can only be found by trial and error, but a good starting point is 6 to 7 metres. Hairtail take hold of a bait gently and move slowly away with it. If a fisherman strikes too early, the bait will be pulled from the fish's mouth. The best strategy is to let out a metre of line, and then strike. Use a wire trace as the hairtail's teeth will quickly sever even heavy nylon line.

Australian bass Australian perch, Estuary perch, Gippsland perch *Macquaria colonorum*
The sturdy fighting bass is found in coastal streams below tidal influence along the eastern seaboard from the Pumice Stone Channel in southern Queensland to the Gippsland lakes in Victoria. Above tidal influence, a similar fish—*Percalates novemaculatus*—can be caught using the same tackle and approach. Two good fishing outfits are a threadline reel spooled with nylon line of 3 to 4 kg breaking strength mounted on a light spinning rod, or a pistol-grip rod with a closed-face or baitcaster reel. The different kinds of bass lure are designed to move like food fish, frogs and insects, or small animals which have fallen into the water. Some lures are made to dive deep when they are reeled in, while others splash across the surface and are more popular for night fishing. Lines are best cast from a boat drifting close to the shore, slowly retrieved, then cast again until there is a strike. The lure should be dropped as close as possible to weed beds, overhanging trees, submerged logs and rocks where bass are likely to be waiting.

John Dory *Zeus faber*
John Dory consistently commands a high price at Australia's fish markets, and is always in demand for restaurants. This greenish brown fish is easily identified by the large dark grey spot on each side of its body just above and behind the small pectoral fins. They can grow to a weight of 4 kg, but most specimens are about 500 g. Their bodies are tall and thin and the head accounts for almost one third of the total length. The huge mouth is capable of wide and rapid extension. The best bait for John Dory is live yellowtail. Use a hook between sizes 3/0 and 5/0, and a light line with a breaking strength of 3 to 4 kg. Rod and reel fishing is usual, and it is worthwhile using a float to keep the live bait in mid-water. John Dory are poor fighters. They are often taken around wharf and jetty piles, in weed beds and over reefs where they feed on small yellowtail, hardyheads, cockney bream, and other bait fish. The fish's skin is smooth and scaleless, so it is only necessary to remove the large head and intestines before cooking.

Prawn family *Penaeidae*, various species
Prawns mature in tidal estuaries and lakes in summer and are caught in shallow water at night as they move towards the sea. Carry a strong light so that prawns stationary on the bottom can be spotted easily, and use a triangular-framed net. Place the net behind the prawn and scoop it up quickly, or startle it with a movement of your foot so that it shoots backwards into the net. Drag longer nets against the current, with one prawner wading into waist-deep water.

Identifying your catch

Of the thousands of species of fish living in the waters around Australia's coast only a small percentage end up in an angler's creel. Many are considered unfit for eating and are simply thrown back into the sea when caught. On the Great Barrier Reef alone there are around 1400 species to be found. Most of these, however, are small fish, more suitable for an aquarium than for the dinner table. Some fish are toxic and if eaten can cause sickness and even death, so it is important to be able to identify your catch. The 22 fish illustrated below are the ones most commonly fished for and caught, either for sport or for eating. Many fish are known by a variety of common names, and these vary from place to place. Even scientific names can change when species are reclassified.

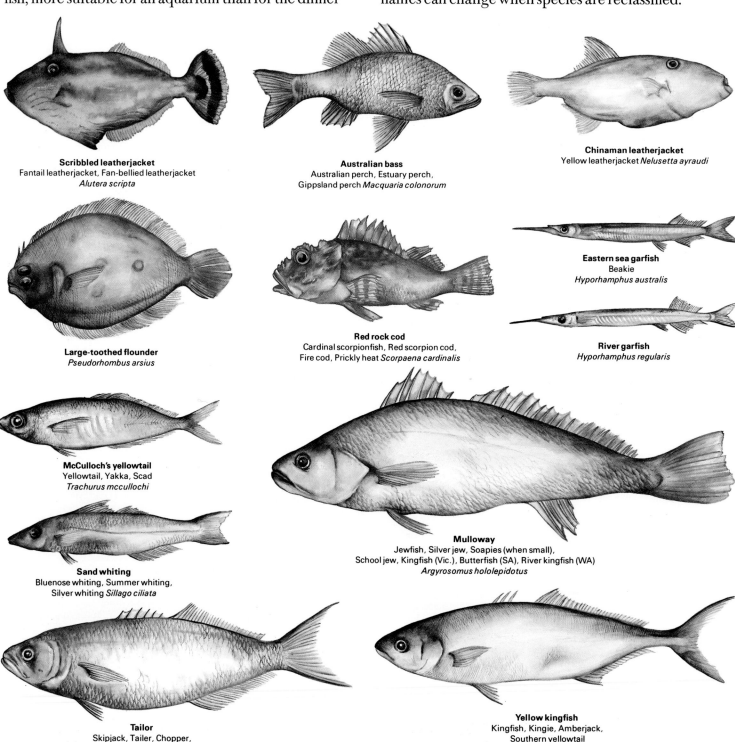

Scribbled leatherjacket
Fantail leatherjacket, Fan-bellied leatherjacket
Alutera scripta

Australian bass
Australian perch, Estuary perch,
Gippsland perch *Macquaria colonorum*

Chinaman leatherjacket
Yellow leatherjacket *Nelusetta ayraudi*

Large-toothed flounder
Pseudorhombus arsius

Red rock cod
Cardinal scorpionfish, Red scorpion cod,
Fire cod, Prickly heat *Scorpaena cardinalis*

Eastern sea garfish
Beakie
Hyporhamphus australis

River garfish
Hyporhamphus regularis

McCulloch's yellowtail
Yellowtail, Yakka, Scad
Trachurus mccullochi

Sand whiting
Bluenose whiting, Summer whiting,
Silver whiting *Sillago ciliata*

Mulloway
Jewfish, Silver jew, Soapies (when small),
School jew, Kingfish (Vic.), Butterfish (SA), River kingfish (WA)
Argyrosomus hololepidotus

Tailor
Skipjack, Tailer, Chopper,
Bluefish *Pomatomus saltatrix*

Yellow kingfish
Kingfish, Kingie, Amberjack,
Southern yellowtail
Seriola lalandi

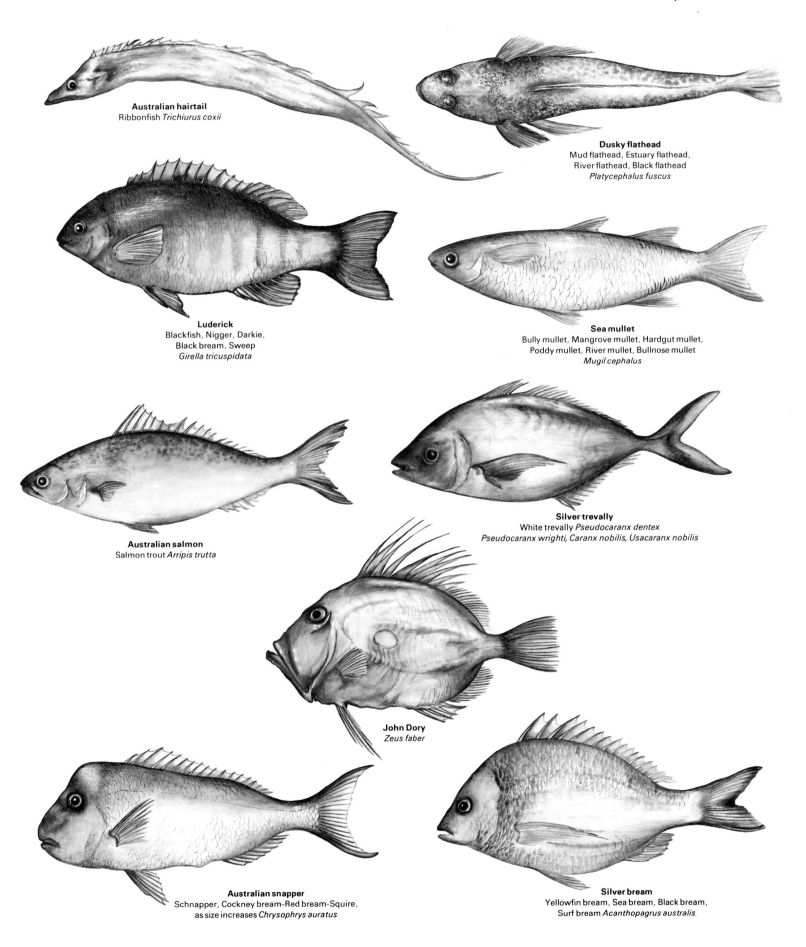

Australian hairtail
Ribbonfish *Trichiurus coxii*

Dusky flathead
Mud flathead, Estuary flathead,
River flathead, Black flathead
Platycephalus fuscus

Luderick
Blackfish, Nigger, Darkie,
Black bream, Sweep
Girella tricuspidata

Sea mullet
Bully mullet, Mangrove mullet, Hardgut mullet,
Poddy mullet, River mullet, Bullnose mullet
Mugil cephalus

Australian salmon
Salmon trout *Arripis trutta*

Silver trevally
White trevally *Pseudocaranx dentex*
Pseudocaranx wrighti, Caranx nobilis, Usacaranx nobilis

John Dory
Zeus faber

Australian snapper
Schnapper, Cockney bream-Red bream-Squire,
as size increases *Chrysophrys auratus*

Silver bream
Yellowfin bream, Sea bream, Black bream,
Surf bream *Acanthopagrus australis*

Inshore boating Vital preparations for a day on the water

Nearly 700,000 Australian families own a craft for sailing, paddling or power boating. Most are small and low-powered, used mainly for weekend recreation on bays and estuaries where boat owners are attracted by fine conditions and placid waters. But behind the apparent safety of sheltered waterways lie potential hazards which must not be disregarded. To prevent a holiday turning into a nightmare, every boat owner must be aware of the problems that can arise, and the steps that may be taken to avoid them.

The anchor, one of the principal pieces of equipment on the boat, is thought by many to be of use only for holding the boat in position while fishing over a favourite spot or picnicking on the shore. But the anchor is more than that—it is a vital safety aid. In the wide estuaries common to most of Australia's big rivers mechanical failure may result in a boat being caught in a strong outrunning tide and swept on to a dangerous bar at the entrance. Because most boats are too heavy or cumbersome to be rowed against such a tide, or against a strong wind, the only way to avoid disaster is to drop the anchor as quickly as possible. With the correct anchor and gear, a boat can be halted and held in position while repair work is carried out, or signals are sent for help.

Anchors of inappropriate design and weight, however, will not catch in the sea bed, and an anchor line which is too short will constantly pluck the anchor out before it can take a firm hold. While a sand-anchor may sometimes hold on a rocky bottom, a reef-anchor will not hold properly in sand or mud. A short anchor line which is quite adequate in a sheltered bay will be insufficient in deep water or against a strong current.

The best anchor lines are made of nylon or other synthetic materials and must be long enough to allow at least five or six times the water's depth to be paid out. The longer and heavier the anchor line, the greater the anchor's holding power. A length of chain about 3 metres long between the anchor and the line adds weight and prevents the line chafing on the sea bed, particularly over reefs. Any reputable dealer will advise on the correct type and weight of anchor for your particular craft.

A boat which is overloaded may appear stable in sheltered nearshore waters, but the wash of a passing vessel or a turbulent rip sweeping around

Long mooring lines must be used in areas where the tide range is large. Secure a boat at both bow and stern so that it can rise and fall with the water level

A long line, with a length of chain attached, helps the anchor to lie on the sea bed and dig in securely. The length of line hanging in the water forms a buffer against the tugging of the boat as it is buffeted by wind and waves—small shocks are absorbed by the line before they reach the anchor

a headland may push a wave aboard. When the boat's stability is upset it may be impossible to avoid further waves and the boat may soon be swamped. All boats should carry a notice indicating the maximum number of people to be carried, and this figure must be sensibly balanced with the amount of gear taken on board.

The effect of bad trimming is much the same as overloading. Move passengers or gear so that the boat is neither down at the bow nor at the stern—conditions which make any craft difficult to handle and impair its performance. A badly trimmed boat will use more fuel, strain the motor and provide an uncomfortable ride. In small boats correct trim is easily achieved by adjusting the positions of passengers or luggage, but larger craft need adjustable trim controls.

Naval charts and boating maps can help sailors avoid the hazards hidden in many deceptively safe waterways. If a boat is grounded on a mud-bank it may result in little more than a scratched bottom, but to hit a reef, particularly at high speed, can cause serious damage to the craft and injury to the occupants. The reefs, sand banks, shoals and channels shown on maps allow sailors to plot a safe course, and prominent landmarks are shown to aid navigation.

For anglers, the location of wrecks and the contours and composition of the sea bed may give a good indication of the sorts of fish likely to be found in an area. Charts produced by the hydrographic office of the Navy are readily available for most major waterways, and boating maps produced by local authorities cover many popular rivers, lakes and estuaries.

In unfamiliar waters boat owners must seek local advice on sand bars and channels, as these may change considerably depending on the weather, the tide and the volume of water flowing into rivers and lakes.

The gradient of any specially constructed launching ramp usually provides sufficient depth of water over a normal range of tides, so that a boat can be launched and retrieved without damage to its hull. Take care not to immerse the trailer's wheel hubs because bearings will rapidly corrode in the salt water, and this is potentially dangerous. Most ramps have areas nearby where preparation for launching can be carried out. Release tie-downs, check the motor, and load all equipment to prevent unnecessary delays on the ramp itself

Nothing has a greater effect on boating holidays than the weather. Apart from comfort, the weather can greatly affect the safety of any vessel. Check the forecast before setting out to avoid being caught in bad weather. This is particularly important for small boats in open waterways such as Melbourne's Port Phillip Bay and Brisbane's Moreton Bay, where choppy seas can quickly develop that will threaten all but the most seaworthy craft. However, local conditions can change rapidly and forecasts can be wrong, so it is wise to learn to recognise threatening weather patterns.

Most dangerous weather conditions give an indication of their approach with unmistakable sky signs. A cold front is usually accompanied by a build up of giant towering clouds. A line squall can appear as a fast-moving roll of cloud stretching across the sky. Local weather patterns may have their own peculiar signs which, if recognised early enough, give sailors time to make for port or for the shelter of a headland. Coast guards, members of yacht clubs and commercial fishermen are always willing to provide helpful information to visitors.

Many of the rules governing safe boating are covered by regulations and enforced by law. Speed limits apply in most popular waterways and around moorings, and boating may be prohibited altogether in swimming areas. One life jacket per passenger is obligatory on all craft, from the smallest dinghies to ocean-going yachts. An anchor, paddles and fire extinguisher may also be considered to be standard equipment in some areas. Alternative means of propulsion—a secondary outboard, sail, oars or paddles—are useful in case a motor fails or winds become too light to propel a yacht. A good sailing day with a brisk breeze can become a dead calm by the middle of the afternoon, and the shore may be a long way off. Carry a spare length of rope to repair rigging, or a shear pin in case the propeller hits an obstruction in the water. Such precautions can mean the difference between getting back to shore on time or spending hours waiting for a tow. Report trips into offshore waters to the water police or coastguard. Detailed plans of the route to be travelled and expected time of arrival are necessary, so that a search operation can be started if a boating party fails to confirm its safe arrival.

Four basic knots that boat owners must master

BOATS must be securely tied to anchors and mooring points for safety. The knots that are used must remain firm whether the rope is wet and taut, or dry and slack. Modern synthetic ropes have a slippery surface and this must also be taken into account. A good knot must release easily when the direction of pressure is reversed, so that a quick reaction to emergencies is possible. Each knot serves a different purpose—everything from mooring a boat to a jetty to joining two pieces of rope together—and all boat owners must be familiar with the four most common ones. These are the reef knot, the clove hitch, the bowline, the round-turn with two half-hitches. Practice tying the knots at home until the sequence of operations becomes second nature.

Reef knot
Joins two pieces of rope of similar size. Will not jam. Release by pushing strands of one rope into the knot

Round-turn and two half-hitches
Safe, efficient way to securely fasten a rope to small fixtures such as jetty rings and nails

Clove hitch
Simple knot used to attach a rope to a fixed object. Release knot by easing pressure on either end of the rope

Bowline
Mainly used at the end of a rope to make a non-slip loop for dropping over mooring posts on a wharf or jetty. Release by pushing rope into knot

Coastal hazards Dangers that can be avoided

Coasts are risky places—mainly because so many people using them are visiting unfamiliar territory and experiencing an unaccustomed climate. Often people are literally out of their element, venturing on and into water that holds its own menace, as well as concealing dangerous creatures. But nearly all trouble can be avoided with some knowledge of where hazards may be found, and the exercise of common sense and caution. The problems that most frequently lead to drowning are discussed earlier in this section, and resuscitation is dealt with overleaf, as are other first aid treatments, including those for many stings and bites. Two special menaces of tropical coasts are saltwater crocodiles, which can kill with a blow from their tails, and box jellyfish, whose stings require trained assistance.

Sun effects—sunburn, sunstroke and heat exhaustion—are characteristic of coasts only because most people wear less clothing and spend more time basking than usual. Screening creams provide the best protection against burning. If washed off by perspiration or bathing, they should be reapplied at once. Sunstroke is a breakdown of the body's heat-regulating system: victims do not sweat. Heat exhaustion is a failure of blood circulation to the extremities, caused by loss of body salt and fluid, and is more common among the chronically ill or elderly. People prone to either sunstroke or heat exhaustion should seek shade and cooler air, and perhaps limit their travelling to temperate regions.

Infections start easily from coral cuts in the tropics, from wounds inflicted by some of the relatively harmless marine stingers or spiked fish, and from insect bites. Shoes should be worn on reefs and in tropical waters. The use of insect repellents is advisable, even by people who are not irritated by itching bites. Mosquito-borne

Cone shells must be left alone—the poison injected by tropical species is usually fatal

diseases include dengue fever in the tropics and the related Ross River fever in subtropical Queensland. And in remote parts on the north coast, pockets of malaria may still be found.

Stinging jellyfish, other than the tropical box jellyfish, are unlikely to cause death. But heavy doses of their venom can cause severe and prolonged pain and may bring about collapse. Corneal scarring may result from a sting across an eye. Swimmers should note that the prevalence of most such jellyfish increases with the water temperature: risks are greatest in late summer. At least six Australian species of *Conus*, the **stinging shellfish,** are known to be dangerous. They shoot out hard, barbed spears that pump venom. The most lethal are found on tropical reefs, where they bury themselves in sand by day. All known species contain some venom and none should be handled before making certain that the living animal is not still inside.

Of dozens of species of venomous **stinging fish,** the deadliest are stonefish, *Synanceia*. Though big—up to 500 mm—and bulky, they are virtually impossible to see in their coral reef or mudflat habitats, because they are coated with slime and algae and sometimes partly buried in sand. They have 13 sharp spines along their backs, each

linked to two venom glands. Stonefish are distributed throughout the tropics and south to Brisbane, most stings occurring at Easter or during the August school holidays. Strong footwear is the best protection. Fishermen should learn to identify stonefish, and not grab too quickly at whatever they hook or net. Stinging fish common in cooler waters—catfish, bullrout, fortescue, cobbler, red rock cod, flathead, goblinfish, old wife and many more—do most harm to anglers and trawlermen handling them accidentally, especially at night. Their venom is much less dangerous than that of the stonefish and other tropical species, but it may cause a collapse leading to drowning. Stingrays, though venomous, do most of their damage by the wound they inflict. Feeding on the sea bed and often motionless, a stingray drives its long, spiny tail directly up at anyone treading on it. Some species are found all around the coast. They are unlikely to feed where many people are swimming, but a close watch should be kept in lonely waters. One species of shark, known as the Port Jackson but

Camouflage renders the stonefish almost invisible

The ocean's most feared menace

THE POSSIBILITY of shark attack probably worries Australian surf bathers more than any other seaside hazard. Yet the chances of being bitten are extremely remote. In the decade from 1970 there were only 20 attacks in Australian waters, of which five were fatal. Many city beaches have now been made even safer by meshing—with a net suspended in the water a few hundred metres from the beach for part of its length. The net is not intended to seal off the beach completely, but to provide a trap for any sharks in the area. Sharks must keep moving so that water can circulate through their gills; if they are caught in a net and immobilised they quickly drown. Nets are retrieved at regular intervals, dead sharks removed and damage repaired. Since meshing was introduced in Sydney in 1937 there has not been a fatal attack on any of Sydney's 60 km of ocean beaches. In recent years the number of sharks caught in nets has declined considerably, in Sydney from 224 in 1951 to 43 in 1969, and some experts think that the nets may discourage sharks from establishing territories. Attacks are very rare in waters where the surface temperature is below 21°C, so the seasonal patterns of water temperature variations are a good guide to the periods when bathing is most likely to be safe.

Shark attacks follow the seasonal warming of southern waters. Bathers should remember that shallow bays are often warmer than the surrounding ocean

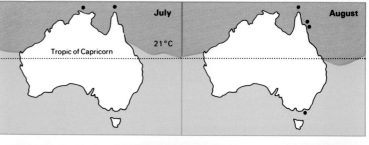

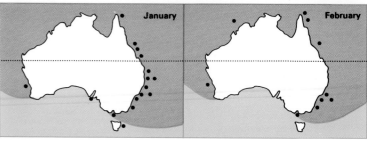

▨ Temperature above 21°C   ☐ Temperature below 21°C   ● Shark attack sites

Vivid circles of colour make the blue-ringed octopus easy to identify. These creatures are very common

When a fish feast may be poisonous

CIGUATERA poisoning, much publicised since the late 1970s, has always been a risk on tropical coasts and islands. Toxins originating in coral reef algae and small marine animals are passed from fish to fish in the reef food chain. The bigger the fish, the greater the accumulation of poison. More than 300 species could have it, but the highest concentrations are believed to be in the liver and other internal organs of red bass, chinaman and paddletail—none of which are permitted to be sold commercially—along with barracouta and moray eel.

Symptoms of ciguatera poisoning usually include numb and tingling fingers, numbness around the mouth, burning or tingling of the skin in cold water, muscle and joint pain, vomiting, diarrhoea and headache. Death is unusual but a lengthy treatment in hospital may be necessary. The disease can have a debilitating effect for months. Fish eaters visiting the tropics should not eat large portions from the bigger reef fish, and they should never eat repeated meals from the same fish. Whatever the species, the internal organs of reef fish should never be eaten.

distributed throughout temperate waters, has a venomous spine in front of each of the two fins on its back. Its struggles when hooked or speared can drive a spine centimetres into a fisherman's flesh. Pain and muscle weakness from the poison may last only a few hours, but the ragged wound is easily infected. Both the tiny southern blue-ringed octopus and its bigger tropical relative have been known to kill humans with the venomous bites of their beaks. The deaths were entirely avoidable. This easily identified animal is harmless in the water—it bites humans only if it is picked up, usually after having been stranded in a rock pool by low tide.

More than 30 species of **sea snake** are found in tropical Australian waters but only two are distributed as far south as Cape Leeuwin or Bass Strait. Their fangs deliver meagre amounts of venom but it can be extremely toxic, causing death by muscle destruction. No one inexperienced in handling snakes should pick one up, and prawning or fishing nets should be handled with care, especially at night.

Coastal **land snakes** in temperate regions include the Western Australian dugite and the Sydney broad-headed snake, both of which are highly venomous though unlikely to cause death. The broad-head likes to hide in dry rock crevices or under boulders and slabs. The taipan—the longest venomous snake in Australia, and invariably lethal with its bite until an anti-venom was developed in the 1950s—inhabits north-eastern and northern coastal areas. Normally timid, it flees when approached, but is likely to strike if cornered, snapping three or four times with fangs up to 13 mm long.

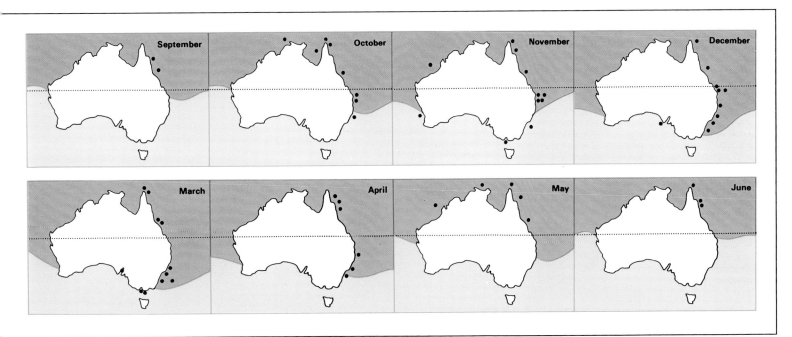

Emergency action Skills to save a life

A drowning person's breathing and heartbeat may stop, but they can still be revived. Resuscitation has to begin as soon as possible—in the water if necessary—to restore the supply of oxygen to the blood, restart the heart and keep the blood circulating around the body. Victims of suffocation, electric shock, heart attack and some poisons and venoms can also be kept alive.

Place the victim on their side on a firm, level surface and clear the throat to prevent any food, blood or mucus going down into the lungs. If the patient is unconscious, make sure the tongue does not fall backwards and block the throat. Use your fingers to scoop out any particles behind the tongue. Take out any false teeth. Tilt the head backwards while supporting the jaw with the other hand, keeping the face pointing slightly down so that any mucus or fluid can drain out of the mouth. Then put the person on their back. Kneel at the head and put the palm of one hand on the top of the victim's head while supporting the chin with the other, and tilt the head back so the tongue will keep out of the way and air will be able to enter freely.

Pinch the victim's nostrils closed with your thumb and forefinger, all the time keeping the head tilted back. Take a deep breath, open your mouth as wide as possible and put it over the victim's mouth, making an airtight seal. Blow into the mouth strongly.

Take your mouth away. If the victim's chest is not rising, check if the airway is clear. Then put your mouth back over the victim's and breathe into the victim five times, as fast as you can.

Check if there is any pulse beat by feeling for the carotid pulse in the neck (as shown). If there is a pulse beat, continue with mouth-to-mouth respiration at 12 breaths a minute. It may be necessary to continue for a long time. Check the carotid pulse every two minutes.

If there is no carotid pulse, mouth-to-mouth respiration should go on and heart massage should begin immediately. Kneel beside the victim. Find the lower half of the breastbone. Put the heel of your other hand over the first hand. With arms straight, lean forward and press down on the breastbone so it goes down about 50 mm. Keeping your hands in position, lean back and release the pressure. Continue the process rhythmically, pressing down *at least* once a second. The best rate would be around 80 times a minute.

If you are alone with the victim, after 15 chest presses move to the head and use your mouth to inflate the lungs twice. Continue with 15 chest compressions then two lung inflations in turn.

If there are two people available they should kneel on opposite sides of the victim. One person does five chest presses, one every second—to get the timing right, count out loud 'one thousand, two thousand' and so on. The other person then makes one chest inflation using mouth-to-mouth.

If the victim is a child, only one hand should be used for chest compressions, and they should be given a little faster. The breastbone should be pressed down only 20 mm. Do not press a baby's breastbone down more than 10 mm.

If breathing begins, put the victim quickly into the recovery position (as shown). Vomiting will often occur now. Keep the throat clear. Watch the person continually to check if the breathing is satisfactory. If not, replace on the back and begin resuscitation again. Check the pulse every 2 to 3 minutes. To stop loss of body heat, cover the victim with a coat or blanket. Stay with the victim until qualified help comes.

How to give mouth-to-mouth resuscitation

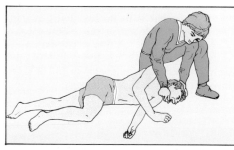

1 Resuscitation can begin in the water if necessary. Once out of the water, place the victim lying on their side on a firm, level surface. Keep the head tilted to help clear the airway

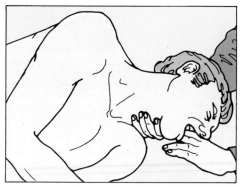

2 An unconscious person cannot prevent food or mucus passing down the throat into the lungs, so clear the mouth behind the tongue

3 Once the airway has been cleared, turn the patient on their back. Supporting the chin, tilt the head so that the tongue is clear and air can enter the lungs

4 While the head is still tilted back, pinch the patient's nostrils. Take a deep breath, hold it, then put your mouth firmly over the victim's and blow strongly

5 When you take your mouth away, check to see if the patient's chest is rising, and listen for any exhalation of air. Repeat resuscitation until breathing resumes

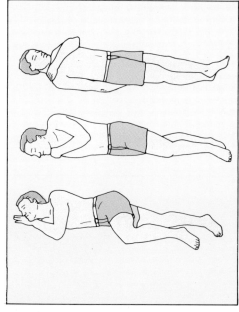

6 The recovery or coma position keeps the airway clear and stops vomit getting into the lungs. If you have given mouth-to-mouth resuscitation and heart massage and restored a victim's breathing and heart beat, they will be lying on their back.

To put the victim in the recovery position, kneel at the victim's side and pull their further leg over the one nearest to you. Then place the arm further from you across the chest to the shoulder area. Position the other arm down along the torso (with the palm upwards). Next pull the victim on to the side that is nearest to you. Pull the underneath arm down behind the back. Bend the top leg. Put the arm of the top hand under the chin, supporting the chin but with the hand clear of the mouth. Tilt the head slightly backwards to keep the airway clear

The technique of heart massage

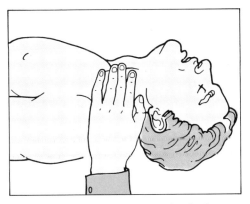

1 To check for heartbeat, place your hand palm downwards across the side of the victim's neck and feel for the carotid artery pulse between the Adam's apple and the neck muscles

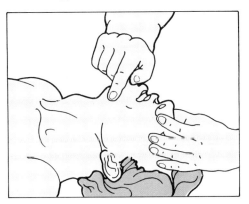

2 Before applying external cardiac compression, place the patient on their back on a flat, firm surface and remove any restricting clothing. Check that the airway is clear, then tilt head well back

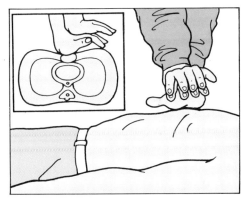

3 Kneeling to one side, place the heel of one hand on the middle half of the patient's breastbone. Keeping palm and fingers raised above the chest, place heel of other hand on top of first hand

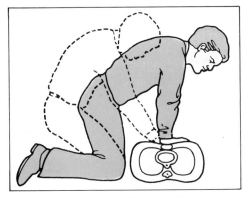

4 Straighten arms and push down on the breastbone, depressing it about 50 mm. Keeping your hands in position, lean back and release pressure on chest. Repeat at least once a second

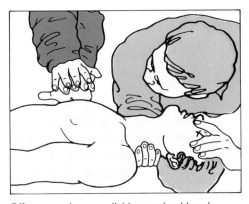

5 If two people are available, one should apply mouth-to-mouth resuscitation while the other continues heart massage, working together at the rate of 1 air inflation to 5 compressions

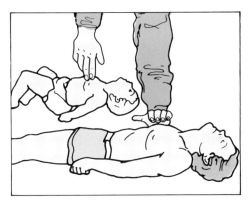

6 On a child, use only one hand and increase the adult rate of cardiac compressions, with less depression of the breastbone. Do not depress a baby's breastbone more than 10 mm

Aiding a shark attack victim

MOST shark attacks are survivable if help is at hand. Rescuers are hardly ever harmed. But people must condition themselves to the horrifying appearance of some wounds, to avoid panic.

Bleeding must be staunched quickly. If the victim cannot be brought ashore immediately, use your fingers to press hard into or just above any point where blood is spurting. Once ashore, do NOT try to get the victim to hospital. Move him only out of reach of waves and lay him on the sand with his head lowermost.

Apply a tourniquet above the wound, over a long bone—not a joint. You can use a belt or a strip of cloth or rubber, but nothing as narrow as string or shoe laces. If heavy bleeding continues, use pressure by hand or pack cloth of any kind over the wound. Do NOT remove blood-soaked dressings—press more cloths on top. Then call an ambulance.

While waiting, cover the victim lightly but give him nothing to eat or drink. If he is wearing a wetsuit, leave it on. Monitor the victim's breathing and be ready to give mouth-to-mouth resuscitation.

Venomous bites and stings

Snakebites and most serious marine stingings can be combated with good first aid. The aim is to slow the spread of venom and the onset of paralysis until qualified medical treatment can be given.

Never cut into a snakebite wound or cut away injured tissue. That does more harm than good. Do NOT try to remove clothing covering the wound—movement will spread the venom. Do NOT wash the wounded area. Surplus venom splashes on the skin cannot hurt the victim and it will help in quick identification of the snake type. Do NOT try to kill the snake at the risk of further bites. And do NOT tie an arterial tourniquet above the wound.

Wrap a wide bandage directly over the bitten area, as firmly as if you were binding a sprained ankle. Extend the binding as high as you can—to the thigh if a foot or leg is bitten—and secure a splint to the whole leg. If the bite is on a hand or forearm, apply bandages and a splint as far as the elbow and place the arm in a sling.

Keep the victim warm and as still as possible.

Check regularly for breathing. If first aid comes too late and paralysis sets in, mouth-to-mouth resuscitation may be necessary. If the victim must be moved, it should be done gently—preferably on a stretcher.

Exactly the same pressure/immobilisation first aid works for funnelweb spider bites. It is not necessary for the bite of the redback spider, which has a slower-acting venom. Pressure on a redback bite only increases pain, and that can be eased by cooling the wound with a mixture of ice cubes and water in a plastic bag—but do NOT apply ice directly to a wound.

Warm water, on the other hand, is often a pain-reliever for the victims of stinging fish. Cone shell stings and blue-ringed octopus bites are dealt with by the pressure/immobilisation method. Jellyfish stings can be neutralised to some extent with vinegar—NOT methylated spirit or other alcohols. The main risk of marine stingings is for a person to collapse and drown—but be as gentle as possible in removing a victim from the water.

PART 4

Discovering the coast

Faced with the immensity of the seaboard, travellers must be selective. For every person who seeks reassuring surroundings and familiar activities at journey's end, there is another who hopes for surprise and challenge.

Fascination may lie in landscapes and wildlife, or the ocean itself may be the lure.

Coastal towns can command attention in their own right, or be seen as mere resting places. Choice is a matter of personal taste and circumstances.

In this part of the book the options are left open. With the widest range of interests in mind, priority is given to solid, serviceable information about scores of localities.

Most of the places described are illustrated with aerial photographs, and wherever possible these have been joined together to give the broadest possible view, even if there is a shift in colour.

These sweeping panoramas could otherwise be photographed only from a great altitude, where atmospheric haze reduces clarity.

The photographs provide a remarkable new perspective of even familiar areas. Mysteries of local topography, access, vegetation and waterways all become clear.

Even individual houses can be easily identified.

Evening clouds gather over a coastal mountain range

Aerial photography A bird's eye view of the shore

Nearly all of the illustrations in the following guide sections are reproduced from specially commissioned vertical aerial photographs. The technique of taking them is a demanding one, calling for exceptional precision in navigation and timing. But nothing else is so effective in showing the positions of ground features in relation to one another. The pictures work as living maps. And some incidental points of information emerging from them could not be conveyed even in the most elaborate formal mapping.

Aerial cameras work the same way as those used in conventional photography. But they are exceptionally big. They take rolls of film on which each frame is more than 225 mm square— almost the size of this page—and each roll has room for more than 100 frames. The film magazine alone is bigger than a typewriter and almost as bulky. High-performance light aircraft are modified—their hydraulic systems and electrical wiring may have to be shifted—so that the camera can be mounted in the belly of the fuselage with a lens cone protruding downwards through the hull. Normal or wide-angle lenses may be fitted. The mounting allows the camera to be swung out of line with the heading of the aircraft, or to be tilted if the aircraft is not in level flight.

The requirements of the picture—always a compromise between the detail that can be shown and the area that can be covered— determine the shooting altitude. Reader's Digest decided on 3000 metres, giving a ground spread of about 4.5 km in each full frame. Each area was plotted on detailed maps, allowing for overlaps where it was intended that pictures be joined up. Then it was up to navigator-cameramen to direct pilots over exactly the right spot while maintaining the right height. Taking their bearings from the most prominent ground features, they set a course to the centre of the plotted area. Sighting instruments enabled them not only to trigger their cameras with split-second timing, but also to

Only the centre of an aerial photograph is a truly vertical view—features at the edges lean outwards

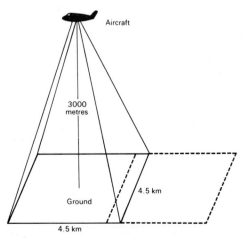

A normal lens used at an altitude of 3000 metres covers a ground area of 20.25 sq km. Pictures are overlapped to reduce the contrast in angles when they are joined

observe wind-drifting or tilting so that camera angles could be adjusted. The precision achieved far excels that of wartime bomb-aiming.

Because the distance between the camera and the ground is greater at the edges of each picture, angles are created that slightly distort the image. Tall features appear to lean out at all sides of a picture—most noticeably in city shots. Angling at the edges may also affect coloration, so that pictures that are joined with a considerable overlap do not match well. Readers will see some pictures that are much more obviously mis-matched: the hues of water and sometimes of vegetation seem to change completely. That is because they were not taken on the same aerial run. Flight plans are subject to sudden change for many reasons—for example, the requirements of air traffic control. And a delay even of minutes means a change in sun angle and perhaps in light intensity. If the delay is extended to days or weeks by bad weather, then water conditions and vegetation will almost certainly be different.

Given that pictures are taken in the desired place, the only yardstick of success in aerial photography is the sharpness of ground details. Good definition requires very strong sunlight. A picture taken in poor light will come out, but ground features do not stand out starkly enough for it to be of much use. So aerial photographers are much more subject to weather limitations than most other aviators, whose only concern is getting safely from place to place. Overcast con-

ditions, even if the air is perfectly calm, mean no work can be done. Just a thin layer of light cirrus cloud above the aircraft softens the details in a picture. Isolated, fluffy cumulus clouds cast shadows that may obscure important features, interrupting or spoiling a run at the last moment. Clouds scattered below the plane may be less of a problem because their positions are more easily observed. But haze or extensive smoke—conditions that other fliers could avoid or ignore —rule out photography altogether.

Angling of the sun shortens an aerial photographer's productive hours, even in totally clear weather. The light cast below the plane is inadequate if the sun is within 30 degrees of the horizon—within three hours, say, of dawn or dusk around the latitude of Adelaide in mid-spring. Mid-winter work is scarcely worth attempting in the far south, not simply because of bad weather but also because the sun passes so far to the north that it is at a poor angle nearly all day.

The time of year is also important if the purpose is to assemble knowledge of vegetation, or to record slight contour variations that could be obscured by vegetation—for example, a flush of tall grass in late spring. In areas such as the far north, where there are big tide ranges and tidal flats kilometres wide, a set of pictures makes little sense unless the tide level is consistent. In that case the photographer can only work on certain days, regardless of weather and light conditions.

What the guide sections do

Information on virtually every place on the coast where travellers are likely to stay has been compiled from on-the-spot reports. In the descriptive material, every attempt has been made to bring out the points that give each place its own character, whether they be aspects of scenery, activity or historical interest. But the guide entries are not intended to amount to recommendations. Personal tastes vary as widely as the places. It is for readers to weigh up their own preferences and judge—from the pictures, from the descriptions and from the details of facilities and access—where the effort and expense of travel may produce the greatest reward.

Key maps are included with all entries. They place each locality in the context of its surrounding district, to assist travellers to find their bearings and to make sure that they do not overlook nearby points of possible interest. Minor roads, except for those essential to reach destinations discussed in the text, are omitted for the sake of

Key to town facilities

Hotel or motel	Holiday letting	Caravan park	Camping ground	Petrol	Chemist	Cinema	Public bar	Licensed club
Restaurant	Takeaway food	Boat hire	Bait	Swimming pool	Golf	Tennis	Bowls	Launching ramp

clarity. All key maps are designed with north to the top of the page. Shaded parts represent the areas covered in the accompanying aerial photographs. Some variation in the scale of the photographs has been dictated by space restrictions. The white northward arrow appearing on each picture indicates not only its alignment with grid north but also its scale: the arrow's length represents an actual ground span of about 250 metres.

Secrets unlocked from above

AERIAL pictures speak volumes to scientists. Botanists use them to classify vegetation—not only the dominant land plants but also seagrass beds and seaweeds. Zoologists can tell what animal life is likely to be found. Geologists are able to distinguish rock types, and by picking out ancient dunes and beach ridges they trace changes in sea level. Oceanographers discern currents, and 'fronts' of different water temperature. From wave patterns they can read the contours of the sea bed.

Laymen, too, can learn more—even of their home shores. Bushwalkers can spot unknown tracks, surfers can note unusual wave breaks, and boat owners can see the twists and turns of channels. Submerged reefs and bars and tricky currents show up. So do flood-prone areas.

Right: Contrasting colours of river and tidal waters at Burnett Heads, Qld, mark a 'front' where fish feed intensively

Travelling sand bars off Busselton, WA, go westward in storms, averaging a few metres each year. Beach sands move with them, perpetually altering the shoreline

Details of motoring access and of public transport availability are not exhaustive. They are based on the usual travel routes and practical requirements of most people. Other routes and services may be found, particularly from inland centres. Some hotels and motels operate pick-up services for booked guests arriving at railway or coach stations and airports. And once in a seaside township, visitors may find that they can avail themselves of local transport arrangements that are too variable to be listed.

Hours stated for surf club patrols, and for some other institutions such as museums and historic buildings, are subject to change, in most cases from year to year but sometimes at shorter notice. Weekday lifeguards, paid from council grants or business donations, may augment the part-time protection afforded by surf club volunteers in some beach towns. The financial basis of such services was considered too uncertain for them to be included in a book which it is hoped readers will use for many years.

Coastal conditions are subject to change, both gradual and sudden. References to the popularity of certain beaches for swimming, or to the suitability of certain spots for boating or fishing, should not be taken as absolute assurances as to their safety. It is always advisable for visitors to take every opportunity to borrow local knowledge, not only to avoid hazards but also to gain the maximum enjoyment from their stay.

The metropolitan sections do not include listings of transport details and other localised information. It can be presumed that all facilities will be found within a reasonable distance of the places dealt with in the text and that ample information on access and public transport will be easily obtainable by visitors.

The introduction to each regional section includes some discussion of general climatic factors, especially those that bear on the times of year when visits are likely to be most enjoyable. Charts showing the year-round averages of meteorological readings are included with some individual entries. They give a guide to seasonal trends in temperature, sunshine, rainfall and 3 p.m. relative humidity. But they have a most limited application. Actual weather conditions vary widely at any time, and quite small differences in distance or altitude from the site of the weather station could produce a markedly different climatic pattern. Figures are given only where they are of some relevance because the weather station is nearby.

Sydney

There can be few cities in the world that offer their residents quite the variety of beaches and waterways that Sydney does. Surfing beaches line over 60 km of the city's ocean coast and houses crowd the convoluted shores of its six harbours. One of the three rivers that reach the coast at Sydney is navigable for nearly 110 km inland.

Spectator craft track the harbour ferry fleet, hotly competing in their annual race

An early-rising optimist near Fort Denison

Barrenjoey Light, guarding Pitt Water

Hawkesbury River

Broken Bay

West Head

Palm Beach

Whale Beach

KU-RING-GAI NATIONAL PARK

Pitt Water

Avalon

Bilgola
Newport

Bungan

Warriewood

Narrabeen

Collaroy

Long Reef
Dee Why

Curl Curl

Harbord
Queenscliff

Manly

Middle
Harbour

North
Harbour

Lane Cove River

Middle
Head

TASMAN
SEA

Parramatta River

North
Sydney

Watsons Bay

Cockatoo Island

Port
Jackson

Vaucluse

Sydney
Cove

Rose
Bay

Sydney

Double
Bay

NEW SOUTH WALES

Bondi

Bronte

Clovelly

Coogee

Cooks River

Maroubra

Long Bay

Botany Bay

Little Bay

La Perouse

Georges River

Kurnell

Cronulla

SOUTH PACIFIC
OCEAN

Hacking River

Port Hacking

Bundeena

ROYAL NATIONAL PARK

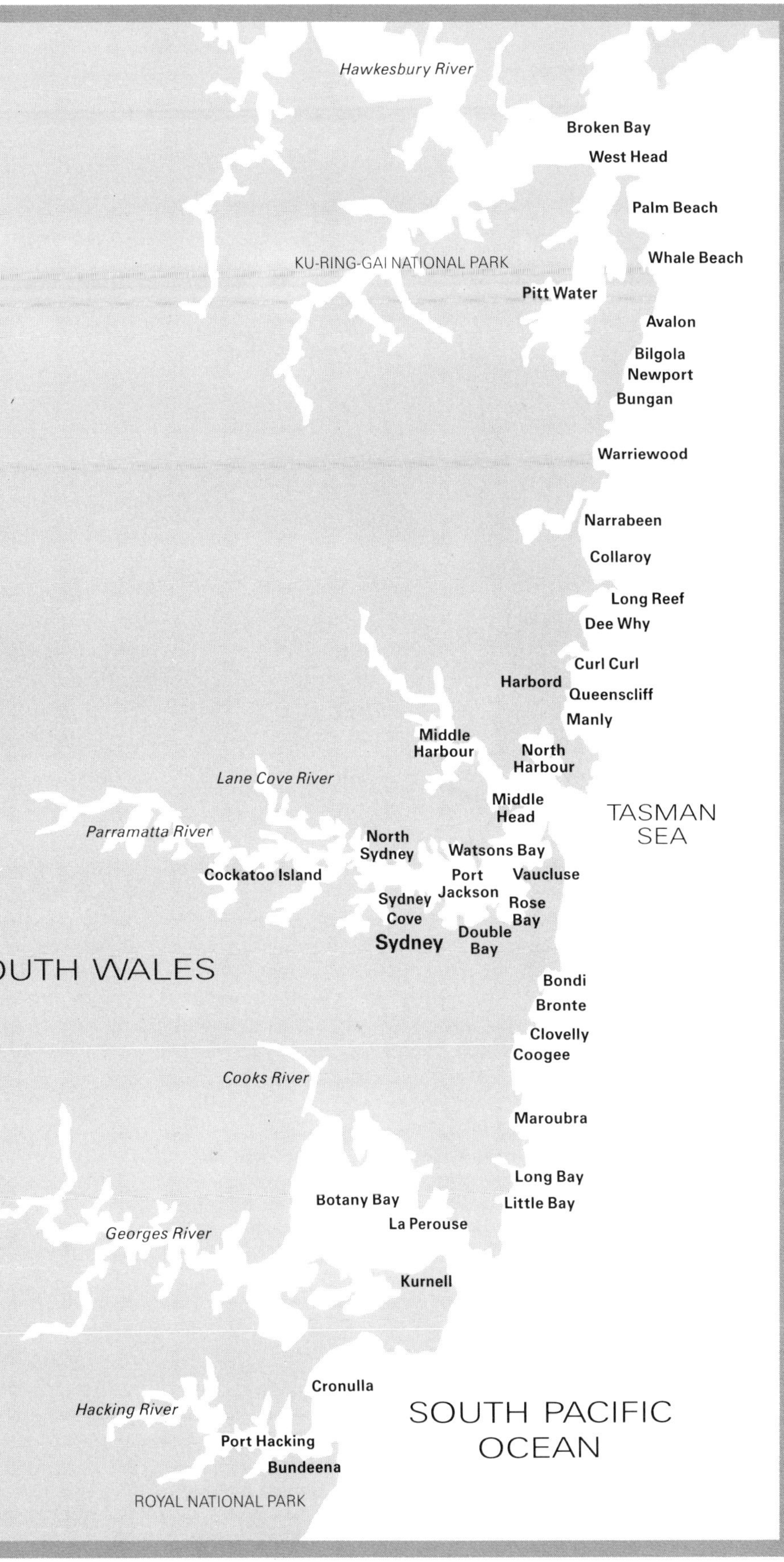

Pre-dawn light across Sydney Harbour throws the banks and islands of the Parramatta River into stark contrast with its twisting waterways

Shores where a nation was born

SYDNEY'S coastline is so complex that some of its twists and turns bewilder even life-long residents. Few can claim familiarity with every one of the ocean surfing beaches, let alone with all the bays and coves of the six metropolitan harbours—Port Hacking, Botany Bay, Port Jackson, Middle and North Harbours, and Pitt Water. Convolutions of the city and suburban shores extend the seaboard distance between Cronulla and Palm Beach—less than 65 km in a straight line—to 350 km. As a result, Sydney is probably unrivalled in the number of its people living, working or playing close to the sea. About 200 000 own registered pleasure boats. More than 10 000 are active in surf lifesaving clubs. Countless more take to the water informally on boards and surf skis, or in canoes and fishing dinghies. The number of anglers trying their luck from beaches, rock platforms and harbour wharves can only be guessed, and marvelled at. But by far the greatest number of Sydneysiders enjoying the sea are content to loll on ocean beaches and occasionally splash in the surf. On an ideal day, given 50 000 at Bondi alone, it is conceivable that half a million people crowd the Tasman shores. Thousands more head for secluded harbourside parks and beaches—some of which are among the unsung delights of Sydney, known only to and used almost exclusively by local residents.

For the visitor attempting an understanding of the city's intricate coastal geography, there is no better starting point than the birthplace of the New South Wales colony—Sydney Cove. Here at Circular Quay are the terminals of all the ferries and most of the cruise boats plying the harbour. Destinations are so varied that a day or more can be devoted, at little expense, to pleasurable discovery. Outside of commuter peak hours and at weekends some of the ferries make touring cruises, with commentaries that touch on facets of Sydney's history and its changing landscape. Surprisingly little attention is paid, however, to Circular Quay itself—though no part of Sydney has undergone greater transformation.

When the First Fleet anchored in 1788, the head of the cove was fringed by mudflats, and angled sharply back to the wide opening of the Tank Stream. Between 1837 and 1844, in an engineering project that was as ambitious in its day as the Harbour Bridge was in the 1920s or the Opera House in the 1960s, convicts built a horseshoe-shaped seawall beyond the low-water mark and reclaimed the mudflats with thousands of tonnes of sandstone rubble, hewn from the Argyle Cut in the Rocks district, from the Tarpeian Rock—a high outcrop on what became the site of Government House—and from Cockatoo and Pinchgut Islands. Wharves lined the curve of the horseshoe, forming 'Semi-Circular Quay'.

The name, absurdly shortened to Circular Quay, became completely nonsensical in the 1900s, when the western and southern side of the cove were straightened for new docks. In the 1950s the Quay skyline, too, was drastically altered with the construction of an overhead railway station, the Cahill Expressway and the first of Sydney's postwar generation of high, slab-sided office blocks of concrete and glass. A further refinement of the area began in 1981 with the

The harbour parks: a legacy of fear

THANKS to Sydney's long preoccupation with the chance of seaborne invasion, Port Jackson is unusually well endowed with coastal parks. High ground, once reserved for military occupation and fortification, has almost all been relinquished, but it remains reserved—for public recreation.

The first defence zone to be dedicated as a park was Bradleys Point, which became Ashton Park in 1908. Taronga Park was carved from it four years later to accommodate a superbly sited zoo. Together with some land at Dobroyd Head, and Shark and Clark Islands, Ashton Park was the first

major acquisition of the Sydney Harbour National Park administration, set up in 1975. Nielsen Park, plus extensive tracts of military land at North, Middle, South, Dobroyd, Georges and Chowder Heads, were handed over between 1978 and 1981.

Economic stringencies followed almost immediately, leaving the park administration short of the funds necessary to replant native vegetation and develop public facilities as quickly as was planned. Eventually, however, Sydney should be able to boast the most spacious and most natural coastal playgrounds of any city in the world.

Redevelopment in the Rocks area west of Sydney Cove has kept some of the original atmosphere

Installations such as this fort at Middle Head saved superb vantage points for the public

MASCOT												
	Jan	Feb	Mar	Apr	May	Jun	Jul	Aug	Sep	Oct	Nov	Dec
Maximum C°	26	26	25	23	20	18	17	18	20	22	24	25
Minimum C°	18	18	17	14	10	8	6	7	10	13	15	17
Rainfall mm	98	111	112	104	98	123	70	84	60	74	80	81
Humidity %	61	61	60	56	53	58	51	51	59	54	55	59
Rain days	11	11	12	11	11	11	9	10	10	11	11	11
Sunshine hrs	Summer 6 +			Autumn 6 +			Winter 6 +			Spring 6 +		

part-conversion of Alfred Street, behind the ferry terminals, into a promenade plaza. East of Circular Quay, past the unmistakable vaulted curves of the Opera House, is the harbourside entrance to the Royal Botanic Gardens.

Enjoyable walks lead around Farm Cove to the Domain and Mrs Macquarie's Point, where a long seat was carved from sandstone 170 years ago so that the governor's wife could rest while taking in her favourite view. Not far south, towards Woolloomooloo, the splendid Andrew ('Boy') Charlton Pool commemorates Australia's swimming hero of the 1920s.

To the west of Circular Quay, on slopes climbing to the Harbour Bridge approaches, is the tourist-oriented Rocks redevelopment, devised in the 1970s. Points of interest, which include the skilful restoration and adaptation of old bond stores and warehouses, are fully detailed at a visitor centre in upper George Street.

Very few private residences in the district are original. Most of its 19th-century houses were overcrowded, unsanitary hovels, pulled down in 1900 after rats from ships in Darling Harbour or Walsh Bay spread bubonic plague among the occupants. Down the hill just west of the ferry wharves, however, is Sydney's oldest home, Cadman's Cottage. It was built in 1816 for John Cadman, a ship's chandler. The lower floor, containing a re-creation of his workshop, faces across lawns to the roadways and distant docks of West Circular Quay. One glance shows how Sydney Cove has changed: boats used to be pulled up at Cadman's door.

Manly Beach—one of the most popular on Sydney's northern ocean coast

Port Jackson south

Wind-blasted shrubbery gives meagre shelter to the steep pathways of Gap Park, high above Watsons Bay village, but Sydney offers no finer coastal vantage-point. Sheer sandstone cliffs screening the harbour entrance rise 50 metres and more from the crashing swells of the Tasman. On one hand, past South Head and the Hornby lighthouse, the dark bulk of North Head looms; on the other, to the south, are Dunbar Head signal station and the Macquarie lighthouse. Ships and yachts pass close by the Gap, a deep indentation in the towering wall of rock. Some have cut their courses too fine—most notably the immigrant ship *Dunbar*, blown broadside into the cliffs in 1857. All but one of the 122 people aboard perished. The survivor, an Irish seaman, clung to a ledge for 36 hours. The *Dunbar's* anchor, recovered in 1907, is set in rock near the park entrance. Less than a kilometre away, inside South Head at Camp Cove, a plaque commemorates Governor Arthur Phillip's landing in 1788 after deciding to found the New South Wales colony in Port Jackson rather than Botany Bay. Camp Cove is popular for calm-water swimming and the slopes of Laings Point are ideal for picnics, but parking is scarce. An easy walk of about 20 minutes from the northern end of the cove follows the cliff line past Lady Bay, where full nudity is permitted, to South Head and up to the Hornby light. The track, dotted with old fortifications, skirts a naval training base, HMAS *Watson*. Visitors may enter the base to worship in the beautiful naval memorial chapel of St George the Martyr, built at the eastern cliff edge in 1961. Watsons Bay, with its usually gentle waters, saltwater baths, big park and playgrounds, beachfront beer garden and an array of eating houses and takeaway shops, has been a favourite family spot for generations. One of the ferries that used to serve the district, the *Greycliffe*, was cut in two by the liner *Tahiti* in 1927. The loss of 42 lives—mostly of school-children—was Sydney's worst harbour disaster.

Parsley and Vaucluse Bays have sheltered pocket beaches backed by shady reserves. Vaucluse Park has as its showpiece Vaucluse House, built between 1828 and 1837 for the explorer-politician William Charles Wentworth. Its front incorporates the wall of an 1803 cottage—the oldest remaining house structure in Sydney. The handsome mansion, well preserved, is open 10.00-17.00 as a historical museum. Greycliffe House, in nearby Nielsen Park, was built in the 1850s for a son-in-law of Wentworth. Already in use as the Sydney Harbour National Park headquarters, it is to be restored as a visitor centre when funds are available. The spacious park extends to headlands enclosing a beach that is netted against sharks in summer and has all facilities. Above it are varied walks and lookouts and an abundance of picnic spots. Hermitage Reserve runs south of the park along the eastern edge of Rose Bay, past many impressive private homes and gardens; jetties or ramps cluttering the shoreline are unauthorised structures and may be crossed without challenge. Rose Bay's waters bristle with yachts and motor boats, and the Woollahra Sailing Club offers tuition. Lyne Park has a public launching ramp.

Point Piper and Darling Point, each side of Sydney's most elegant shopping and dining area at Double Bay, have the city's greatest concentrations of opulent houses. Duff Reserve, a grassed lookout on Point Piper wedged between two big waterfront homes in Wolseley Road, is known to few outsiders: locals use it to view harbour yacht races. To the south, Seven Shillings Beach is dominated by Redleaf Sea Pool. The surroundings make a pleasant picnic area but parking is limited. The western side of Darling Point, on Rushcutter Bay, has a charming waterside reserve, while the inner shores of the bay are occupied by playing fields and the extensive but little-shaded lawns of Rushcutter Bay Park.

Moored yachts crowd the waters just offshore. A steep path from the western end of the park leads up over Macleay Point to the slopes of Elizabeth Bay. Onslow Avenue loops around stately Elizabeth Bay House, which was regarded as the finest private residence in Sydney when it was completed in 1838 for Alexander Macleay, the colonial secretary. After his descendants disposed of the mansion in the 1920s, it suffered neglect, conversion, reconversion and dilapidation until public authorities took it over in the 1960s. Restored to its original grandeur and furnished in 1840s style, the building is open from 10.00 Tuesday-Saturday and from 12.00 on Sundays. Below, at the waterline, the palm-fringed lawns

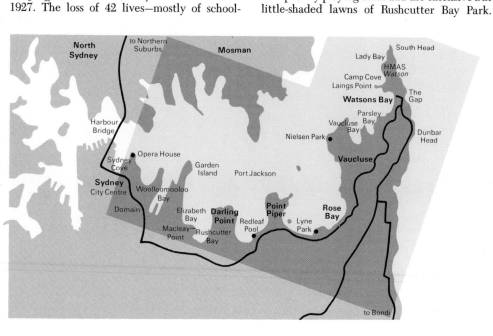

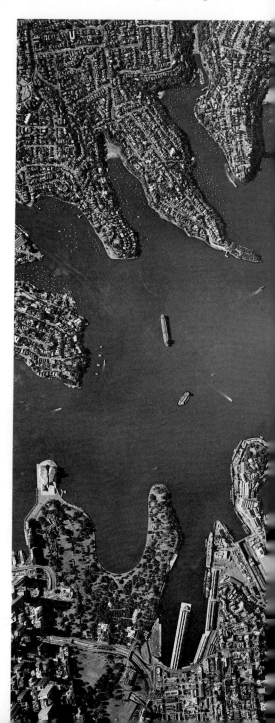

of Beare Park lie at the feet of luxurious apartment blocks. To the north, most of Potts Point is occupied by naval dockyards, extending to the RAN depot at Garden Island. Challis Avenue, almost above Elizabeth Bay House, short-cuts across the point to steps descending a cliff face to Woolloomooloo Bay. Old mercantile wharf sheds obscuring the narrow bay were demolished in 1982 after the site was transferred to RAN conrol as a further fleet berth. The land has been largely left clear, and a multi-storey car park has been built against the cliff with a public roof garden affording good views to the Domain.

Some of Sydney's most exclusive suburbs overlook the northern foreshores and busy waters of Port Jackson, between Elizabeth Bay and Watsons Bay

North Shore

Taronga Park, only 6 km from the heart of Sydney, occupies the finest position of any zoo in the world. Sloping down to the blue waters of Athol Bay, its terraced walks commanding a panorama of the harbour and city, the 24-hectare site was an inspired choice when the zoo was moved in 1912 from cramped and unhealthy quarters at Moore Park. Taronga Park quickly became much more than a place to inspect animals—its vistas are so arresting that the exhibits are often of secondary interest. But although the setting is priceless, it is not unique. Shores all the way to Middle Head are free of suburban development. North of Chowder Bay they are largely bare of vegetation. The land was Commonwealth military reserve until it came under Sydney Harbour National Park control in 1981; regeneration and the provision of public facilities will be a slow process. Cobblers and Obelisk Beaches, accessible on foot, are sheltered and secluded. Between them, the slopes of Middle Head are riddled with defence works—gun posts, tunnels, ramps and underground chambers, most of them excavated from solid rock.

Parks and beaches line the convoluted northern coast of Port Jackson. Much of Sydney's extensive waterfront has been set aside for public enjoyment

South of Chowder Bay, nature holds sway. An 8 km coastal walk of fascinating variety can be made around Chowder and Bradleys Heads and past the zoo into Little Sirius Cove. Starting to the south of the beach at Clifton Gardens, the track meanders among rocks and bush around Chowder Head to parkland and a stretch of quiet beach in Taylors Bay. The promontory reaching to Bradleys Head is occupied by Ashton Park, one of Sydney's earliest and biggest reserves of native bush. An easy walk continues past a tiny, unnamed beach to picnic grounds on the head-land. The slopes are pitted with old gun emplacements. Nearby is the mainmast from the first HMAS *Sydney*, which won distinction in 1914 by sinking the German raider *Emden* near Cocos Island. North from the head, the main track climbs into bushland but the waterline can be followed to Athol Bay. Steps above the wharf lead to Athol Reserve, where there are playgrounds and a pavilion which in the late 19th century was a dance hall. Revellers came by the ferryload, and behaved so scandalously that local residents forced its closure. The track merges with a road opposite the zoo aquarium, but resumes after the Taronga Park ferry wharf and continues to Whiting Beach and Little Sirius Point. Where it comes closest to the zoo wall a steep, rough trail drops to the water's edge and the remains of a camp occupied last century by an artists' colony. Opposite a nearshore rock, levelled off to make a boat landing, are overgrown stone steps, a wall and a pick-hewn rock face. Sirius Park, backing a pleasant pocket beach at the end of the walk, has an adventure playground, picnic tables and sea baths that are usable at high tide. The whole walk, with stops to examine its features, can be made at an easy pace in about three hours.

To the west, Cremorne Point is fringed by public parkland and gardens from Great Sirius Cove to Shell Cove. At Reid Park, behind an enclosed bathing beach, a roomy play area leads into a gully of native bush. Another playground with picnic sites occupies the tip of the point. An agreeable walk between the two, along sealed pathways linked by steps, is easily taken by get-ting off a harbour ferry at one wharf—Mosman or Cremorne—and returning from the other. Parks and lookouts on each headland of Neutral Bay are also most easily reached by ferry. Careening Cove accommodates the Royal Sydney Yacht Squadron. It is backed by Milson Park, a shady spot to picnic and watch the bustle of boat preparation. Kirribilli Point to the south is occupied by Admiralty House, the Governor-General's Sydney residence, and Kirribilli House, which is available for the Prime Minister or for high-ranking guests of the federal government. The grounds are opened on rare occasions for charity fêtes; otherwise both buildings are best seen from the harbour. Bradfield Park on Milsons Point is an ideal place to watch major shipping movements, though trains overhead on the Harbour Bridge make a disconcerting din. Lavender Bay, downhill to the west, is bordered by North Sydney Olympic Pool—heated in winter—and the year-round funfair of Luna Park, revived in 1982 after a three-year closure because of a fatal 'Ghost Train' fire. A reserve on Blues Point offers the closest views of mercantile shipping activities to the south in Darling Harbour. Balls Head Reserve, because of its greater height, commands the best inner-harbour views of all. It has varied picnic spots—some with barbecues and a free supply of gas—hilly bushwalks, and tracks by which the adventurous can descend to the waterline. More recreation reserves extend generously around Balls Head Bay, Gore Cove and Greenwich, where the Parramatta and Lane Cove Rivers meet at the head of Port Jackson.

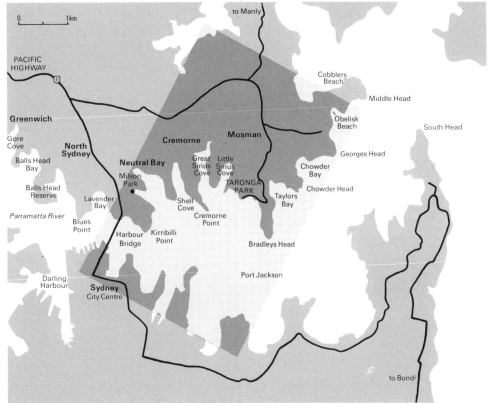

North and Middle Harbours

North Harbour holds two of Sydney's best-kept coastal secrets—Forty Baskets and Reef Beaches. While sands on the Manly Cove side of the harbour are carpeted with people during summer weekends, the western shores are virtually deserted. They are accessible only on foot, but not difficult to reach from Balgowlah Heights or Fairlight. A walkway from Manly winds through Esplanade Park, past Fairlight Beach and its swimming enclosure to grassy North Harbour Reserve—known to locals as the Old Dairy, because of its former use. A track through the bush of Wellings Reserve leads to Forty Baskets Beach. Its grass verges are shaded by trees, and a barbecue and firewood are provided. A small swimming enclosure is unusually free of rubbish: water movements along this stretch of the harbour seem to have a clearing effect. The track leads on through native bush to Reef Beach, in the Dobroyd Head section of Sydney Harbour National Park. Nude bathing is permitted here. On around the headland the shore is rocky, and walkers have to cope with dense bush and steep grades. An easier way to enjoy the splendid views from the headland is to take the Dobroyd Scenic Drive, which loops past three lookouts arranged around Tania Park. On Crater Beach, below the steepest cliffs, can be seen the shacks of a commune of squatters who subsist on seafood and vegetables and rarely leave the area.

Grotto Point, at the entrance to Middle Harbour, is perhaps the least-frequented part of the metropolitan coastline. Its steep and exposed terrain is daunting, and most people are content with the views to be had from a car park lookout at the end of Cutler Road, Clontarf. But the more energetic can scramble down a rough track to the lighthouse at the end of the point, or to secluded Washaway Beach. Ancient Aboriginal designs are carved into some of the rock faces; national park rangers guide walking parties to them once a fortnight. At low tide it is possible to walk from the point to Clontarf Beach, which has a swimming enclosure and a big, sheltered park at its southern end. Better-known walks start from the Spit, south of its lifting bridge. A particularly pleasant one leads around Pearl Bay and Beauty Point to Quakers Hat. Near the start, under the steep bank of Spit Road, are huge sandstone outcrops pitted by caves. Past Pearl Bay the shoreline route is rocky and sometimes strenuous, but full of variety. Shorter sections of this walk, which takes more than an hour each way, may be sampled by descending footpaths and steps from Bay Street or Delecta Avenue. On the other side of Spit Road is Parriwi Park, where native bush is being regenerated under National Trust auspices. A lookout at the top of the steep park is a favourite spot for watching Middle Harbour's summer evening yacht races. Chinamans Beach, to the south in Shell Cove, is backed by spacious Rosherville Park and makes an ideal picnic place. Some swimmers avoid it, however, because of the cove's bad reputation for sharks. Edwards Beach, on round Wyargine Point, has a

shark-proof pool and shady waterfront park with picnic tables. Rocky Point, virtually an island joined to the northern end of Balmoral Beach by a sandspit and footbridge, makes another pleasant picnic spot. The Balmoral waterfront, with its stately trees and old-established houses and shops, is dominated by huge sea baths splitting the beach that curves round to HMAS *Penguin* naval depot. To the east, Cobblers Beach marks the start of a chain of reserves from Middle Head to Mosman (*see* North Shore, previous page).

To the west of the Spit, Middle Harbour points fiord-like fingers surprisingly deep into the suburban heartland of the upper North Shore. Its longest reach extends past Roseville Bridge to East Killara, and its tidal effects are observed in creeks as distant as Frenchs Forest. Easily accessible bush reserves and picnic grounds occupy both shores, from Forestville to Killarney Heights and from East Killara to Castle Cove. Beaches and sandy shallows are found from Roseville Chase to the bridge, where there is also a swimming enclosure. One of the finest areas of natural bushland on the harbour can be found around Bantry Bay. Boat owners can inspect, from a distance, the remains of an old explosives complex built in 1915, but landings are not per-

mitted at the moment. South of Castle Cove, Sugarloaf Bay splits into two arms around the forested heights of Middle Cove. Short tracks from a central parking and barbecue area in Harold Reid Reserve reach a wide choice of rock shelves perched high over the water. The long promontory of Castlecrag—its maze of looping streets laid out by Walter Burley Griffin, the designer of Canberra—is fringed to the south by charming waterline reserves east of Sailors Bay Park. A smaller park on the opposite flank of Sailors Bay has a swimming enclosure. Clive Park, on the Northbridge headland, and Tunks Park and Primrose Park, at the heads of the two southernmost arms of Long Bay, off Cammeray, are busy boating centres. All the sheltered reaches of Middle Harbour are heavily used by boat enthusiasts and anglers, and there is intense competition for private moorings. Pressure was mounting in 1982 to have mooring rights limited to the residents of adjacent suburbs. There are public launching ramps at Roseville Bridge and at Tunks, Primrose and Clontarf Parks.

The complex waterways of North and Middle Harbours offer many possibilities for recreation. Some of the best spots are used only by locals

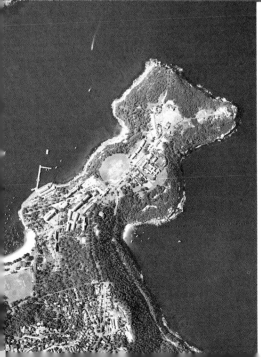

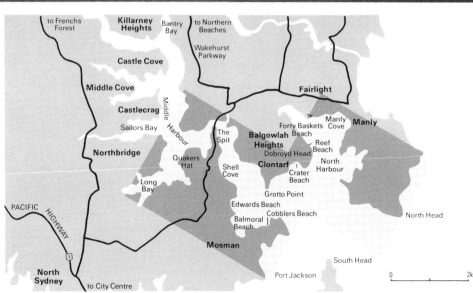

to Frenchs Forest

Killarney Heights

Bantry Bay

to Northern Beaches

Wakehurst Parkway

Castle Cove

Middle Cove

Fairlight

Castlecrag

Sailors Bay

Middle Harbour

The Spit

Forty Baskets Beach

Manly Cove

Manly

Balgowlah Heights

Reef Beach

Dobroyd Head

North Harbour

Northbridge

Quakers Hat

Clontarf

Crater Beach

Shell Cove

Long Bay

Grotto Point

Edwards Beach

Cobblers Beach

Balmoral Beach

PACIFIC HIGHWAY

Mosman

North Head

South Head

1

North Sydney

to City Centre

Port Jackson

0   2km

to Narrabeen
0
1km
Collaroy
Long Reef Point
Long Reef Beach
Dee Why Lagoon
Pittwater Road
Dee Why
Brookvale
Harbord Lagoon
Harbord
Curl Curl Beach
Manly Lagoon
Queenscliff
Freshwater Beach
Curl Curl Head
to North Sydney
Manly
Fairy Bower
Shelly Beach
Little Manly Cove
Spring Cove
North Harbour
North Head

North Head's rocky plateau affords spectacular cliff-top views of the harbour entrance

Manly to Dee Why

The beaches between Manly and Dee Why are almost the only remaining parts of this closely settled coastline not covered by houses

Manly Corso, crammed with shops and eating houses and part-closed to traffic to allow open-air dining and entertainment, is little more than 300 metres long. Yet it separates two worlds—a sweeping ocean coast of limitless seas and boisterous surf, and a harbour cove of constrained and gentle waters and old-fashioned amusements. Both aspects of the city have their adherents, in swarming numbers. Manly is the only coastal resort served by Sydney's harbour ferries, offering beachgoers the delight of the crossing itself as well as relief from crowded roads and car parks. 'Seven Miles From Sydney—A Thousand Miles From Care' is Manly's perennial sign. Since 1931 a funfair has greeted passengers on one side of the ferry wharf. On the other side a sandy beach and calm-water swimming enclosure extend towards Marineland, where big sharks are fed daily at 11.15 and 15.15, and a waterslide. An art gallery and museum nearby is open every afternoon except Monday. Waterline walks head west (see North Harbour, previous page) while residential streets to the east reach secluded beaches in Little Manly Cove and Spring Cove, where the North Head section of Sydney Harbour National Park starts. Tracks climb to the North Head Scenic Drive, which motorists and bus passengers reach by Darley Road. A level path loops from a car park to a

number of lookouts around the high headland, where native heath is being regenerated on what until 1979 was a military reserve. Water is available but there are no picnic facilities.

On Manly's ocean coast, Cabbage Tree Bay forms a sheltered corner with a sealed pathway leading to a little beach and rock pool at Fairy Bower, and a deep pocket of sand and a headland nature reserve at Shelly Beach. But views are overwhelmingly dominated by the long lines of green rollers mounting into surf off the beach that stretches to Queenscliff. Lining the ocean promenade are tall Norfolk Island pines, a symbol of Manly for more than a century—though some are by no means that old. Heedless of local protests, the army in 1942 ordered the felling of certain trees that were considered a potential navigation aid to Japanese invaders. Replacement saplings, planted immediately, have since grown to maturity. Whatever their age, most of the trees have become sickly because air pollution destroys their resistance to salt. The Queenscliff end of the beach cannot match Manly for shops and amusements, but it offers more scope for non-surfers: grassy parks surround Manly Lagoon, and a big rock pool is set into the base of Curl Curl Head. Freshwater Beach, over the hill at Harbord, gets its name from a creek—now replaced by a stormwater

pipe—which used to flow beside it. The surfing beach, the most sheltered on Sydney's northern coast, is bordered by a picnic area to the south and a rock pool to the north.

Curl Curl Beach has a notorious rip beside the rock pool at the southern end; surfers call it 'the Express'. Waters are far safer to the north, where there is another rock pool. An attractive, leafy park with barbecues surrounds Harbord Lagoon. Dee Why Beach is backed by a much more extensive lagoon, also ringed with recreation reserves. Wildlife Service signs help indentify the waterfowl and reptile species breeding in the lagoon. Its outlet, to the north, marks the start of Long Reef Beach, reaching past a headland golf links to good rock fishing ledges at Long Reef Point. The beach is particularly exposed to southerlies, but popular with board-riders when big swells break over reefs and offshore rocks. Swimming outside the flagged area near the lifesaving clubhouse can be decidedly dangerous; so can the lagoon outlet after prolonged rains. Stony Range Flora Reserve, open daily except public holidays on Pittwater Road 1.5 km south of Dee Why Lagoon, has short walking trails through three hectares of native vegetation. Picnic facilities and lavatories are provided and a kiosk operates in spring, when blossoming orchids and boronias draw most visitors.

Long Reef to Mona Vale

The untidy suburban sprawl that has crept along the narrow coastal strip from Collaroy north to Mona Vale has not improved an already flat and unpromising area. Where houses and apartment blocks have been kept back from the shore the beaches retain some of their natural charm, but where suburbia meets the sea the result is disastrous. Visitors can get a good idea of the geography of the district from Turimetta Head. To the south, beyond Narrabeen Head, is the long sweep of Narrabeen and Collaroy Beaches stretching away to Long Reef; to the south-west is Narrabeen Lagoon; to the north are the headlands and bays marching up towards Palm Beach, with the expanse of Pitt Water in the distance. All of the beaches, except Turimetta, have surf clubs with regular patrols in summer. Hotels, motels and holiday flats abound, and

North Narrabeen has a large camping ground and caravan park. All the headlands are capped by grassy reserves with good views—ideal places for a picnic, but lacking conveniences and water.

Long Reef Point, formerly an island, is surrounded by a wide rock platform and now linked to the mainland by a sandspit. Its summit feels pleasantly isolated because urban development has been kept at bay by a spectacularly situated golf links. The reef shore and its underwater face for 100 metres seawards are an aquatic reserve: no reef creature may be disturbed. Angling and spearfishing are permitted, however. The end of the reef is popular with board-riders because it often produces surf when other areas are flat. The 100-metre-high headland is also one of only three places on Sydney's north coast where hang-gliding is allowed—the others are Turimetta

Long, open beaches at Mona Vale and Narrabeen dominate this section of Sydney's northern coast

Head and Barrenjoey. A small car park, half-way up the hill, is reached through the entrance to the golf course. A broad track runs to the summit and down to the rock platform beyond. Another car park just beyond the golf clubhouse gives access to tiny Fishermans Beach (sometimes called the Basin). This protected cove is the base for the beach rescue helicopter, and is much used by windsurfers when conditions are right.

Dunes behind Collaroy and Narrabeen Beaches were 20 metres high at the turn of the century, when experimental aviators used to launch themselves from the summits suspended beneath flimsy contraptions of wood and fabric. Those mounds are long gone—removed as building material—and the shore is edged instead by houses, units and the occasional tower block. Collaroy and Narrabeen are arbitrary divisions of the one stretch of sand, nearly 5 km long, that runs from Long Reef to Narrabeen Head. Each section has its surf club and flagged swimming area, but on summer weekends when the ocean is quiet, swimmers and surfboard-riders dot the water along the entire length of the beach. Below Narrabeen Head, just beyond the point where Narrabeen Lagoon enters the sea, is one of the most famous surfing spots in Sydney. The area has been a nursery for many of Australia's best surfers, and the competition for waves is always fierce at any time of year.

Narrabeen Lagoon is making a slow recovery. A few years ago it was badly polluted, criss-crossed by powerful speedboats towing water-skiers, and facing the prospect of becoming a base for sea-plane flights. Thanks to the sewering of its catchment area and the permanent opening of its sea entrance, pollution has been considerably reduced and the birds and fish are returning. A speed limit of 8 knots has been imposed, so power boats have been replaced by canoes, small sailing boats and sailboards. The operations of a sand mining company in part of the lagoon are increasing the area deep enough for boating. Of many access points along the Wakehurst Parkway, the most popular is at the extreme western end of the lagoon, beside a National Fitness Camp. Catamarans and sailboards can be hired. Clean, calm and shallow water is found just inside the lagoon mouth, east of the Ocean Street bridge. This spot is particularly popular with people staying at the large caravan park on the northern shore of the lagoon.

Turimetta Beach is a pleasant surprise—a secluded spot in the centre of suburbia. It is well away from the main road and can only be reached on foot; access tracks descend to both ends. The beach, short but roomy, is backed by cliffs. Houses above are built well back from the cliff edge, so only a small portion of the southern end of the beach is overlooked. Turimetta has no surf patrols: swimmers must rely on common sense. If seas are too rough, big swimming and wading pools at the northern end of adjoining North Narrabeen Beach can be reached over the headland rocks. Extensive platforms both north and south of Turimetta are popular with anglers; fish are attracted by a sewer outfall 50 metres off the northern headland. Warriewood Beach, at the north-western base of Turimetta Head, is ringed by steep hills surmounted by a row of high-priced houses, providing shelter from all but a north-easterly wind. Mona Vale Beach is backed for most of its length by low dunes and a golf links. The nearest units and houses are a comfortable distance to the north, giving the beach a pleasant, open feeling. However, on days when a strong southerly blows, it can be exposed and bleak. North of the main beach, and tucked away between the rocky mass of Mona Vale Headland and a large rock platform that juts into the sea, is the Basin. Its little beach is protected and quiet, though overlooked by units and houses. A swimming pool has been built into the southern platform, which is also a favourite spot of local fishermen.

Warringah beaches

Rugged headlands march up the ocean shore of the Warringah Peninsula to Barrenjoey Head and Broken Bay. Small beaches between the headlands are popular weekend destinations for city dwellers

Two results in a recent survey of Sydney suburbs sum up life on Warringah Peninsula—they placed Palm Beach first in prestige and last in disposable income. But, apart from its social aspects, the area also has some of Sydney's cleanest and prettiest beaches. At its widest the peninsula is only about 2.5 km across. Nearly all available land has been built on, but most development is low-density and there are still plenty of parks, reserves and trees. Recreation revolves around the water. All the ocean beaches have surf clubs—Palm Beach has two—so there are flagged areas and regular patrols in summer. All the beaches, except Bungan, also have salt-water swimming pools. Holiday accommodation is limited mainly to flats and houses for rent. The only licensed hotel is at Newport. Church Point, Palm Beach and Newport have motels, and there is a guest house at Palm Beach. The nearest camping and

caravan park is well to the south at North Narrabeen (previous page).

Bungan Beach's chief asset is that it is difficult to reach, and therefore not as crowded as other spots. Visitors have to clamber down one of two paths that drop steeply from the road. Parking above the beach, on suburban streets, is strictly limited. Houses are set well back from the cliff edge, so a large part of the beach is overlooked only by a steep, grassy hillside. This apparent privacy encourages nude sunbathing, and every year the local paper reports sporadic prosecutions. There are no shops at the beach—the nearest are at Newport or Mona Vale.

Behind Newport Beach, Barrenjoey Road epitomises the seaside resort shopping centre—an untidy string of stores and fast-food outlets clamouring for the attention of passing motorists. In winter it is drab, in summer gaudy and

brash. The beach is popular with surfers. The best board-riding surf is generally at the northern end, but locals guard it jealously—they are intolerant of outsiders. Newport has a bad reputation for bluebottle swarms in summer. Bilgola Beach, a short drive north, is tucked away at the base of a fold in the hills. The beach is small, overlooked by some precariously placed waterfront houses, and flanked at both ends by tall cliffs. Bilgola has very little car parking, and no shops except for a kiosk at the southern end.

Avalon is one of the few beaches around Sydney to have retained its sand dunes almost untouched. It is more popular with surfboard-riders than with swimmers. Experienced surfers can catch the steep, hollow waves that form over a submerged rock ledge at Little Avalon, 100 metres south of the swimming pool. There is a good shopping centre behind the southern end

of the beach, with supermarkets, restaurants and take-aways. Hills rise behind Whale Beach to form a natural, green amphitheatre, with the beach as its stage. The sands stretch only 500 metres or so, but when the sea is calm it is possible to walk for some distance along the rock platforms at both ends of the beach. There is a kiosk at the beach and a small general store nearby. Parking can be difficult in the summer.

Palm Beach is prestigious, expensive and very popular. Every weekend in summer thousands of people flock to the area, but it still manages to retain an air of almost rural calm. Hidden among trees and lush shrubbery, houses cling precariously to the hillsides, craning for views of bushland and water. The commercial heart of Palm Beach—a handful of shops, a garage and an RSL club—is near the end of Barrenjoey Road. Just beyond the shops are a public wharf, a park and a large car park. Ferries leave the wharf for trips across Pitt Water to the Basin—a popular spot for picnicking and camping—and for cruises up the Hawkesbury River. More intrepid sight-

seers can take sea-plane flights from the wharf at the end of Governor Phillip Park. There is a small general store there, and the car park is a popular place for launching small boats over the sand into Pitt Water. The water beside the car park is shallow for some distance from the shore—ideal for children—and the broad sweep of North Palm Beach is only a two-minute walk away. When a strong southerly wind makes most of Palm Beach too rough for swimming, there is a protected corner behind the headland at the southern end of the beach. There, at Cabbage Tree Boat Harbour, the water is almost always calm. Beyond the northern car park a low isthmus of sand—only 100 metres wide in places—connects the mainland to the rugged mass of Barrenjoey Head. Views from the top are well worth a steep, 113-metre climb. From the lighthouse the entire expanse of Broken Bay is laid out like a map. The path to the lookout starts beside the boatshed at the extreme northern end of the beach on the Pitt Water side. The walk from the car park to the summit and back takes an hour.

Pitt Water and Hawkesbury River

Luxuriant vegetation spills from the high spine of Warringah Peninsula to the broad expanse of Pitt Water. To the west across this deeply carved southern arm of Broken Bay loom even more commanding heights on Lambert Peninsula, forest-fringed and topped by dense heathland scrub. The sea between, completely sheltered, is a boating paradise. Governor Arthur Phillip, who led the exploration of Pitt Water in March 1788, preferred it to Port Jackson and to any harbour he had visited in his naval career. He called it 'the finest piece of water I ever saw'. A multitude of modern seafarers agree: small boats crowd anchorages in every bay and inlet, and during summer weekends the whole 9 km reach of water, up to 2 km wide, is peppered with craft ranging from dinghies to big luxury cruisers. Public wharves are plentiful and there are launching ramps at Church Point, Bayview, Careel Bay and Palm Beach. It is also possible to launch over sand at other points along the shore. Fuel is available near the constructed ramps and at Newport, at the head of the inlet. The Royal Motor Yacht Club has its headquarters in Horseshoe Cove at Newport, and the Royal Prince Alfred Yacht Club is a little to the south at Green Point. Pitt Water holds no major boating hazards except for the usual inshore problems of shallows and rocks. An 8-knot speed limit applies on all bays and inshore waters from Careel Bay south to Elvina Bay. From Taylors Point a torpedo firing range, stretching north for 3 km and marked by pontoons, is a prohibited anchorage and must be kept clear when red flags are shown or when sirens are sounded. Seaplanes based at a wharf north of Palm Beach golf course sometimes take off and land to the north of Observation Point.

Shores along both sides of the northern end of Pitt Water are dotted with small, sandy beaches, but many on the western side can be reached only by boat, or on foot through Ku-ring-gai Chase National Park. Beaches at the southern end of Pitt Water are made less attractive by mangroves and mud. The most popular on the eastern side are Long Beach, Clareville Beach and Paradise Beach. The water is shallow and calm at the shore, although it can be murky and is sometimes polluted by the moored boats. Parking at all the beaches is very limited. Long Beach has a small shop. Most of the western shore is in the national park but some private land adjoins the water. Small settlements, dotting the shore at various points, rely on boat access. So

Many hundreds of pleasure craft dot the sheltered upper reaches of Pitt Water. Some settlements on the western shore can only be reached by boat or on foot

do the residents of Scotland Island, which retains a good cover of trees in spite of the number of houses on it. Many tiny coves and beaches on the western shore of Pitt Water can be reached on foot from the national park road to West Head. Other trails descend the opposite slopes of Lambert Peninsula, to Cowan Water. The starting points of all tracks are signposted with numbers, keyed to maps obtainable at park entrances or at the Kalkari visitor centre, near Bobbin Head. Some trails are rough and extremely steep in parts—the shortest are often the most strenuous. Any of the accessible shores make good impromptu picnic spots, but facilities are provided only at the Basin, on Pitt Water. This is also the only permitted camping site in Ku-ring-gai Chase's area of nearly 15 000 hectares. Other equipped picnic grounds on Lambert Peninsula are at high level along the West Head road and near a display centre above the headland loop. Short nature walks of varying difficulty start near a lookout commanding superb views of Broken Bay and Palm Beach. Travellers from the Pitt Water side also pass delightful picnic spots beside waterfalls at McCarrs Creek, just before entering the national park. Across the base of the peninsula, the road descends to Coal and Candle Creek, one of the busy boating inlets of Cowan Water. Clippers Anchorage at Akuna Bay is a well-planned complex of marine service facilities, shops and a restaurant centred among moorings, marina walkways, a huge boat-stacking shed and an ample car park. Luxury cruisers and ocean racing yachts can be examined at close quarters, along with houseboats and launches available for hire for trips into Broken Bay or up the Hawkesbury River. Not far west at Illawong Bay, well-equipped picnic grounds are wedged in the shelter of steep hillsides, covered in varied native bush. More boat-hire facilities and a kiosk are found at Cottage Point, a less-frequented spot reached by a narrow road branching from the westernmost loop of the main route.

Ku-ring-gai's oldest-established boating centre, at Bobbin Head on Cowan Creek, has a separate access route connecting with the

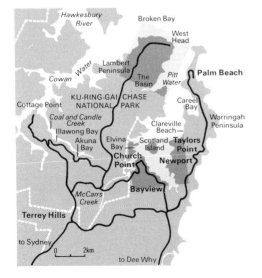

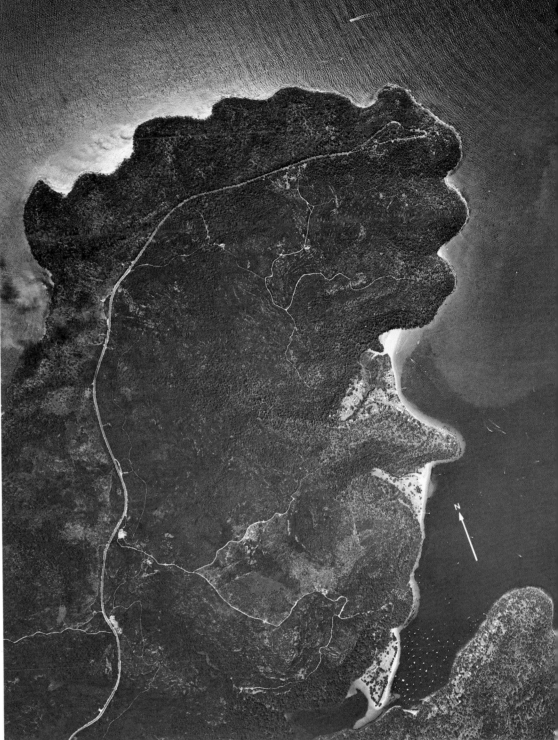

Tiny sandy beaches around the shores of rugged Lambert Peninsula make ideal picnic spots

Pacific Highway at Turramurra and Mount Colah. Its extensive picnic grounds, near Halvorsens' boatyards and marina, are frequently crowded; quieter sites may be found a little downstream at Apple Tree Bay. Both places have food and drink stalls and shark-netted swimming areas. The only other netted enclosure on the park shores is at the Basin camping ground on Pitt Water. At the Basin a net across the narrow entrance to a lagoon provides a large, safe swimming area. Apple Tree Bay and Akuna Bay have public boat ramps. Just outside the park's northern boundary is the town of Brooklyn, yet another major boating base. It can be reached by the old section of the Pacific Highway now superseded by the F3 Freeway, or by train to Hawkesbury River station. Brooklyn's boat harbour in Parsley Bay is backed by a pleasant park with picnic facilities. Commercial wharves and slipways, near the railway station, include the berths of ferries which run scheduled services and cruises to the islands of the lower Hawkesbury. Dangar Island has many private homes, Milson Island upriver is a penal detention centre. Spectacle Island and Long Island, closest to Brooklyn, are nature reserves.

Bondi to Long Bay

Bondi is the closest ocean beach to central Sydney and is the city's most popular, regularly attracting more than 50 000 people on hot summer days. Crowds using the wading pools, playground, baths, park, pavilion and beach spill over onto an esplanade lined with restaurants, shops and hotels. Sydneysiders discovered the pleasures of Bondi long before its beachfront cattle pastures became a public park in 1882. As early as the 1850s coachloads of city-dwellers arrived to take in the sea air and stroll along the shores—fully clad. Soon after its acquisition as a reserve, baths were constructed on the southern promontory and the rows of sprawling sandhills were contained by a seaside promenade. By 1894 the horse-powered trip from the city to the coast was replaced by steam trams which careered down the slopes leading to the beach at a hairraising 65 km/h—giving rise to the expression 'shoot through like a Bondi tram'. Australia's first official surf lifesaving club was formed at Bondi

in 1906. Two clubs now patrol the beach and there are usually three sets of flags to indicate safe areas free of rips. Rock ledges under Ben Buckler, the beach's northern headland, attract anglers and at low tide snorkellers can explore big rock pools teeming with marine life. Just north of Ben Buckler an outcrop of rock, left uncovered by the rolling fairways of Williams Park golf links, bears weathered carvings of fish and corroboree dancers cut by the Biddigal Aboriginal tribe, who inhabited the Bondi district until the early 1800s. At the northern end of the golf links a sewage outfall spills tens of thousands of litres of effluent into the sea every day. Beaches may be closed if swells drive the waste onshore, or if industrial disputes allow it to be discharged untreated. Anglers know it as the Murk, and are grateful for the fish it attracts.

Around the cliffs south of Bondi a pathway climbs past the rocky surfing beach of Mackenzies Bay to Tamarama. At the turn of the century,

funfair roller-coasters sped on high tracks between the headlands. Today, although parking is scarce and rips are strong, Tamarama is a popular sunbathing and surfing spot. At Bronte Beach, lawns sweep down from a wooded gully to pine trees and palms shading a park dotted with picnic tables. Sheltered swimming areas at the southern end of the beach are enclosed by arcs of rocks and overlooked by baths built well above the sea's wash. Southerly swells can produce rideable waves at the northern end of Bronte, but a strong rip can develop to the south. Clovelly, south of Bronte past the slopes of Waverley Cemetery and the playing fields and bowling greens of Burrows Park surrounds a long inlet of shallow water, well protected by its rock-strewn entrance. Wide concrete platforms lining the sides of the inlet, with steps down to the water, make it seem like a mammoth swimming pool. The calm waters make an excellent training area for snorkellers, skindivers and swimmers. Toddlers

Bondi Beach has achieved international fame, although it is only proximity to the city that distinguishes it from any of Sydney's many other ocean beaches

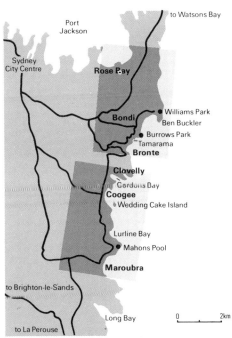

can paddle in a wading pool on the southern platform. The small pocket beach of Gordons Bay is a 500-metre walk from the car park flanking Clovelly Beach. The path hugs the edge of high cliffs above popular sunbathing positions on massive rocks lining the bay. A bombora off the southern headland produces consistently rideable waves for surfers, but rips are dangerous.

The open parks on the headlands around Coogee Beach and its series of surf-fed rock pools incorporate a fitness track covering just over 2 km, with stops at 12 sets of exercise equipment. The beach is partly sheltered by Wedding Cake Island and board-riding waves develop only in heavy swells. Smaller waves are popular with body surfers and children on light boards. Earlier this century Coogee was Sydney's foremost pleasure resort, and boasted shark-proof netting, floodlit night surfing and a dance hall on an amusement pier. The dome of an old aquarium still dominates the northern beachfront. Between Coogee and the long sweep of Maroubra Beach a break in the sheer cliff face provides

local residents with a secluded sunbathing spot at Lurline Bay. Intrepid swimmers dive from the rocks into deep water and wait to be pushed back up onto the rocks as the sea surges in, but this is not a place for the faint-hearted—or for anyone at all in rough conditions. Farther south, safer swimming is found at Mahons Pool. The wide, tiered rock ledges surrounding the pool provide an amazing seascape as the waves wash over them and cascade in foam around the placid surface of a big rock basin.

Waves commonly 2-3 metres high draw boardriders year round to Maroubra Beach; a large part of the bay is set aside for the use of surf craft. Plans to replace the old wooden dressing sheds and rickety picnic pavilions will change the face of Maroubra's long beachfront walkway with well-appointed club buildings and public amenities. Gunfire reverberates from the rifle range which occupies the barren promontory between Maroubra and Long Bay, a sheltered inlet backed by a small park, playgrounds, barbecues and picnic tables near a launching ramp.

Busy inner-city suburbs ensure dense crowds at Clovelly, Coogee and Maroubra beaches in summer

Botany Bay

Rolling lawns, bush reserves and golf links spread along the ocean coast and over the headlands of Botany Bay, just a short distance from the wide land reclamations of Port Botany and the massive tanks of Kurnell's oil refinery. Within sight of the refinery jetty are monuments and plaques commemorating Lieutenant James Cook's first landing in Australia. A designated historic site of 324 hectares covers all the eastern extremities of Kurnell Peninsula. Near the park headquarters, visitors can wade out to the rock onto which the first man ashore in 1770, Mrs Cook's young cousin Isaac Smith, is thought to have leapt. A small museum exhibits relics of Cook's voyages and of HMS *Endeavour*, along with Aboriginal artefacts. Shaded lawns outside, furnished with picnic tables and barbecues, slope towards the bay. Inland, the Muru and Yena tracks combine to make an easy bushwalk of about 45 minutes through low scrub and woodland to the ocean coast. The Cape Solander Scenic Drive sweeps along the park's ocean cliffs and a road branches off near the eastern end of the Muru track to a pebbly beach with picnic spots and low rock ledges popular with anglers. The Cape Baily walking trail strikes out from the southern end of the scenic drive along heath-covered clifftops. It passes the narrow cleft of Tabbagai Gap, where the remains of weekend fishing shacks perch on the southern cliff face.

Industrial developments have claimed much of the woods and wetlands surrounding the park on Kurnell Peninsula. Removal of sand for building purposes has altered an extensive area of high dunes which until the mid-1970s spared the beaches at Cronulla from views of a conglomeration of smokestacks, factories and storage tanks. Silver Beach, on the bay shores below Kurnell township, is broken by a series of groynes designed to stabilise the beach sand. Shark netting strung between two of the long, rocky arms forms a swimming enclosure. To the west are the sandspits, mudflats, dunes and mangrove swamps of Towra Point, set aside in 1982 as part of the proposed Botany Bay Headlands National Park. Plans for the point are aimed at conservation of migratory bird habitats, with limited public access for educational use. The new national park will incorporate Bare Island, reached by a plank bridge from La Perouse. Two massive cannon which guarded the entrance to Botany Bay in the 19th century remain housed in deep pits dug into the island's fortified terraces. A maze of trenches and passageways leads between the guns and up to vantage points with sweeping views of the bay and its entrance. On the grassy knoll of the La Perouse Historic Site is a French-donated monument to Rear-Admiral La Perouse, who arrived in Botany Bay eight days after Captain Arthur Phillip's First Fleet in 1788. His party stayed six weeks to replenish supplies and repair their two frigates. Since the

Two road bridges span the mouth of the Georges River and link Sydney to its far southern suburbs

Botany Bay Heads have escaped the development that dominates the rest of the bay

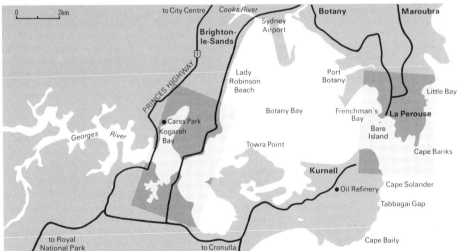

monument's construction in 1828, the crews of many French ships have added plates commemorating their visits; they fill a small plot around the original obelisk. The site is maintained with funds from the French government. Other buildings on the hillock are a customs watchtower, erected before 1820, and a cable station—later a Salvation Army hostel—built by the company which laid the first telegraph line to New Zealand in 1876. The beach of Frenchman's Bay, stretching north from La Perouse to Yarra Bay and the long concrete breakwater wall of Port Botany, has a launching ramp, a boat-hire depot and a summertime food kiosk. A rugged stretch of coast, popular with walkers and rock fishermen, reaches around steep slopes east of the La Perouse monument. Paths worn through low scrub skirt three golf courses past Cape Banks to the sheltered beach of Little Bay.

From Cooks River to Georges River, the long, grassy stretch of Cook Park rises behind an unbroken beach. Shark-proof swimming enclosures, playgrounds, boat ramps and an abundance of shady picnic spots make Lady Robinson Beach as popular as any on the ocean coast in summer. The wide lower reaches of Georges River, flowing into the south-west corner of Botany Bay, are indented with inlets and bays, well-equipped with launching ramps, jetties and yacht clubs for the thousands of boating enthusiasts who crowd the bay on weekends. An Olympic-size pool, playing fields, picnic grounds and a large swimming enclosure occupy the banks of Kogarah Bay below the thickly wooded slopes of Carss Bush Park. Walking and cycling tracks cross the park and a small cottage museum, open 13.00-17.00 on Sundays and public holidays, has a variety of interesting displays.

Wanda Beach sweeps around to Cronulla on the north side of Port Hacking. It is only 1 km across the water to Bundeena, but 32 km by road

Cronulla and Port Hacking

Cronulla Peninsula's wide finger juts between pounding ocean surf and the sheltered waters of Gunnamatta Bay, one of Port Hacking's many tranquil inlets. The great popularity of Cronulla can be partly attributed to its having the only beaches reached by suburban trains. The journey from Sydney first became an easy day trip in 1911, when steam tram services were inaugurated from Sutherland. Even before then, the small beach settlement had been a popular haunt of young men who would hike or ride down for surfing, and well-to-do families kept cottages along the wooded banks of Gunnamatta Bay. The peninsula's eastern shores present a rocky face to the sea, with reefs hiding under the waves just offshore. A concrete promenade skirts the bottom of low cliffs close to water level, and large parks open up between waterfront houses which cram the peninsula from shore to shore. At Shelly Beach an avenue of palms leads across lawns shaded by groups of Norfolk Island pines to barbecues and a picnic pavilion on the rocky beach platform. A big rock pool draws crowds of children to its calm waters while small waves forming over a nearshore reef attract young surfers.

From the wide, sandy arena of South Beach and its park, picnic grounds and changing sheds, a pathway flanked by tall apartment buildings threads around a promontory past two tidal rock pools to North Beach, just a short distance from the town centre. Farther to the north, Bate Bay's beaches stretch around a continuous sandy crescent almost 5 km long. Surfing waves can form along most the bay, depending on current and winds, but board-riders and sunbathers mainly gather around the surf clubs at Cronulla Point, North Beach, Elouera and Wanda. High, bare dunes north of the road access to Wanda Beach reach up to 1 km inland; in spite of the extensive removal of sand for the building industry, they retain the appearance which suited them as the location for the 1940s desert war film *Forty Thousand Horsemen*. Persistent onshore winds continue to strip the dunes of vegetation, but a successful conservation project has been carried out on a narrow strip along the beach, where frontal dunes have been fenced and planted with marram grass to stop sand-drift.

Merries Reef shelters the northern end of Bate Bay, creating a calm stretch of beach separated by a wide sandspit from the shallow and placid inlet of Boat Harbour Bay. A cluster of weather-beaten weekend cottages shelters at the head of the bay and the small circular inlet has been a haven to many boats caught between Port Hacking and Botany Bay at the onset of rough weather. On private land around Boat Harbour a network of tracks made by the uncontrolled use of off-road vehicles has led to severe erosion of the clifftops and secondary dunes. The state government plans to resume a strip reaching for 300 metres behind the beach, with provision for its conservation, revegetation and use as a recreation reserve.

On the eastern banks of Gunnamatta Bay, gnarled eucalypts shade a wide grassy park sloping to the water's edge. Picnic pavilions, changing sheds, an amphitheatre for music and drama and a kiosk lie behind the bay's sandy beach. A broad pier hung with shark-proof netting encloses a large swimming area and provides a popular base for anglers. Boats are launched from a ramp in the northern corner of the bay, and small outboards can be hired at a nearby boatshed. From the Gunnamatta wharf launches leave for Bundeena, which is situated at the northern entrance of Royal National Park. This is an irregular service, so it is advisable to check with the relevant authorities before making plans. The large bays and arms of the northern shores of Port Hacking, generously equipped with boat ramps, jetties and fuelling points, are mostly occupied to the backshore by suburban residences. Much of the southern shore is part of the national park, providing a large expanse of natural bushland which makes for excellent cruising and shore picnics. However, navigating between sand bars can sometimes be tricky.

Sydney to Eden

A climate preferable to their own draws residents of inland New South Wales, Canberra and even Melbourne to the stretch of coast from Royal National Park to Eden. Its many attractions include superior boating and fishing—and the world's whitest sands at Jervis Bay.

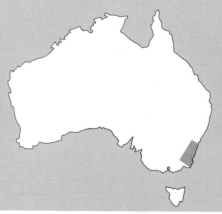

Australia's highest sea cliffs, towards St George Head, south of Jervis Bay

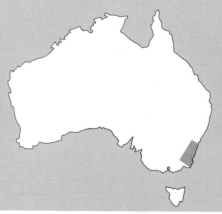

Unloading the catch at Eden

The Glasshouse Rocks, near Narooma

Sydney

Royal National Park • Marley
Garie
• Stanwell Park

• Wollongong
Port Kembla • Windang
Shellharbour •
• Kiama
• Gerringong
• Shoalhaven Heads
Shoalhaven River

• Orient Point

• Currarong

Huskisson • Jervis Bay
St Georges Basin • Wreck Bay
Sussex Inlet •

• Conjola Lake
• Ulladulla
Burrill Lake • Tabourie Lake

• Bawley Point
• Kioloa
Clyde River • Depot Beach
Durras Lake

Batemans Bay •
• Malua Bay
• Broulee
Moruya •

• Tuross Head
Potato Point •

NEW SOUTH WALES   • Dalmeny
• Narooma

• Bermagui

• Canberra

AUSTRALIAN
CAPITAL
TERRITORY

SOUTH PACIFIC
OCEAN

• Tathra

Merimbula •
• Pambula Beach

Eden •
Twofold Bay

VICTORIA

Cape Howe

Cool seas yield a fishing bonanza

CITY INFLUENCES are interrupted only briefly by the Hacking River and the high, cliffed heathlands of Royal National Park. They resume to the south, extending at least to Kiama. The Illawarra region, drawing on rich coal measures and heavily dominated by industrial Wollongong and Port Kembla, is closely tied to the Sydney economy. Rural production from a broad coastal plain is aimed at Sydney consumers. Most tourists and holidaymakers come from the state capital.

From Shoalhaven on, the South Coast establishes a quiet, slower-paced character of its own. Rolling foothills of the southern tablelands, separated by a succession of river valleys and narrow flats, reach close to the Tasman Sea. Bays alternate with rounded granite headlands. Each sheltered river estuary has its shipping port, dating back to the heydays of hinterland timber-getting and gold mining, or of bay whaling. Now these harbours are bases for Australia's most intensive commercial and sporting fisheries. Because major urban centres are remote, more fish is canned than is marketed fresh. And in dairying, the region's other mainstay, producers concentrate on cheese-making rather than fresh milk or butter supply.

The climate has year-round advantages, its mildness appealing especially to people from Canberra, inland New South Wales and Victoria—even Melbourne. In summer this coast is cooler than their home districts, and for the rest of the year it is markedly warmer. Many houses, on early subdivisions sprawling over prime tracts close to the ocean, see their owners only at holiday time. But resident populations are swelling, often creating a sharply rising market for desirable building sites.

Fishing remains the favoured pastime, not only in the cool and frequently storm-roughened waters of the Tasman but also in the rivers and the coastal lakes that characterise so much of the region. Townships tend accordingly to be peaceful places, offering little that glitters for tourists seeking to buy their fun. That is bound to change in at least one place—Jervis Bay, destined in the 1990s to take over from Sydney as the Royal Australian Navy's principal fleet base. Environmental watchdogs will strive to ensure that the bay's rare natural qualities are preserved. Not least of these is the remarkable colour of its powdery silica sands—acknowledged in the Guinness Book of Records as the whitest in the world—and the vibrant turquoise hue that they lend to nearshore waters.

Point Perpendicular lighthouse marks the northern tip of Jervis Bay

A surf ski rider at Rosedale, south of Batemans Bay

Drawing the line in no man's land

TERMINATION of New South Wales at Cape Howe makes geographical sense. Here the coastline veers westward, giving Victoria's shores a clearly different climate and structure.

In fact the choice of a border point was made simply to avoid political argument. This corner of Australia was, and still is, unpopulated. Beyond Eden, nature reserves occupy an area greater than the whole urban district of Sydney.

A cairn of boulders was erected on the cape in 1850, a year before Victoria's territory was carved from NSW. But not until 1870 did surveyors attempt to define the boundary inland, in a straight line from Conference Point to the nearest headwater of the Murray River. Alexander Black and Alexander Allan spent two years on this survey, struggling to the distant and remote heights of the Snowy Mountains.

In 1985 the Black-Allen line was checked with modern techniques and found to be near-perfect. But a few markers were obscured. A 50-year-old border sign near Genoa, Vic, was found to be out of place. NSW had been maintaining some of Victoria's share of the Princes Highway…14 metres of it.

Planted grasses bind the sand at Stanwell Park

Royal National Park

On Sydney's southern doorstep a richly varied coast—free of housing and commercial development for most of its length—stretches for more than 20 km. Behind it Australia's first national park, declared in 1879, covers almost 15 000 hectares of forest, bushland and heath. Roads give easy access to most of the park's natural attractions, and to picnic areas and lookouts. The only serviced camping and caravan ground, near Bundeena at Bonnie Vale, has lavatories and washing facilities but no power outlets. A long sand bar provides suitable swimming for children. Bush camping is allowed in most of the park, except within 1 km of roads and picnic grounds or in areas that are closed from time to time for conser-

vation purposes. Permits are issued at the park headquarters at Audley.

Well-developed walking trails lead to the rugged headlands and secluded coves of the coast. Beaches at Marley, Curracurrang, Era, Burning Palms and Hell Hole can be reached only on foot. They and the busier beaches with road access are linked by a coast track from Bundeena to Otford. Low-lying at first, it rises in the south to the rims of high cliffs, giving views as far as Port Kembla.

Marley is a 45-minute walk east from Bundeena Drive, through thick bush past Deer Pool, a pleasant swimming hole. The longer routes from Bundeena lead to the open sandhills of Marley Beach. Sandstone bluffs shelter the

beach, but the surf is considered dangerous. The track leads on through scrub above the rocky shoreline to Little Marley, where there is a grassy area and the waves are more gentle. Wattamolla can be reached by car. It offers picnic spots and walks with spectacular high-level views, as well as beach and lagoon swimming and fishing along the shore. Nearby Curracurrang is a 3 km walk from parking areas and has a rocky foreshore, but its waterfall and swimming hole make it an attractive picnic place.

Garie, the most popular surfing beach, has ample parking space near the lifesaving clubhouse. Picnic spots with barbecues are scattered around the area, which is also favoured by rock

Varied beaches and camping spots between Burning Palms and Garie can be reached by roads or foot tracks from the Governor Game Lookout

N

Marley Beach's deep wedge of sand penetrates to the edge of Marley Lagoon; at left is Little Marley

fishermen. From the road down to Garie, just short of the Governor Game Lookout, an unsealed road branches south to a parking and picnic area at Garrawarra. Foot tracks descend the cliffs to patrolled beaches at North and South Era and Burning Palms. The final leg of the coast track to Otford leads through the thickets of Palm Jungle and along a rocky shore past Werrong Point and Hell Hole and Bulgo Beaches.

ROYAL NATIONAL PARK east of Princes Highway or F6 Southern Freeway 30-50 km from Sydney (turn off at Loftus, Waterfall or Helensburgh).
TRANSPORT: trains Sydney-Royal National Park daily; ferry Cronulla-Bundeena daily; no beach transport.
NEAREST SERVICES: Bundeena or Helensburgh.
SURF CLUB PATROLS: October-Easter, at Garie Saturday 13.00-16.00, Sunday and public holidays 09.45-17.30; at Era and Burning Palms Saturday 11.30-15.30, Sunday and public holidays 09.00-16.00.
YOUTH HOSTEL: Garie Beach, open year-round.

Houses that die with their owners

NEARLY 300 privately rented weekend cabins remain in Royal National Park, out of more than 400 which the National Parks and Wildlife Service inherited when it took control in 1967. Many date from the 1930s Depression, when people squatted in the park and built their own shelters. Owners registered in 1966 were granted occupancy licences. These cannot be transferred to other people or passed to descendants. So when a registered occupier dies, the cabin is demolished. Ultimately all are to go.

Bonnie Vale, at the northern end of the park, had more than 60 such cabins left in 1982, rented for $832 a year. Occupants have the use of camping ground showers, lavatories and laundry facilities. The remainder of the cabins, lacking piped water or sewerage, are near southern beaches from Little Garie to Bulgo. They cost only $447 a year. Pensioners are charged half the rent in both cases.

Sports grounds and parks form a buffer between North Wollongong Beach and a bustling city

Stanwell Park to Wollongong

High up on the cliffs enclosing Stanwell Park, hang-gliding pilots hurl themselves into the wind and go soaring out over the Tasman. Minutes later, the last spiral of their brilliantly coloured craft brings them swooping in to the beach—often to the astonishment of motorists rounding the final bend on their approach to the bay. These cliffs, now a hang-gliding mecca, were where Lawrence Hargrave—the aviation pioneer who is honoured on $20 notes—conducted many of his early experiments. In 1894, he was lifted 5 metres from the ground by a train of four box kites. Bald Hill, where a monument to Hargrave stands, commands a remark-

able view south-west along the Illawarra coast. The vista of rocky headlands and wide, sandy beaches reaches beyond Wollongong, to the chimneys of Port Kembla. Because the steep cliffs of the district are subject to landslides, development below them is sparse. Stanwell Park has no tourist accommodation. But the beach, with its gentle slope and long-running surf, is popular. The lifesaving club was founded by coalminers from Helensburgh, who began using the beach before the turn of the century.

Coalcliff, just south of Stanwell Park, has a smaller surf beach with a saltwater pool set in rocks at one end. Seams of coal glisten in the cliff

face behind. They drew attention to the industrial potential of the Illawarra region as early as 1797, when they were reported by a survivor of the wrecked *Sydney Cove* and verified by the naval explorer George Bass.

Wollongong's sprawling northern suburbs reach all the way to Scarborough. Broad, flat surfing beaches separated by small rocky bluffs stretch for more than 25 km. They include major swimming spots at Coledale, Austinmer, Thirroul, Woonona and Bellambi. The main city beaches are Corrimal, Towradgi, Fairy Meadow, North Wollongong and Wollongong—the latter dominated by the towering smokestacks of Port

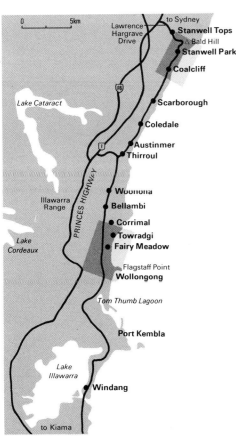

Kembla to the south. Inside Port Kembla harbour, which handles all the district's cargo work, is Tom Thumb Lagoon, where George Bass and Matthew Flinders put in during their first voyage of exploration south from Sydney, in 1796.

Wollongong, the third-largest city in New South Wales and the seventh in Australia, owes its growth to the coalmines of the Illawarra Range to the west. As well as contributing substantially to exports, they have provided fuel for one of Australia's areas of heaviest industrial development, concentrated around the artificial harbour at Port Kembla. Wollongong's own peaceful harbour, older and smaller than Port Kembla, shelters at the northern base of Flagstaff Point. Its deep-water moorings, wharves and concrete ramp are used mainly by commercial fishing boats and offshore pleasure craft. Three saltwater pools, including one for children, are built on the rocks near the northern breakwater. On grassy Flagstaff Point, shingled wooden shelters with tables and benches give rest and shade for visitors to picnic and take in the view from Port Kembla to Sandspit Point. The district was first settled in 1816, and a town proclaimed in 1843. Many historic buildings and other reminders of colonial days can be seen in the central city area. The Illawarra Historical Society museum is open 14.00-17.00 on Wednesdays, Saturdays and Sundays.

STANWELL PARK east of Princes Highway 58 km from Sydney (turn off 53 km south of Sydney along Lawrence Hargrave Drive).
TRANSPORT: trains from Sydney and Nowra daily.
SURF CLUB PATROL: October-Easter, Saturday 10.00-14.00, Sunday and public holidays 09.00-17.00.

WOLLONGONG (pop. 208 601) on Princes Highway 80 km from Sydney.
TRANSPORT: trains from Sydney and Nowra daily; coach Melbourne-Wollongong most days (17 hrs).
SURF CLUB PATROLS: October-Easter, at Wollongong, Saturday 10.00-13.00, Sunday and public holidays 09.00-17.00; Fairy Meadow, Saturday 10.00-13.00, Sunday and public holidays 09.00-17.00; Towradgi, Saturday 12.00-16.00, Sunday and public holidays 09.00-17.00; North Wollongong, Saturday 12.00-16.00, Sunday and public holidays 08.30-17.30.

WOLLONGONG												
	Jan	Feb	Mar	Apr	May	Jun	Jul	Aug	Sep	Oct	Nov	Dec
Maximum C°	25	25	24	23	20	17	17	18	21	22	22	26
Minimum C°	18	19	17	14	11	9	9	9	11	13	14	17
Rainfall mm	267	207	123	82	44	76	24	65	23	101	108	155
Humidity %	73	71	67	60	57	56	52	50	50	57	61	66
Rain days	16	18	16	8	8	7	7	9	5	12	13	11
Sunshine hrs	Summer 6 +			Autumn 6 +			Winter 6 +			Spring 6 +		

Twisting roads above Stanwell Park descend to the coast at Coalcliff, marked by black mine dumps

Windang to Shellharbour

Inside the Windang bridge at the entrance to Lake Illawarra, fishermen in dinghies jam the channels on a summer afternoon while paddlers strain the shallows for bait. Children jump from the bridge crossbeams as traffic rumbles overhead. The northern surroundings of Lake Illawarra are virtually part of Wollongong. Windang Peninsula, however, with easy access to lake and ocean, has the district's heaviest concentration of holiday services.

Windang Beach, wide and clean, is screened off from industrial Port Kembla by sandhills. Windang Island, opposite the lake entrance, is connected with the mainland by a sandspit. It has wide rock ledges for fishing, and its grassy centre makes a pleasant picnic spot. But the spit is exposed to heavy seas, and should be crossed only at low tide. Warilla Beach is limited in width and access by housing. Fishermen make

for Barrack Point at the southern end, with its generous expanses of rock. The twin arms of Little Lake join and feed into the sea just north of the point, providing sandy shallows.

Shellharbour's rocky little horseshoe bay, centred between two surfing beaches, has good rock fishing, a concrete saltwater pool and a sheltered harbour suitable for offshore fishing boats of shallow draught. A shoreline park has playground equipment, and the pitted rocks opposite can be explored for sea eggs and other marine life. The breakwaters, dating from the 1830s, and the quarries to the south at the base of Bass Point recall the town's beginnings as an outlet for bluemetal shipments. For a time, the beach sands were also mined for gold. The port lost most of its trade after the South Coast railway was built. But the township, overlooking the Tasman, has survived as a quiet holiday spot.

South of the open ocean beach at Windang (right), headlands shield generous scoops of sand that draw holidaymakers seeking a quieter time

WINDANG east of Princes Highway 96 km from Sydney, 950 km from Melbourne (turn off at Kembla Grange racecourse).

TRANSPORT: trains from Sydney and Nowra to Wollongong with connecting buses to Windang and Shellharbour daily; coach Melbourne-Wollongong most days (17 hrs).

SURF CLUB PATROLS: October-Easter, at Windang Saturday 12.40-16.40, Sunday and public holidays 09.00-17.00; at Warilla Saturday 10.00-14.00, Sunday and public holidays 08.45-17.00.

SHELLHARBOUR east of Princes Highway 4 km south of Windang.

TRANSPORT: as for Windang.

SURF CLUB PATROL: North Shellharbour Beach October-Easter, Saturday 12.00-16.00, Sunday and public holidays 09.00-17.00.

Lake Illawarra

BUDDING sailors can find all they need on Lake Illawarra—boat hire and tuition are specialties of the district. Power boats also have their zones on the 4200-hectare lake. Anglers prefer creek mouths on the west side, particularly Macquarie Rivulet and Mullet Creek. To the north, Gooseberry and Hooka Islands are nature reserves where rare examples of Illawarra rainforest remain.

Lakeside in winter

Kiama and Gerringong

Sightseers peering from the railed viewing platforms at Kiama's Blow Hole Point come away, more often than not, wondering what all the fuss was about. In strong south-easterly swells, seas surging under the dark volcanic rock used to explode more than 50 metres into the air through a natural funnel. But since the 1960s the blowhole has lost much of its force. The water action that carved the funnel has continued its work, enlarging the hole so that pressure has fallen. By the 1980s the blowhole was performing on only

about one day in ten, and seldom spouting more than 20 metres above its outlet. Some businessmen, concerned at falling tourist income, were advocating an artificial lining to reduce the size of the hole.

Near the base of the point, the eastern cove of Kiama Harbour has a jetty and boat-launching ramps. On the northern flank of the harbour, across the oily sands and dark waters of Black Beach, a swimming pool is set in the rocks of Pheasant Point. Just south of the town centre, the

tiny surf beach in Storm Bay is evenly divided for board-riding and swimming—100 metres to each. Kendalls Beach and Easts Beach, farther south and hemmed in by camping and caravan grounds, are more spacious but the surf is disappointing. Between them, on the southern prong of Marsden Head, are the Endeavour Lookout and a smaller blowhole.

Twenty minutes' drive west from the town centre, a good road climbs past the pioneer dairying village of Jamberoo to the Minnamurra Falls,

Dairy pastures embracing Werri Beach and Gerringong reach right to the edges of the headland cliffs; rock fishermen find challenging sport below

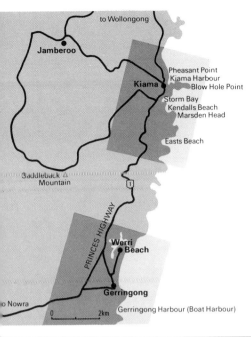

which spill 50 metres into a rocky gorge surrounded by dense rainforest. Near the foot of the falls, a nature reserve rich in bird life has a kiosk and picnic facilities. The run to Saddleback Mountain, 7 km south-west of Kiama, is shorter but steeper—it ascends more than 600 metres among the remnants of old volcanoes. Saddleback, too, has fully developed picnic grounds, with lookouts which command remarkable views of the valleys inland and the coast from Sydney to Ulladulla.

South of Kiama, on the approach to Gerringong, dairy pastures reach almost to the sea at Werri Beach. Surfers can exploit long, straight breakers while there is swimming for children in a rock pool at the southern end, past an extensive caravan park. Gerringong's boat harbour, in the little bay south of the pool, is exposed to the east but otherwise sheltered by rocky headlands and high ground. Near its parking area and launching ramp are a grassy picnic area and playground.

Kiama's intricate coastline creates a variety of surfing conditions at the town's sheltered beaches

KIAMA (pop. 7716) on Princes Highway 120 km from Sydney, 926 km from Melbourne.

TRANSPORT: trains from Sydney or Nowra daily; coach Melbourne-Kiama most days (16 hrs).

SURF CLUB PATROL: Surf Beach October-Easter, Saturday 09.00-13.00, Sunday and public holidays 09.00-17.00.

GERRINGONG (pop. 1776) on Princes Highway 129 km from Sydney, 915 km from Melbourne.

TRANSPORT: trains from Sydney or Nowra daily; coach Melbourne-Gerringong most days (16 hrs).

SURF CLUB PATROL: Werri Beach October-Easter, Saturday 09.00-13.00, Sunday and public holidays 09.00-17.00.

KIAMA												
	Jan	Feb	Mar	Apr	May	Jun	Jul	Aug	Sep	Oct	Nov	Dec
Rainfall mm	109	112	130	131	119	121	95	82	70	83	82	98
Rain days	13	13	13	12	11	11	8	10	8	12	12	11
Sunshine hrs	Summer 6 +			Autumn 6 +			Winter 6 +			Spring 6 +		

Shoalhaven Bight

A splendid sweep of wide, deserted sand stretches south from Gerroa, where a monument marks the start of the first commercial flight to New Zealand by Charles Kingsford Smith. The shore is backed by the heavily wooded dunes of Seven Mile Beach National Park. No camping is allowed, but a parking area 3 km from Gerroa has water, barbecues, lavatories and access to the beach. At the Shoalhaven end the beach is patrolled during summer weekends and there are sandy shallows for swimming inside the protected mouth of the river. Boats launched here find good fishing and interesting cruising in the delta, where the Shoalhaven River spreads around islands and into mangrove creeks before meeting the Crookhaven Estuary.

Greenwell Point, on the western side of the estuary, is the base for a small fishing fleet which ties up by a grassy waterfront playground. There are launching ramps and a jetty for visitors' boats. Orient Point is only 300 metres across the Crookhaven from Greenwell Point, but more than 20 km away by road. It has a concrete ramp just inside the protected river mouth, where a deep channel gives all-weather passage between Shoalhaven Bight and the delta waterways.

At Currarong, in the southern hook of the bight, Peels Reef shelters a narrow, rocky beach and a boat ramp. Seas can be extremely dangerous, however: the 50-year-old wreck of the steamer *Merimbula* rusts away on Whale Point. Abrahams Bosom Beach and other tiny alcoves of sand on the rocky northern shore of Beecroft Peninsula offer secluded swimming and good rock fishing. South of Currarong, nature trails lead off roads down the peninsula. But the area includes a naval gunnery range—weekday access is usually prohibited.

CROOKHAVEN HEADS												
	Jan	Feb	Mar	Apr	May	Jun	Jul	Aug	Sep	Oct	Nov	Dec
Rainfall mm	91	101	108	114	116	120	98	67	67	65	61	78
Rain days	11	12	13	13	12	11	10	10	10	11	11	11
Sunshine hrs	Summer 6 +			Autumn 6 +			Winter 6 +			Spring 6 +		

East of the beach township of Currarong, the coast is inhospitable and seas can be dangerous

SHOALHAVEN HEADS (pop. 1547) east of Princes Highway 152 km from Sydney, 902 km from Melbourne (turn off at Berry southbound, Bomaderry northbound).
TRANSPORT: train Sydney-Nowra with connecting bus weekdays; coach Melbourne-Nowra most days (15 hrs); flights Sydney-Nowra daily.
SURF CLUB PATROL: Seven Mile Beach October-Easter, Saturday 09.00-13.00, Sunday and public holidays 09.00-17.00.

GREENWELL POINT (pop. 944) and **CULBURRA-ORIENT POINT** (pop. 2067) east of Princes Highway 174-179 km from Sydney, 900-905 km from Melbourne (turn off at Nowra).
TRANSPORT: as for Shoalhaven Heads; buses from Nowra weekdays.
SURF CLUB PATROL: Warrain October-April, Saturday 09.00-13.00, Sunday and public holidays 09.00-17.00.

CURRARONG (pop. 518) east of Princes Highway 200 km from Sydney, 926 km from Melbourne (turn off at Nowra).
TRANSPORT: as for Shoalhaven Heads; buses weekdays.

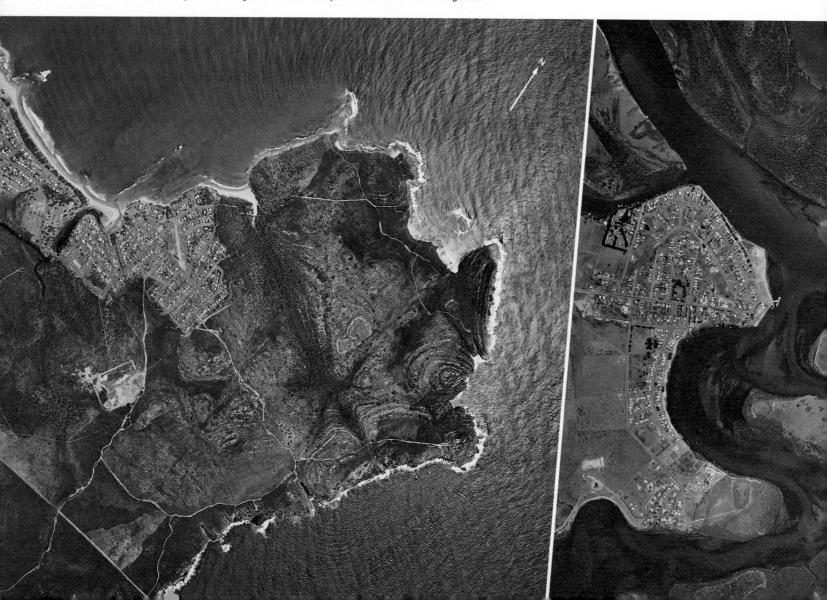

First Coolangatta

Queensland's Coolangatta, the high-rise, high-price southern hub of glittering Gold Coast City, owes its name to unassuming Shoalhaven. A peak 2 km west of Shoalhaven Heads was called Coolangatta by the Aborigines of the region, and in 1822 the first British settler, Alexander Berry, adopted the name for his convict-built homestead.

By the 1840s Berry's business interests extended to Sydney and the Moreton Bay settlement—now Brisbane—and he had his own ships to serve them. One, a brigantine built on the Shoalhaven River, was also called *Coolangatta*. It was wrecked in 1846, just north of the Tweed River heads, and this deserted stretch of sand became known as Coolangatta Beach. A tourist village on the Shoalhaven-Nowra road incorporates some of the outbuildings of Berry's original Coolangatta homestead.

Shoalhaven River waters join the Crookhaven to find an outlet at Orient Point (below); an earlier course (right) is barred by advancing sand

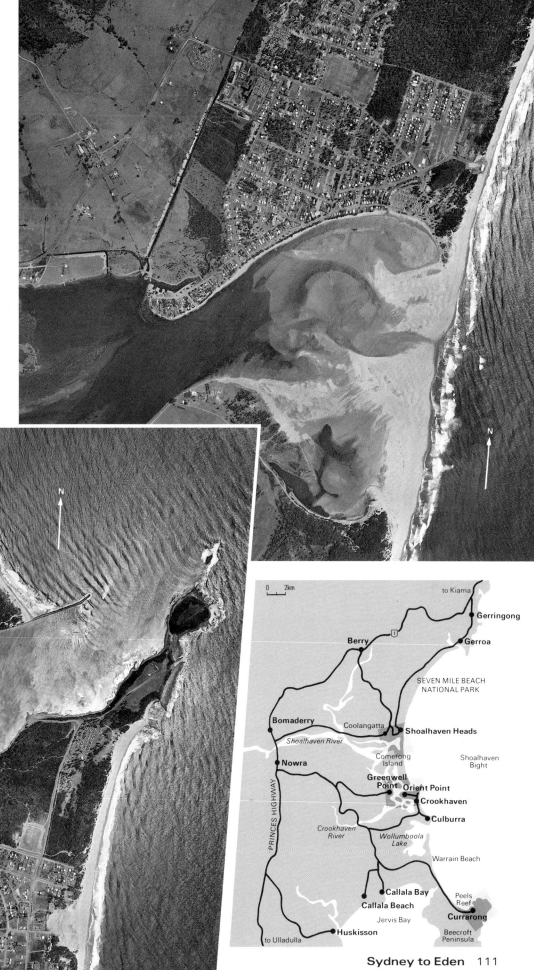

Jervis Bay inner shores

Huskisson people claim that Jervis Bay, with one and a half times the water volume of Sydney Harbour, is twice as good. They say the yachtsmen who call in every January, after the Sydney-Hobart race, come to see what a real harbour is like. No haven on the New South Wales south coast is more enhanced by untouched bushland. Much of the bay's 45 km shoreline has been declared as reserve and left in its natural state.

From the reef-sheltered deep-water moorings and large launching ramp at Callala Bay in the north, Callala Beach sweeps round to the mouth of Currambene Creek at Huskisson, although there is no direct road between the two. A rock pool overlooks the creek entrance, and a ramp and jetties just south of it serve pleasure craft along with the Huskisson fishing fleet. South of Tapalla Point, by the mouth of Moona Moona Creek, is a natural platform for rock fishermen. Vincentia, centred around Plantation Point, is a southern extension of Huskisson, mostly of recent development. It has a ramp for small craft and good beaches to the south-east. Orioan and Barfleur are rocky, and favoured by divers. Nelsons Beach is a pleasant stretch of sand backed by grass, with an imposing view of the naval college at the foot of the bay. Blenheim Beach, sheltered in a tiny cove, attracts families with young children. The finest view of the bay, taking in Bowen Island and Point Perpendicular, is to be had from the hill behind Vincentia, leading to the bush-fringed golf course.

The beach road from Huskisson to Vincentia is called the Wool Road—all that remains of a plan in the 1840s to develop a port for the Monaro wool trade. The idea of installing port facilities was revived in 1915, when the land behind the southern shores of the bay was proclaimed as part of the Capital Territory, to give Canberra its own sea access. Jervis Bay was expected to become a major shipping and commercial centre by the 1930s. Visitors rejoicing in its natural beauty and peace can be thankful that the forecasts were wrong.

HUSKISSON-VINCENTIA (pop. 2296) east of Princes Highway 183 km from Sydney, 887 km from Melbourne (turn off 2 km south of Falls Creek).
TRANSPORT: train Sydney-Nowra with connecting bus weekdays; coach Melbourne-Nowra most days (15 hrs).

	POINT PERPENDICULAR											
	Jan	Feb	Mar	Apr	May	Jun	Jul	Aug	Sep	Oct	Nov	Dec
Maximum C°	24	24	23	21	18	16	15	16	18	20	21	23
Minimum C°	17	18	17	15	12	11	9	10	11	13	14	16
Rainfall mm	98	97	119	128	128	127	110	95	74	86	79	89
Humidity %	70	72	69	64	62	64	60	61	60	65	67	70
Rain days	11	11	12	12	12	12	11	10	10	11	10	11
Sunshine hrs	Summer 6 +			Autumn 6 +			Winter 6 +			Spring 6 +		

Deep but gentle waters lap the fine, talc-like sands of Huskisson (right) and Vincentia

Jervis Bay Commonwealth Territory

Thanks to a political about-turn, visitors to the southern reach of Jervis Bay ramble in tranquil bushland instead of the railway yards of a major seaport city. Of the 7200 hectares proclaimed in 1915 as Commonwealth territory, to give Canberra a sea access, 4420 hectares were declared a public park in 1971. Except for the Royal Aus-

tralian Naval College grounds and the naval air station, HMAS *Creswell*, the rest of the territory is also managed as if it were a nature reserve. The college is not generally open, but on weekend afternoons motorists can see the parade ground and stately buildings during 20-minute 'windscreen tours'. Close to the college,

a sandy beach runs south-east to a popular picnic and camping area at Green Patch. A grassy hill, shaded by tall eucalypts and generously equipped with tables, slopes to the turquoise waters of the bay. Other picnic grounds are nearby—inland at Iluka and east on Bristol Point.

At Lake McKenzie, off a dusty dirt road to

Caves Beach, is a park with luxuriant native bush, kangaroos and parrots. This is the Jervis Bay annex of the National Botanic Gardens, established for native plants that cannot withstand Canberra's frosts. The gardens have walking trails through wet gullies, sandstone heath, swampland and dunes, with many spots suitable for picnics. To preserve the peace of Caves Beach and the developed camping ground behind it, the parking area is 300 metres back from the fenced and stabilised dunes. There are limestone caves at the western end of the beach and the eastern end is protected by a tiny reef.

Wreck Bay village, with its small general

East of the naval airfield, dense bush reaches from Jervis Bay to Summercloud Cove

store, is an Aboriginal community. Shell dumps indicate 6000 years of settlement in the area. Fish-hooks of shell and tools of worked stone have been found among the refuse. Summercloud Cove, just down from the village, is well known for its excellent surf and has a car park, picnic ground and boat ramp. Bush trails ranging from 2 to 13 km start nearby. Scuba divers are trained in the clear waters of the cove. Walking trails lead to St George Head, in the south, and to Steamers Beach—a popular fishing spot flanked by Australia's highest sea cliffs, which reach 135 metres. Other trails or roads in the east of the reserve give access to Cape St George, with its ruined lighthouse, to Stony Creek—also noted for good fishing—and to Murrays Beach at the entrance to the bay. This beach was the centre of controversy in the early 1970s when excavations were started for Australia's first nuclear power station. The project was deferred, but the area is still designated for that purpose.

JERVIS BAY VILLAGE east of Princes Highway 194 km from Sydney, 887 km from Melbourne (turn off 2 km south of Falls Creek southbound, at Grange Road, south of Tomerong, northbound).
TRANSPORT: train Sydney-Nowra; connecting bus some days; coach Melbourne-Nowra most days (15 hrs).
NEAREST SERVICES: Hyams Beach.

Shape up or ship out

DEMANDING standards are enforced at HMAS *Creswell*, the Royal Australian Navy's college for new officers. They are the best-paid students in the country. 'But they're also the hardest-worked,' a navy spokesman says. 'As well as excelling in professional techniques, they have to develop strength of character and the aptitude for leadership. If they can't, they don't last long here.'

The college's sparkling buildings, in immaculate grounds sloping to the waters of Jervis Bay, were established in 1915 as HMAS *Franklin*. Depression spending cuts forced a closure in 1930, when the training facility was incorporated into Flinders Naval Depot, near Melbourne. The Jervis Bay complex reopened in 1957 as *Creswell*—named to honour the 1880s cattle drover who became skipper of a South Australian colonial gunboat and went on to head the national navy when it was formed in 1910.

All newly admitted officers attend the college to learn the complicated arts of running and supplying modern fighting ships. Most are school-leavers with good HSC passes and records of other outstanding activity. Older entrants, including promoted naval ratings and some candidates who already have professional qualifications, take the usual roll of students to about 150. An executive and tutoring staff of 30 officers is supported by 150 sailors.

A typical day for the main intake of youngsters—midshipmen, or 'snotties' as sailors call them—starts around 6 a.m. Physical training comes before breakfast, and marching drill after. Professional classes are held from 8 a.m. to 4 p.m., followed by team training routines or sport. A taxing schedule reaches its climax in a harsh evening inspection of 'cabins', which the trainees must keep in perfect order. Extra duties, handed out in abundance, include manning guard posts, supervising the boatshed and running the college library.

Leave is not allowed for the first eight weeks. For the rest of year, duties are assigned on one weekend in every four. Free time is cut further by ceremonial parades on some Sundays, and by compulsory attendance of the officers at major sports tournaments.

Motorists are permitted to tour the college grounds on weekend afternoons

Finding a ship's position with a sextant

Up and away into Jervis Bay

Behind the college and Jervis Bay village lie nature reserves and a naval airstrip

Over the side for lifeboat drill

Immaculately kept since 1915

Sussex Inlet (right) gives a boating outlet from St Georges Basin; Swan Lake, to the south, is usually closed by sand

St Georges Basin

St Georges Basin is muddy or swampy around much of its shore, but there are also short sandy beaches and rocky points backed by steep, wooded country. Roads skirt the north of the lake, passing through the villages of Basin View, St Georges Basin, Sanctuary Point and Erowal Bay—all with their small beaches and boat ramps. At Palm Beach, on Sanctuary Point, fire-places and tables are scattered on casuarina-shaded banks. Rowing boats, canoes and catamarans are for hire nearby. Shore-level rocks on the point attract anglers, and snorkellers can explore the rocky shallows to the east.

Man-made canals have turned the central part of Sussex Inlet fishing resort into an island, joined to the rest of the town by three bridges. Mosquito-infested swamps, drained by the canals, are replaced by landscaped waterfront gardens and parks. Shorter canals have been dug into the island to provide water frontages for holiday homes and caravan parks. The inlet flows around the eastern shores of the town and is lined with narrow sandy beaches and grassy banks suitable for picnics. Small boats can be run on to the beach or tied up at one of many small jetties. Major facilities for boating are found in the cen-tral waterfront area of Sussex Inlet and down-stream at Tralee. Fishing opportunities abound in the channel, from rocks at the entrance, and offshore around Flat Rock—though the bar can be tricky—as well as in the vast basin lake.

Swan Lake has no swans. Nor, after sand closed the inlet in 1979, did it have the prawns for which it used to be noted. Whether open or not, the lake is suitable for shallow-draught boating. Small craft can be launched over firm sand at many spots, or across gravel ramps at Swan Haven or north of the Cudmirrah bridge. Both locations have parking nearby and open but shaded banks. The dunes at the inlet give ac-cess to Cudmirrah's fine surfing beach and to a reef which makes a good fishing base. To the south, beyond a nature reserve, there is usually challenging surf at Bendalong.

Sanctuary Point has muddy shallows, but boats are easily launched into the basin

ST GEORGES BASIN-SANCTUARY POINT (pop. 1881) east of Princes Highway 190 km from Sydney, 878 km from Melbourne (turn off at Grange Road, south of Tomerong).

TRANSPORT: train Sydney-Nowra daily; bus Nowra-Sanctuary Point weekdays; coach Melbourne-Nowra most days (15 hrs).

SUSSEX INLET (pop. 1290) east of Princes Highway 205 km from Sydney, 867 km from Melbourne (turn off 3 km south of Wandandian).

TRANSPORT: as for St Georges Basin.

CUDMIRRAH-BERRARA east of Princes Highway 212 km from Sydney, 874 km from Melbourne.

TRANSPORT: none beyond Sussex Inlet, 7 km away.

Conjola Lake and Ulladulla

Swimmers have an easy choice on the sand bar which all but blocks the entrance to Conjola and Berringer Lakes. It forms a broad, two-sided beach, dropping steeply to the inlet or sloping gently to the ocean surf. The mouth, though shallow enough to walk across, has closed only once in 30 years: prawns running in season bring visitors out at night with torches and scoop nets. The channel is narrow and Berringer Lake in particular is extremely shallow. But much of Conjola Lake, with its numerous arms reaching between forested hills, is suitable for boating. There are three ramps on the south side of the estuary and many pleasant picnic spots along the shores. Green Island can be reached on foot at mid-tide and is popular with rock fishermen. Beaches to the north—Cunjurong, Manyannah and especially Bendalong—are noted for surfing. Car access is by Red Head Road.

Ulladulla's little harbour is the centre of a thriving fishing industry. On the south side, visitors can see the bustle at the end of the day as incoming trawlers land their catches. Every Easter, during the Fleet Festival, the harbour fills with boats to be blessed in a colourful cere-mony introduced by Italian fishermen. A natural haven has been improved by two break-waters, sheltering a large area for the trawlers and a busy crowd of pleasure craft. A concrete ramp and a public wharf are situated inside, with a large car park nearby and a clean sandy beach for those not heading out to sea. A short distance away, an Olympic-size pool juts into the waves. In front of Warden Head, the southern promont-ory of the natural harbour, a long reef guards the headland rocks, and fishermen can walk to the edge of the inner shelf. The headlands of the narrow bay immediately north of the harbour offer more rock or offshore fishing. There is surfing in the bay north of Ulladulla Harbour and along Mollymook Beach, where an 18-hole public golf course overlooks the sea. At the northern end of Mollymook Beach, Bannisters Point provides generous views to the north. Shallow, sandy channels in the Narrawallee Creek inlet provide safe areas for children to swim and canoe. A grassy park by the entrance is shaded and pleasant, and there is a playground 300 metres upriver. The inlet has a concrete ramp, but sand build-up often makes it useless.

CONJOLA LAKE east of Princes Highway 220 km from Sydney, 840 km from Melbourne (turn off at Yat-teyattah).

TRANSPORT: train Sydney-Nowra with connecting bus Nowra-Milton daily; none beyond Milton, 15 km away.

ULLADULLA-MOLLYMOOK (pop. 6016) on Princes Highway 226 km from Sydney, 820 km from Melbourne.

TRANSPORT: train Sydney-Nowra with connecting bus daily; coach Melbourne-Ulladulla most days (14 hrs); buses Ulladulla-Mollymook weekdays.

SURF CLUB PATROL: Mollymook October-Easter, Saturday 09.00-13.00, Sunday and holidays 09.00-17.00.

	ULLADULLA											
	Jan	Feb	Mar	Apr	May	Jun	Jul	Aug	Sep	Oct	Nov	Dec
Maximum C°	24	24	24	23	19	17	17	18	19	22	22	23
Minimum C°	17	17	15	13	11	9	7	8	9	11	13	15
Rainfall mm	98	116	116	120	129	143	68	90	79	109	96	102
Rain days	15	16	12	6	6	4	3	5	3	5	10	17
Sunshine hrs	Summer 6 +			Autumn 6 +			Winter 6 +			Spring 6 +		

Warden Head, shielding Ulladulla's near-circular boat harbour, bends the ocean swell to produce fine surf just to the north at Mollymook

Green Island, linked by a spit except at high tide,
marks the entrance to Conjola and Berringer Lakes

to Nowra
to Princes Highway
Red Head
Yatteyattah
Conjola Lake
Manyannah Beach
Conjola Lake
Green Island
PRINCES HIGHWAY
Narrawallee Creek
Bannisters Point
Mollymook
Ulladulla
Ulladulla Harbour
Warden Head
Burrill Lake
0   2km
Burrill Lake
to Tabourie Lake

Sydney to Eden   121

Burrill and Tabourie Lakes

Passing motorists catch a glimpse of Burrill's superb surf beach, and a cluster of children and fishermen in the reedy shallows of the lake inlet. Buildings, some of them shabby, crowd near the highway bridge and present an unpromising scene. The true beauty of Burrill Lake is hidden almost a kilometre inland. Its brilliant blue waters, with sandy bays and tree-lined inlets, can be fully discovered only by boat. Small boats can be launched or hired at ramps on both shores of the inlet, west of the bridge. Larger craft are launched from Kings Point, which is reached by sealed road from a turn-off about 1 km north of the bridge. Water-skiing is well established on the lake, but sailing craft, too, find plenty of room round its varied shores. On the southern side,

past Bungalow Park, small craft can be launched over firm sand.

South of the narrow lake entrance, which is rarely open to the sea and never navigable, the Tasman Sea shore rises from a rocky ledge, popular with anglers. An open, grassy reserve occupies the headland above. It is equipped with good picnic facilities.

At Tabourie Point, the green-topped, rocky knob of Crampton Island rises out of a reef at the entrance to Tabourie Lake. The island is connected to the wide entrance beach by a spit of sand. It is surrounded by rock ledges where fishermen gain some protection from the turbulent surf breaking around them and on to the beaches stretching north and south. Immedi-

Woodburn State Forest reaches to the sandy fringes of Tabourie Lake; the winding inlet of the lake cuts off a strip of scrub-covered dunes behind the generous sweep of Wairo Beach

Burrill Lake township has acquired a twin settlement, Bungalow Park, across the lake outlet

ately south of the island is a reef popular with skindivers. It curves in towards the beach, forming a pocket of calm water where children can enjoy sheltered ocean swimming. At the camping ground just inside the inlet, colourful native birds are tame enough to be fed by hand.

Tabourie Lake is well stocked with prawns and fish when the inlet is open and the water level high. Then it is possible to launch small boats over the firm, sandy edges of the lake, though in places access is hampered by the thick

bush of Woodburn State Forest, which almost surrounds the lake. When the lake is low, canoes are the most suitable craft. Even they may have to be hauled over the sand at times.

Exhibits at the Lake Tabourie Museum, open 09.00-17.00 daily on Princes Highway, just south of the lake turn-off, range from Aboriginal tools and weapons to a furnished bedroom and kitchen of the late 1800s. Some of the Aboriginal artefacts came from a midden discovered at Murramarang Point, 10 km to the south.

BURRILL LAKE on Princes Highway 231 km from Sydney, 815 km from Melbourne.
TRANSPORT: train Sydney-Nowra with connecting bus daily (5 hrs); coach Melbourne-Burrill Lake most days (13½ hrs).

TABOURIE LAKE on Princes Highway 238 km from Sydney, 808 km from Melbourne.
TRANSPORT: train Sydney-Nowra with connecting bus daily (5 hrs); coach Melbourne-Tabourie Lake most days (13½ hrs).

Bawley Point and Kioloa Beach

Rocky headlands from Bawley Point to Murramarang Point, separated by golden pocket beaches, provide a secluded stretch of coastline for swimmers and fishermen. One motel, some holiday rentals and several camping and caravan sites make it possible to set up a base in this quiet area, with the busy towns of Ulladulla and Batemans Bay close at hand.

A boat ramp sheltered on the northern side of Bawley Point leads into a narrow channel, enabling fishermen and skindivers to reach the brilliantly clear water, sandy bottoms and reefs offshore. Another ramp is in the caravan park at Merry Beach and small boats can be launched over the sand at Kioloa Beach. The sea may be difficult in anything but calm conditions, but the fishing is superb for those with sufficient seamanship. Ledges surrounding the headlands, especially at Bawley Point, Snapper Point and the rocky pier south of Pretty Beach, are excellent for rock fishing, and when open to the sea, Willinga Lake has seasonal prawns and crabs.

West of Murramarang Road, at Nundera Point, old farm buildings house an Australian National University geography and biology research station. In the first week of January it is open to the public, admission free, for displays and lectures on the local environment.

South of Merry Beach lies the largely undeveloped northern section of the long, fragmented Murramarang National Park. Between Bawley Point and Batemans Bay the park occupies 27 km of coastline, 2 km across at its widest,

South of O'Hara Head and the disjointed settlement of Kioloa, secluded little beaches are accessible only on foot through Murramarang National Park

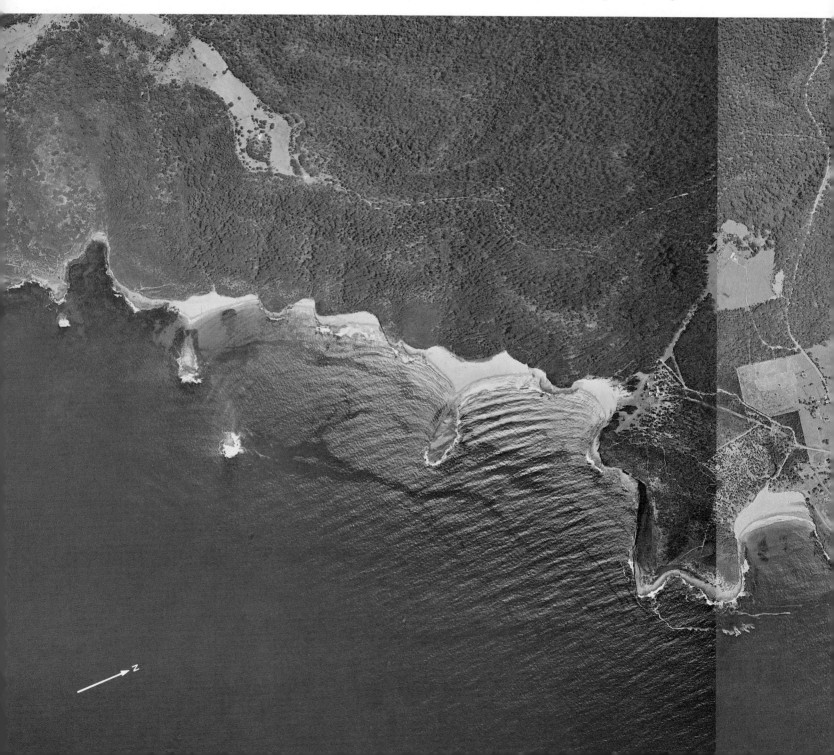

Murramarang Point, an ancient Aboriginal campsite, is protected for its archaeological importance

with Brush and Belowla Islands set aside as reserves for sea birds—muttonbirds, albatrosses, terns, gannets and oyster-catchers. Old forestry roads make good tracks for bushwalking through the park and there are extensive views from the lookout at an abandoned farm on Durras Mountain, the 903-metre peak of the Murramarang Range. It is reached through tall stands of wet eucalypt forest and gullies of rainforest.

BAWLEY POINT east of Princes Highway 252 km from Sydney, 806 km from Melbourne (turn off at Termeil).
TRANSPORT: train Sydney-Nowra with connecting bus to Termeil daily (5 hrs); coach Melbourne-Termeil most days (13½ hrs); none beyond Termeil, 6 km away.

KIOLOA 5 km south of Bawley Point (unsealed road).
TRANSPORT: as for Bawley Point.

Durras

A scenic drive through wet eucalypt forest, thick with vines and burrawang cycads, leads from East Lynne to the access roads for Pebbly Beach Depot Beach and Durras North. The dirt roads through Kioloa State Forest and Murramarang National Park are rough, but they are periodically graded and negotiable by car. At Pebbly Beach and Depot Beach, kangaroos and wallabies come out of the park to feed on the dune grasses, and are tame enough to take food from visitors' hands. These beaches are excellent spots for picnics, with sandy stretches for swimmers and rocky ledges around the headlands for fishermen. At low tide and in calm conditions walkers can explore the caves and rock pools carved into the headland cliffs by the sea. Old forestry roads criss-crossing the area make good bushwalking tracks. One of them strikes out west from Durras North along the shores of Durras Lake to meet up with Mount Agony Road. After heavy rain, however, swollen creeks may make the paths difficult to follow.

The calm waters of Durras Lake can be seen in glimpses between the trees from the sealed road leading through Benandarah State Forest to the twin settlements of Durras Lake and Durras, which residents call collectively South Durras. Activities on the lake are governed by the level of water and the condition of the entrance, which can be closed for long periods. At the southern end of the sandy curve of Beagle Bay, a well-equipped caravan park is sited behind a shady avenue of pine trees and eucalypts, while just offshore the sea boils over shallow reefs around Wasp Island. Line fishing is good and skindivers can explore the scattered reefs which protect the bay. A boat ramp crosses the southern end of the beach in front of the caravan park. Walking tracks branch out into the southern section of Murramarang National Park. During the summer school holidays, ranger-led bushwalks depart from the Beagle Bay caravan park to explore the forests and rocky coastline.

DEPOT BEACH east of Princes Highway 273 km from Sydney, 789 km from Melbourne (turn off at East Lynne).
TRANSPORT: train Sydney-Nowra with connecting bus Nowra-East Lynne daily (5¼ hrs); coach Melbourne-East Lynne most days (13¼ hrs); none beyond East Lynne, 8 km away.

🏠 🚐 ⛺ 🚻

DURRAS LAKE east of Princes Highway 277 km from Sydney, 783 km from Melbourne (turn off at Benandarah).
TRANSPORT: train Sydney-Nowra with connecting bus Nowra-Benandarah daily (5¼ hrs); coach Melbourne-Benandarah most days (13¼ hrs); none beyond Benandarah, 17 km away.

🏠 🚐 ⛺ 🚿 🚻 ⚓ 🎣 ⛵

Sand building up on Beagle Bay blocks the entrance to Durras Lake

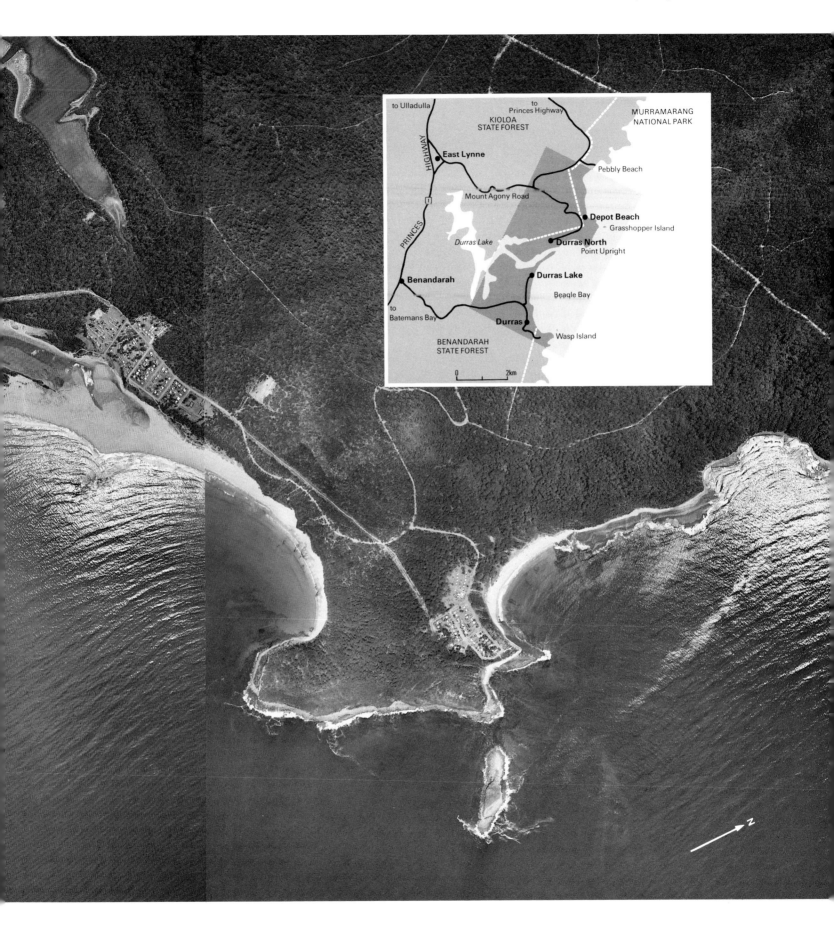

to Ulladulla

to Princes Highway

KIOLOA
STATE FOREST

MURRAMARANG
NATIONAL PARK

HIGHWAY

East Lynne

Pebbly Beach

PRINCES

Mount Agony Road

Depot Beach

Grasshopper Island

Durras Lake

Durras North

Point Upright

Benandarah

Durras Lake

Beagle Bay

to
Batemans Bay

Durras

Wasp Island

BENANDARAH
STATE FOREST

0   2km

Batemans Bay and Clyde River

Punt ramps just upstream of the Princes Highway bridge at Batemans Bay are relics of the town's sleepy years BC—before Canberra. Ferry punts provided the only means of crossing the Clyde River until well into this century. Steam packets occasionally plied the river as far as Nelligen, to bring out dairy produce and timber. Now the bay and river are favourite playgrounds for people from the landlocked national capital. Even the hitch-hikers are likely to be bureaucrats or academics.

The town is geared for visitors, and the bay shores are developed with every facility to meet their needs. Surfside hardly lives up to its name, but Surf Beach does. Caseys and Denhams Beaches, south of Batehaven, have good family swimming. So do Wimbie and Circuit Beaches and Lilli Pilli, at the southern extremity of the bay. Observation Head, where a lookout commands fine views of the bay and its islands, is equipped with barbecues. North of Batehaven, behind Corrigans Beach, is Birdland, a 2-hectare patch of rainforest where a wide variety of caged and free-flying birds and other wildlife is exhibited. Fishing boats tie up at the public wharf near the centre of town. The commercial fleet is one of the few in New South Wales permitted to sell direct to the public. To the south-east, a long sea wall shelters the small-boat harbour, overlooked by a picnic ground. Private boats of shallow draught can be launched from ramps in the harbour or near the bridge, and boats are for hire in both places—but they are not allowed seaward of the harbour. The bar between Square Head and Observation Head is dangerous without local knowledge.

Upstream, the Clyde River wanders through the richly timbered countryside of a chain of state forests. The river is deep for much of its course and navigable in a runabout as far as the weir at Shallow Crossing, more than 30 km up. The lift-span bridge at Batemans Bay can be opened by arrangement, but tall-masted yachts cannot pass the bridge at Nelligen. River cruises are run from the town wharf at Batemans Bay.

BATEMANS BAY												
	Jan	Feb	Mar	Apr	May	Jun	Jul	Aug	Sep	Oct	Nov	Dec
Rainfall mm	98	94	96	97	103	102	71	63	59	73	74	83
Rain days	10	9	9	8	7	8	7	7	8	9	9	9
Sunshine hrs	Summer 7 +			Autumn 6 +			Winter 6 +			Spring 6 +		

Past the long wall shielding Batemans Bay boat harbour, a chain of beaches extends to Lilli Pilli

BATEMANS BAY (pop. 3463) on Princes Highway 279 km from Sydney, 767 km from Melbourne, 147 km from Canberra.
TRANSPORT: train Sydney-Nowra with connecting bus daily (5½ hrs); coach Melbourne-Batemans Bay most days (13 hrs); flights Sydney Moruya with connecting bus daily.

BATEHAVEN south-east of Princes Highway 4 km from Batemans Bay.
TRANSPORT: frequent buses from Batemans Bay.

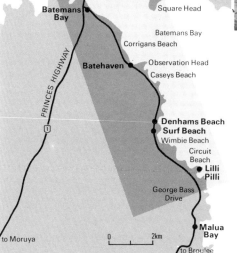

Malua Bay to Broulee

Completion in the 1970s of George Bass Drive has given tourists a new connection between the southern heads of busy Batemans Bay and the quiet resorts of Broulee Bay. It is a winding scenic route which alternately skirts secluded ocean beaches and veers off into the bush. Malua Bay, with its shops, bowling club and playground, is a town beach. In contrast, the little bays south of Pretty Point are reached by dirt tracks off the main road, and forests extend right to the sand. MacKenzies Beach is clean and open, with eucalypts surmounting white cliffs in the north and shrubbery cascading down from the summit. Rosedale is reached by a hill stairway plunging between dense bush and private houses to a long, sandy surf beach. South of Rosedale,

another track branches east to a beach and tiny inlet at Guerilla Bay. There are no facilities for visitors, so although the new coast road has made access easier, the bay retains an atmosphere of isolation and peace. Guerilla Bay is an excellent spot for picnicking, and small boats can be launched over firm sand in a protected area at the northern end of the bay.

At Mossy Point, the sluggish Tomaga River flows to the sea past a tiny wooden jetty and a concrete launching ramp. In spite of a dangerous bar and numerous rocks outside, it is the best spot for launching a sea-going boat between Moruya and Batemans Bay. On the river, pelicans vie with fishermen trying their luck from the rocky banks or from boats in the lower reaches, where

the waters are free of mangroves. Mossy Point's lookout has an attractive view of the Tomaga River wandering around the ochre sandbar and the craggy rocks of the headland, extending half-submerged out into the bay. To the south, past a long, deep surf beach, the thick bush of Broulee Island rises out of the sea. At the feet of sightseers visiting the lookout is an anchor believed to be from the *Scotia*, wrecked off the point in 1884.

Over the bridge of Candlagan Creek is the township of Broulee—a more important port than Batemans Bay when the region was first settled in the 1830s. Sydney timber ships and Jervis Bay whalers kept it in constant use. Broulee Island, a nature reserve, can usually be reached across a sandspit for picnics or rock fishing.

Candlagan Creek and the Tomaga River, both all but choked by sand, trickle into Broulee Bay each side of Mossy Point, north of the main township

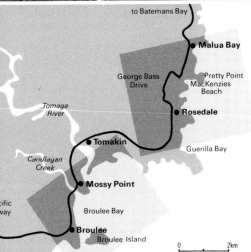

Malua Bay and Rosedale share a complicated coast of coves, headlands and steep inland ridges

MALUA BAY south-east of Princes Highway 290 km from Sydney, 778 km from Melbourne, 158 km from Canberra (turn off at Batemans Bay).
TRANSPORT: as for Batemans Bay, previous page; bus Batemans Bay-Malua Bay daily.
SURF CLUB PATROL: October-Easter, Sunday and public holidays 09.00-16.30.

BROULEE east of Princes Highway 298 km from Sydney, 754 km from Melbourne, 166 km from Canberra (turn off 10 km north of Moruya).
TRANSPORT: as for Batemans Bay, previous page; bus Batemans Bay-Broulee daily.
SURF CLUB PATROL: October-Easter, Sunday and public holidays 09.30-16.00.

Inn lost its guests

HIDDEN under the dense bush of deserted Broulee Island are the foundations of an inn. It did a roaring trade in the 1830s, when Broulee was the main port for Batemans Bay. The island had its own jetty, and the sandspit to the mainland was high and broad enough for stores and cargo to be carted across. Timber-getters and whalers used the pub regularly, and early settlers rested in preparation for their treks inland. But as soon as a port was established at the Clyde mouth—modern Batemans Bay—ships ceased to call at Broulee Island. Eventually the hotel building was dismantled and taken to Moruya, and its foundations were overgrown. The only trace of settlement is a grave—thought to be that of the publican's daughter.

Moruya Heads and Moruya River

Moruya, once a rip-roaring entry port for Australia's third-richest goldfield, is today a tranquil rural centre giving visitors a handy base for fishing, swimming and forest drives. In the 1850s, when more than 15 000 miners were drawn to the diggings between Kiora and Araluen, Moruya's private houses were outnumbered by its stores, pubs, courthouse and jail. When the gold ran out, dairy farms spread on land cleared by timbergetters. Pastures now line most of the Moruya River. In town, parkland occupies the south bank on both sides of the Princes Highway bridge. Riverside Park to the east, shaded by pines and fig trees, has a playground, electric barbecue and lavatories. Beside it is a swimming pool, with a public wharf and boat ramp beyond giving easy access to the river. Weeping willows overhang the river—called the Duea above its tidal limit at Kiora—as it winds through farmland down to the town. The water upstream of Moruya is extremely shallow and not recommended for boating. East of the town bridge a safe navigation channel runs almost to the sea, but hired boats are not permitted to approach the dangerous bar

at the entrance. A fishing jetty and a second launching ramp are sited at the start of a long rock wall which separates the channel from estuary shallows and mudflats to the south.

On the north bank, halfway between the town and the heads, is a quarry from which granite was cut for Sydney's Cenotaph and for the pylons of the Harbour Bridge. From the northern side of the river entrance at Sandy Point, a good beach stretches in an unbroken arc all the way to Broulee. But the surf is more reliable south of Moruya Heads. Toragy Point, the outermost tip of the southern headland, has spectacular views and a century-old cemetery.

The town has retained a strong historic identity and preserves some of its past in the museum which occupies an old two-storey terrace house in Campbell Street. The museum is open 10.00-16.00 on weekdays during school holidays, otherwise 10.00-14.00 on Fridays and 10.00-12.00 on Saturdays. The Courthouse in Vulcan Street, with its wide verandas, high windows and pillared steps, is a striking example of mid-19th-century architecture in a thriving commercial centre. The building is open to the public Monday to Friday.

The navigable stretch of the Moruya River runs 6 km from the old port to a tiny beach settlement

MORUYA (pop. 2003) on Princes Highway 306 km from Sydney, 740 km from Melbourne, 174 km from Canberra.
TRANSPORT: train Sydney-Nowra with connecting bus daily (6 hrs); coach Melbourne-Moruya most days (12½ hrs); flights Sydney-Moruya daily.

MORUYA HEADS 6 km east of Moruya.
TRANSPORT: none beyond Moruya.
SURF CLUB PATROL: South Heads Beach October-Easter, Sunday and public holidays 09.30-16.30.

MORUYA HEADS												
	Jan	Feb	Mar	Apr	May	Jun	Jul	Aug	Sep	Oct	Nov	Dec
Maximum C°	23	24	23	22	19	17	16	16	18	20	21	22
Minimum C°	16	16	15	12	9	7	6	6	8	11	12	14
Rainfall mm	97	90	102	81	85	85	55	54	60	74	74	74
Humidity %	72	74	73	67	63	64	60	61	62	67	70	73
Rain days	10	9	10	8	8	8	7	7	8	10	10	10
Sunshine hrs	Summer 7 +			Autumn 6 +			Winter 6 +			Spring 6 +		

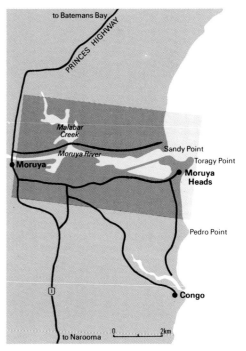

Tuross Lakes and Potato Point

Twin lakes, Tuross and Coila, glitter on each side of the narrow-necked peninsula running down to Tuross Head. The road is lined with Norfolk Island pines—the work of a former landowner, Hector McWilliam. Before he died in 1974, aged 97, he had devoted 50 years to nursing and planting pines. Now they bristle on the headland like needles in a pin-cushion.

Both lakes are best suited to shallow-draught boats. Along with a wide range of fish for anglers, prawns abound in season and oysters thrive on the rocks and in the trays of commercial leases. Small boats can negotiate the twisting, weedy inlets of Tuross Lake or penetrate the attractive dairy country up the Tuross River. One Tree Point, surmounted by its small, solitary pine, is a favourite haunt of rock fishermen. In heavy seas the waves erupt around the point, making a spectacular setting for the caravan park fronting the beach beside it. Good surf fishing and swimming can be found at Bingie Beach.

Potato Point, shown on some maps as Marka

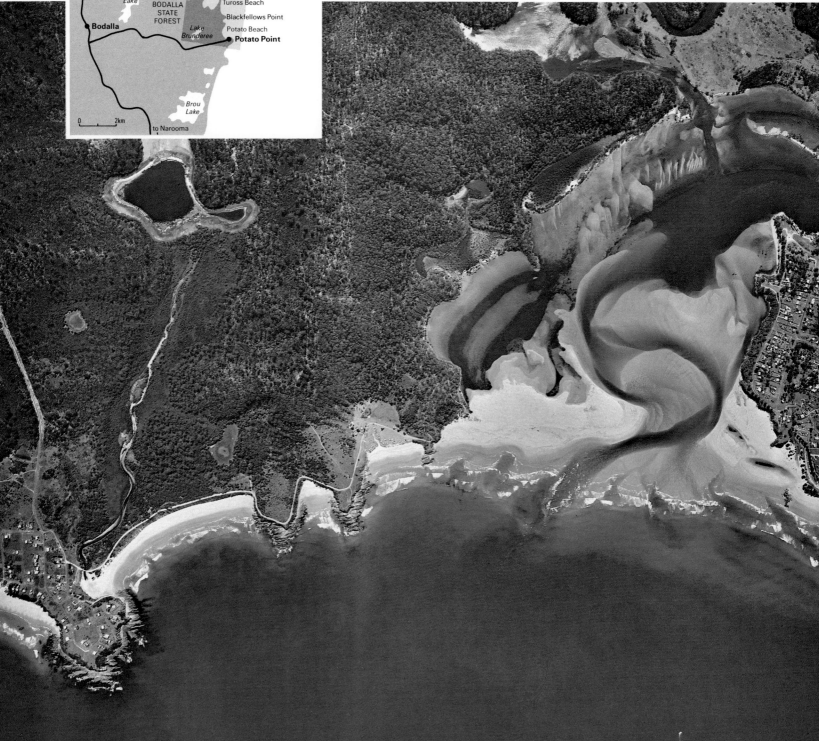

Point and often referred to locally by that name, is a quiet little settlement without even a shop. But the dirt road north from it takes visitors to a jewel of a coast—a natural playground for sunbathers, surfers, skindivers and anglers. Potato and South Tuross Beaches are long and open; Piccaninny Beach, between them, is well sheltered. At Blackfellows Point, the camping area and caravan park are immediately behind a beach without sandhills. Waves run almost to the park fence when the tide is full.

Holidaymakers in the South Tuross area replenish their supplies at Bodalla, where they can also see cheese being made at the factory started by Thomas Mort in the 1860s. It is open on weekdays 06.30-17.00, but the best time to watch production is 09.30-11.00. The town was established in 1870. Other historic buildings remaining there include a hotel where Mort, a temperance advocate, ordered beer to be sold dearly and lemonade was unusually cheap.

Tuross Head township sprawls over a peninsula framed by Coila and Tuross Lakes; Bodalla State Forest backs the beaches to the south, surrounding a scattering of homes on Potato Point

TUROSS HEAD (pop. 835) east of Princes Highway 325 km from Sydney, 731 km from Melbourne, 193 km from Canberra (turn off 14 km south of Moruya).

TRANSPORT: none beyond Moruya (previous page), 19 km away.

POTATO POINT east of Princes Highway 338 km from Sydney, 724 km from Melbourne, 206 km from Canberra (turn off at Bodalla).

TRANSPORT: train Sydney-Nowra and bus Nowra-Bodalla daily (6¾ hrs); none beyond Bodalla, 8 km away.

Narooma's harbour is on the inland side of town —a long trip upriver for ocean fishermen

Narooma and Dalmeny

Beside the Wagonga River bridge at Narooma, the scene is as charming as any to be found in a major Princes Highway town. Boats slide from a wide launching ramp into mirror-clear waters, and pelicans glide among mangroves with the dark hills of Bodalla State Forest as their backdrop. The town, clean and well-appointed, lives up to the promise of its appearance.

Just north of the bridge, a road to the river mouth plunges into the remnants of a rainforest,

matted with ferns, vines and palms. Inside the river entrance, screened from sharks, is a little beach for sheltered swimming. North of the entrance breakwaters, a string of ocean beaches interspersed with rocky knolls and grassy parks is accessible by a gravel road. The popular town surfing beach is south of the river, past the headland with its golf greens jutting out over the rocks. Snorkellers comb the rocks in mint-green waters outside the river entrance, and on

summer mornings the breakwaters are thronged with anglers. Since the 1930s, when the American author Zane Grey drew attention to the marlin to be found off Montague Island, 6 km east, Narooma has also gained status as a game-fishing base. But its boat harbour, west of the town centre, is a long way upriver and the entrance bar can be tricky, so the skippers of most big launches prefer Bermagui.

Bodalla State Forest can be explored along the

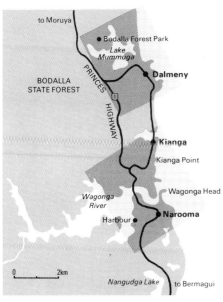

scenic drive around the Wagonga estuary, beginning at a right turn off the highway south of Narooma. North of Narooma, on the eastern side of the highway, the Bodalla Forest Park has easy walks around the shores of Lake Mummuga, where visitors can fish or net prawns in season. There are also full picnic facilities. Dalmeny, at the lake entrance, has a wide boat ramp with reasonable parking nearby. A natural channel leads between rocky promontories to the sea. It is well protected from southerlies but is of limited use in a heavy sea. Expensive new houses in spacious gardens overlook the lake entrance: Dalmeny is feeling the pressure of development and is no longer a place to get away from it all.

NAROOMA (pop. 2758) on Princes Highway 349 km from Sydney, 697 km from Melbourne, 217 km from Canberra.
TRANSPORT: train Sydney-Nowra with connecting bus daily (7 hrs); coach Melbourne-Narooma most days (12 hrs).

SURF CLUB PATROL: October-Easter, Sunday and public holidays 09.00-16.30.

DALMENY (pop. 670) east of Princes Highway 8 km north of Narooma (turn off 6 km north of Narooma).
TRANSPORT: none beyond Narooma.

	NAROOMA											
	Jan	Feb	Mar	Apr	May	Jun	Jul	Aug	Sep	Oct	Nov	Dec
Maximum C°	24	24	23	21	18	16	15	16	18	20	21	23
Minimum C°	15	16	15	12	9	7	6	7	8	11	12	14
Rainfall mm	94	88	95	81	79	85	50	52	54	67	70	76
Rain days	10	10	11	9	8	10	7	8	9	12	11	11
Sunshine hrs	Summer 7 +			Autumn 6 +			Winter 6 +			Spring 6 +		

New subdivisions at fast-growing Dalmeny spread around the southern shores of Lake Mummuga, Bodalla State Forest reaches to the opposite banks

Bermagui and Wallaga Lake

Bermagui owes everything to fish. Commercial trawling sustained the town after a fleeting, boom-and-bust gold-rush to Wallaga Lake in the 1880s. Half a century later, game fishing put it back on the map. Thanks to its convenient, enclosed harbour and all-weather inlet, Bermagui outranks Narooma as a base for chasing marlin and tuna near Montague Island. In the season from January to May, luxurious launches compete for space with rust-stained work boats.

Beside the river entrance is a sharkproof swimming enclosure. Horseshoe Bay, the town beach, is a pleasant stroll across lawns fronting the main shopping area. On the headland to the east, below a car park and lookout, steps lead to the natural, ocean-fed Blue Pool, which includes a shallow basin for children. South along the signposted Marine Drive, below another lookout and a shady park, a track gives access to a second rock pool, named Zane Grey after the author who first publicised the quality of game fishing off this coast. At the Baragoot Lake entrance, the Three Brothers Rocks lie just off a spacious surfing beach. The road continues to Bega, but is unsealed for the 35 km beyond Cuttagee Lake. North of the town, the inland road is connected with both ends of Haywards Beach and with remnants of the former beach road—swamped and eroded during severe storms in 1975 and 1978. Backing the sands at the popular northern end, near Camel Rock, is a shady park with fireplaces and picnic tables.

Wallaga Lake, deeply indented with bays and creek inlets, has a shoreline of more than 100 km which can be explored by road on the eastern and northern sides. The old Montreal gold diggings can be seen at Beauty Point, next to one of the lake's four caravan parks. The western and southern shores are occupied by Wallaga Lake National Park—1141 hectares of woodland backed by the steeply rising slopes of Mount Dromedary (806 metres). The park is best approached by boat. Princes Highway forms its western boundary, but tracks to Dignams Creek and the lake shore are not suitable for vehicles. Camping is not permitted and there are no facilities for visitors. Boat-hire services and launching ramps are available on the eastern side.

Storm erosion of Haywards Beach has destroyed most of an old coast road running north from Bermagui, but the harbour is ideally protected

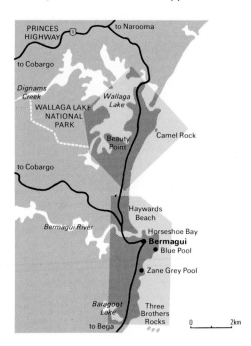

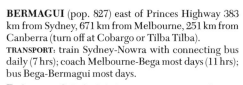

BERMAGUI (pop. 827) east of Princes Highway 383 km from Sydney, 671 km from Melbourne, 251 km from Canberra (turn off at Cobargo or Tilba Tilba).
TRANSPORT: train Sydney-Nowra with connecting bus daily (7 hrs); coach Melbourne-Bega most days (11 hrs); bus Bega-Bermagui most days.

BERMAGUI												
	Jan	Feb	Mar	Apr	May	Jun	Jul	Aug	Sep	Oct	Nov	Dec
Rainfall mm	74	91	90	84	90	92	48	61	52	68	75	77
Rain days	7	8	8	7	7	7	5	5	6	8	8	7
Sunshine hrs	Summer 8 +			Autumn 6 +			Winter 5 +			Spring 6 +		

WALLAGA LAKE 8 km north of Bermagui.
TRANSPORT: none beyond Bermagui.

Homes and camping grounds on the eastern shores of Wallaga Lake are enviably placed for a choice of quiet boating or surfing from a spacious beach

Wallagoot Lake, a playground for Tathra-based boat enthusiasts, can scarcely find an outlet past the wedge of sand piling up on Bournda Beach

Tathra and Wallagoot Lake

Tathra's wharf, built in 1862 and extended twice in the heyday of coastal shipping, was so dilapidated by 1981 that its demolition was ordered. But a local fund-raising campaign, aided by a grant of $160 000 from the NSW Heritage Council, enabled restoration to start in 1982. A national appeal was launched to complete the work—estimated to cost $500 000—as an important example of the old character of the coast. Even as carpenters hammer in new decking planks or rip decayed timbers from the two-

storey storehouse, anglers throng the wharf. Without it they would have only the rocks of the nearby headland, where huge seas claimed the lives of fishermen in three successive years. The headland road, now barred to traffic, was damaged by waves breaking 20 metres above normal sea level. The safest place for boat owners is south of Tathra Head, in sheltered Kianinny Bay. It has a tiny beach and a swimming hole that is popular in calm weather. The Amateur Fishing Club's launching ramp and other facilities,

including a picnic area and playground, are available to visitors for a small fee.

Tathra Beach is patrolled for 1 km north of the town. At the far end a pleasant picnic area overlooks Mogareka Inlet, the entrance to the wide lower reaches of the Bega River. Private boats can be launched beside the road bridge, and hired craft are available nearby. Nelson Lagoon is reached by a rough dirt road starting just over 1 km north of the bridge. It branches east through the southern fringes of Mimosa

Destructive seas can mount against the craggy coast south of Tathra Head, within earshot of the restored wharf on the northern side of the point

Rocks National Park, where tags identify the tree species. Near the sea the road breaks into a network of tracks which cars can negotiate in dry conditions. They lead to Moon Bay, with its secluded beach, to a lookout at Wajurda Point and—through a mass of palms and eucalypts—to the lagoon entrance. Boats can be launched over sand but the water is mostly shallow and access to the sea is dangerous. Wallagoot Lake is more popular with the owners of small boats. Its northern shores can be reached by a sealed road which leads to a picnic area with a boat ramp and jetty. On the southern side, past a camping ground with modern facilities, a dirt road leads to Bondi Lake, which has freshwater swimming, and to surf at Bournda Beach.

TATHRA (pop. 1007) east of Princes Highway 445 km from Sydney, 635 km from Melbourne, 313 km from Canberra (turn off at Bega).
TRANSPORT: train Sydney-Nowra with connecting bus to Bega most days (8½ hrs); bus Bega-Tathra daily; coach Melbourne-Bega most days (11 hrs).
SURF CLUB PATROL: October-Easter, Saturday 13.00-16.30, Sunday and public holidays 09.30-16.30.

	TATHRA											
	Jan	Feb	Mar	Apr	May	Jun	Jul	Aug	Sep	Oct	Nov	Dec
Rainfall mm	82	72	75	78	74	77	57	51	47	55	68	72
Rain days	6	6	6	5	6	6	4	5	6	6	6	6
Sunshine hrs	Summer 8+			Autumn 6+			Winter 5+			Spring 6+		

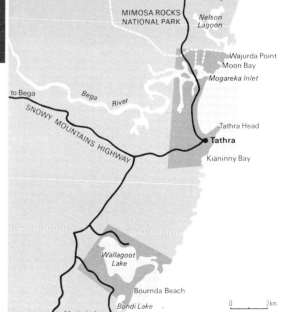

West of rocky Merimbula Point a narrow channel winds among sand bars, opening past the town and its highway bridge to the broad boating waters of Merimbula Lake

Merimbula Bay

Fingers of rock tinged by red ochre stand out like danger signals at both ends of Merimbula Bay's smooth arc. To seafarers the warning is apt: treacherous sand bars hinder access to the sheltered waterways beside each headland. In 1851, however, when the first town sections were sold at Pambula, the Pambula River was navigable. It flowed where the Imlay racecourse is now. But disastrous floods followed, and the river changed course and silted up. Pambula owed its survival to the establishment of Merimbula in 1855, initially as the private port and village of the Twofold Bay Pastoral Association. Merimbula thrived as an outlet for agriculture and forestry over a wide area to the north and west, and boomed with the discovery of gold in the Snowy

Mountains and the Pambula district. But the steamers which brought diggers and took out produce had to stand offshore, relying on flat-bottom boats to serve them, until a wharf was built outside the Merimbula bar in 1901. Relics of the early history of the district are on display in the Merimbula museum, built as a schoolhouse in 1872. It is open 14.30-17.00, Tuesday to Friday in summer and Tuesday and Thursday only for the rest of the year.

Since the 1950s, when the port trade ended, tourism has become the focus of the two towns' activities. The old wharf was demolished in 1980, but an angling platform has replaced it. Other good fishing is available from beaches and headlands or in the shallow, meandering lakes. The

upper reaches of Merimbula and Pambula Lakes are deep enough for boating—though oyster leases must be avoided—and both have launching ramps. Boats and tackle can be hired at a jetty north of the Merimbula bridge, or down a dirt road at the western edge of town. Prawns are prolific in Merimbula Lake and Back Lagoon.

Ocean beaches at each end of the bay, from Merimbula's popular Short Point to Pambula's Little Beach, offer surfing in a variety of conditions. There are also many safe, sheltered places for river or lake bathing, with playgrounds and picnic facilities. For bushwalkers, a trail leads around Merimbula Lake's western shore to a beach at the outlet of Boggy Creek. Kangaroos, wallabies, lyrebirds, parrots and waterfowl

MERIMBULA												
	Jan	Feb	Mar	Apr	May	Jun	Jul	Aug	Sep	Oct	Nov	Dec
Maximum C°	24	25	23	21	18	16	16	17	18	20	20	23
Minimum C°	15	16	13	10	7	5	3	5	6	9	11	13
Rainfall mm	132	129	50	24	36	22	23	63	34	50	166	79
Humidity %	72	73	67	65	64	63	59	61	61	65	72	71
Rain days	13	12	9	8	8	7	8	8	4	13	12	9
Sunshine hrs	Summer 8			Autumn 6 +			Winter 5 +			Spring 6 +		

Haycock Point, the northern limit of Ben Boyd National Park, shields Pambula Beach township

abound in the area. Haycock Point, cut off by the entrance to Pambula Lake, is accessible from the south, by a dirt road through Ben Boyd National Park. The point has fireplaces but no lavatories, and camping is not allowed.

MERIMBULA (pop. 2899) on Princes Highway 461 km from Sydney, 585 km from Melbourne, 32 km from Canberra.

TRANSPORT: train Sydney-Nowra with connecting bus most days (8½ hrs); coach or train and coach Melbourne-Merimbula weekdays (10 hrs); flights from Sydney and Melbourne daily.

PAMBULA BEACH east of Princes Highway 9 km south of Merimbula (turn off at Pambula).

TRANSPORT: as for Merimbula; buses to Pambula daily.
SURF CLUB PATROL: October-Easter, Sunday and public holidays 10.00-16.00.

Eden and Twofold Bay

Glaring white and grandiose, the Seahorse Inn seems out of place behind quiet Boydtown Beach. Up a slippery track nearby is a ruined church. Together, facing out across undisturbed sands and empty waters to the flourishing port of Eden, they symbolise the folly of Twofold Bay's most ambitious pioneer. Benjamin Boyd, using the funds of an investment company he had floated in London, made up his mind in 1843 to build a city to rival Sydney. The church and inn were started as its centrepieces. Soon he had more than 500 men working for him—building houses in Boydtown, tending flocks on his vast pastoral holdings inland, running the whaling station he bought, or manning the steamship service he founded. By 1849 he had over-reached himself financially and the company collapsed. Boyd fled to California, then disappeared in the Pacific Islands. His town was forgotten. Meanwhile Eden had been settled with colonial government support. It prospered first on whaling, then trawling. Wood-chip and canning industries have added to its recent growth, along with tourism. It is a major holiday resort for swimming, offshore and lake fishing, skindiving and water-skiing. Information on its facilities and points of interest is readily available in the town.

Flanking Twofold Bay are the two sections of Ben Boyd National Park. The northern part lies east of Princes Highway between the Pambula River and Worang Point. It has a long surf beach, lookouts and nature walks, but camping is not permitted. Access is by a gravel road off Princes Highway, 10 km north of Eden. From a parking area, a 400-metre trail leads through a knee-high carpet of ferns, emerging at the Quoraburagun Pinnacles, an eroded rock formation. Steps lead down to Long Beach for swimming and beach fishing. The southern section of the park has two camping areas on the coast and scenic drives through the forest. Access is off Princes Highway 20 km south of Eden. The road also leads to the wood-chip mill at Jews Head, and a rough vehicle track branches off to Boyd's Tower, a ruined lighthouse. Forest roads bordering the park are used by logging vehicles, so extreme care should be taken. Bittangabee Bay and Saltwater Bay, the two camping areas, can be reached by rough tracks. There are picnic facilities at both, but little fresh water at Saltwater Bay and none at Bittangabee.

Eden's promontory divides the twin lobes of water which gave Twofold Bay its name

EDEN												
	Jan	Feb	Mar	Apr	May	Jun	Jul	Aug	Sep	Oct	Nov	Dec
Rainfall mm	86	84	83	77	80	86	57	61	60	70	75	75
Rain days	8	9	9	9	9	10	8	9	9	12	10	9
Sunshine hrs	Summer 8 +			Autumn 6 +			Winter 6 +			Spring 6 +		

EDEN (pop. 3107) on Princes Highway 487 km from Sydney, 559 km from Melbourne, 255 km from Canberra.

TRANSPORT train Sydney-Nowra with connecting bus most days (9 hrs); coach Melbourne-Eden most days (9½ hrs); flights Sydney-Merimbula with connecting bus daily, Melbourne-Merimbula daily.

BOYDTOWN 9 km south of Eden.
TRANSPORT: none beyond Eden.

Whaling made easy

TOOTHLESS southern right whales, breeding in Twofold Bay, used to be harpooned for blubber oil and for the horny baleen (whalebone) plates through which they sieved their food. Orcas—the so-called killer whales—also visited the bay during their annual migration. And hungry orcas have a grisly habit of trapping toothless whales and tearing out their tongues.

Eden's whalers, aided by having their quarry killed for them, imagined that the orcas were consciously co-operating. They claimed to recognise old friends on return visits, and fondly gave them names. A myth grew up that the orcas' behaviour was peculiar to Eden. In fact it was observed in other places when both species of whale were more numerous.

Sydney to Tweed Heads

More people live on the central and northern coasts of New South Wales than on any similar stretch of the Australian seaboard. The attractions are obvious. An almost continuous ribbon of sandy, surf-swept beaches lines the shore, while broad river estuaries and extensive coastal lakes provide sheltered water for boat owners and fishermen.

Pipers lead Ballina's Kingsford Smith parade

Yuraygir National Park reaches north from Red Rock

Prawn trawlers ply the maze of waterways behind Yamba

QUEENSLAND

Tweed River
Tweed Heads
Kingscliff
Murwillumbah
Pottsville
Brunswick Heads
Byron Bay
Broken Head
Lismore
Lennox Head
Ballina
Richmond River

Evans Head

Iluka
Yamba
Angourie
Clarence River

Wooli
Red Rock
Mullaway
Woolgoolga
Emerald Beach
Sapphire Gardens
Coffs Harbour
Sawtell
Bellinger River
Urunga
Valla Beach
Nambucca Heads
Scotts Head
Grassy Head
South West Rocks
Macleay River
Hat Head
Kempsey
Crescent Head

NEW SOUTH WALES

Port Macquarie
Lake Cathie
Camden Haven
Laurieton
Crowdy Head
Manning River
Harrington
Taree
Old Bar
Hallidays Point

Forster
Wallis Lake
Pacific Palms
Smiths Lake
Seal Rocks
Myall Lakes

Hawks Nest

Nelson Bay
Port Stephens
Anna Bay
Hunter River
Newcastle
Redhead
Lake Macquarie
Swansea

Toukley
Tuggerah Lake
The Entrance
Gosford Terrigal
Forresters Beach
Umina
Avoca
Bouddi Peninsula
Broken Bay

SOUTH PACIFIC OCEAN

Sydney

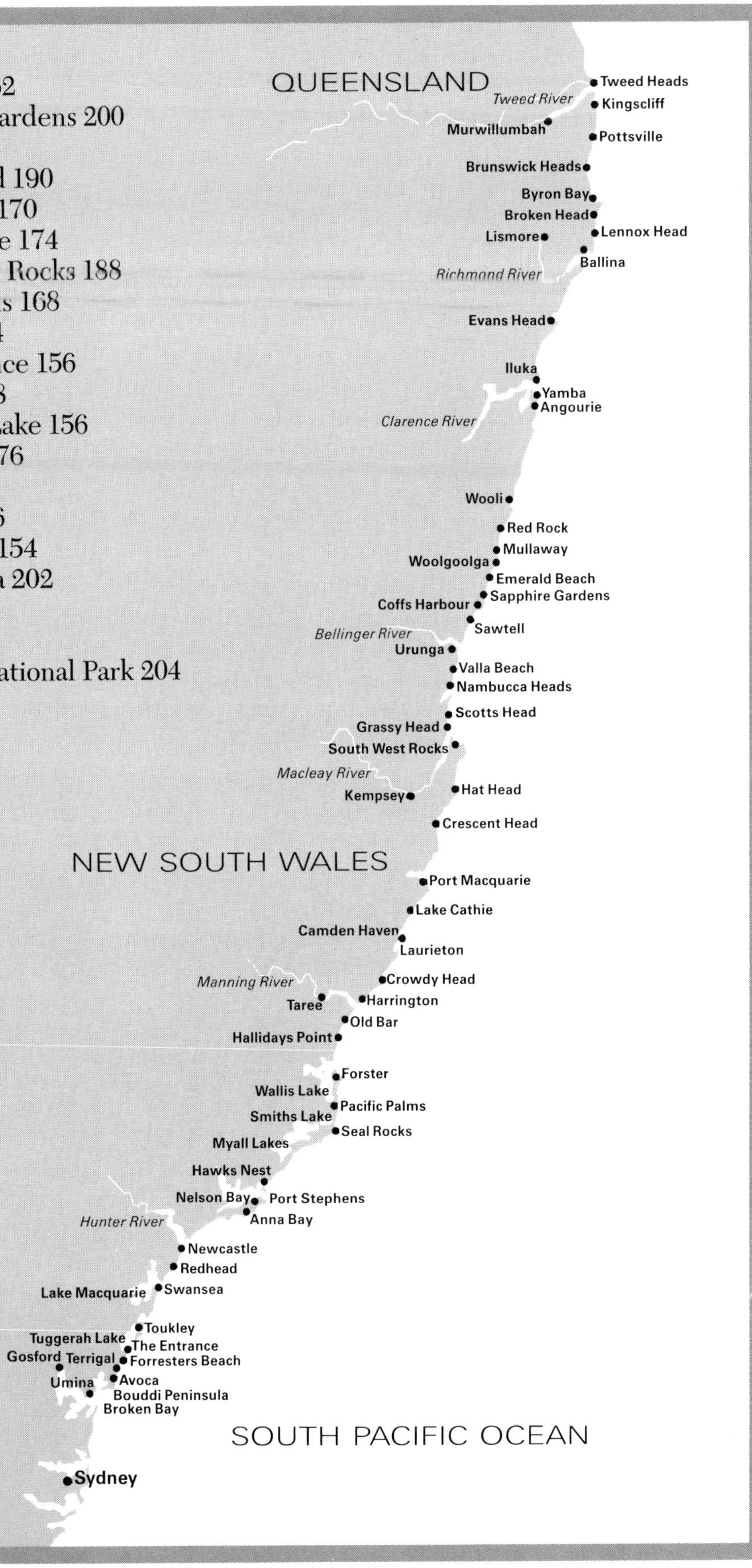

Beaches at the ocean's mercy

NORTH of Sydney's metropolitan boundary, the 700 km reach of the New South Wales coast is more consistently populated than any comparable span of seaboard in Australia. Yet in all this distance the only industrialised centre and major port is Newcastle. The towns beyond are by no means insignificant—soaring property values and rapid commercial expansion testify to that. Nor are they young, raw towns. Most have been settled for at least a century, some for 150 years. But in nearly every case their principal economic contribution is fishing, and their most visible advances are spurred by the necessity to cater adequately for tourism.

Reasons for the seemingly arrested development of old towns on the state's central and northern coasts can be found in their origins. They grew up in subservience to busier centres inland. The important towns were established on big rivers at the limits of commercial navigation: Casino and Lismore in the Richmond Valley, for example, served by Ballina as their seaside satellite, or Grafton and Maclean up the Clarence River, lording it over little Yamba at its mouth. The magnet for river shipping was red 'cedar', *Toona australis*. Its timber, soft and easily worked yet durable, was prized in furniture for its rich appearance and pleasant odour—reminiscent of the true cedars of the Northern Hemisphere. Between 1820 and 1890 every forest accessible by river was stripped of *Toona* along with silky 'oak', *Grevillea robusta*, and hoop pine, *Araucaria cunninghamii*. Timber-getters were followed on to the cleared land by farmers, and settlements which had sprung up on milling sites became substantial agricultural centres. But few of their ocean ports, surrounded by salt marshes or barren dunes, served as more than pilot stations or transshipment points.

Coastal shipping used to link the river mouth towns with Sydney and Brisbane. Services languished in the 1930s and vanished in the 1950s. Commercial traffic on the rivers has gone, too, with the exception of sugar freighters on the Maclean. To compensate, offshore prawning and fishing fleets have expanded, their prosperity made less uncertain by advancing technology. And holidaymakers have come in ever-increasing numbers—though not without some difficulty. The Pacific Highway and main trunk railway follow inland routes for most of their length. Access to beach resorts is often by winding secondary roads beside rivers or around lagoons. The lie of this coast, largely north-easterly, means that most winds and ocean swells approach it more or less at right-angles. Sand is forced back to form long lines of high dunes. Behind there is usually low ground— the result of earlier wave action on soft rock—at various stages of being filled with silt and wind-blown sand. Rivers, barred from direct drainage to the sea, spread in lagoons or swamps. Often lagoons form extensive chains, as they do from Tuggerah Lake to Lake Macquarie, and in the Myall Lakes.

With broad surfing beaches backed by quiet expanses of fresh or brackish water, such formations offer the widest possible range of leisure activities. But the dunes on which they rely have also been attractive to sand miners. While the scars of these mining operations have been, or will be, largely repaired, the original dune vegetation is unlikely to return.

Ocean beaches throughout the region are subject to severe erosion by storm-driven seas. For the most part the problem is temporary: a gradual longshore movement of sand from south to north ensures that lost beach material is naturally replaced. But beyond Ballina, where the coast turns more exactly north, prevailing winds and swells from the south-east strike it obliquely. Erosion is more consistent and a more massive—and permanent—transport of sand sets in. The volume of material scoured from this coast at various levels, virtually without cease for two million years or more, is beyond estimation. The result is clear enough, however, in South Queensland's chain of enormous sand islands, which includes Fraser—the longest sand island in the world.

Winters are mild and sunny in the south of the region, and reliably warm in the north. Rainfall is generally in the moderate range but tends to increase northward—especially in summer—as is evidenced by the scale of sugar-cane planting on the Maclean River and beyond. In summer this northern section is strongly under the influence of tropical weather systems, so high temperatures can be accompanied by extreme humidity.

Trial Bay Gaol, at South West Rocks where the Macleay River meets the Pacific, was built in 1879 and attracts many visitors

The pleasures of rock fishing can be enjoyed around the rugged coastline adjoining industrialised Newcastle

Where fish are caught in cages

Trapping is big business in offshore fishing

MANY offshore fishermen in northern New South Wales never touch a net or a line. They work with traps. Some of the most sought-after species—for example, snapper, pearl perch and John Dory—abound here. But they are bottom feeders, and the seabed is rocky. Hooks or trawling nets are soon snagged. Instead the professionals load their boats with wire-mesh cages, usually the size and shape of large wardrobes.

The traps have funnel-shaped entrances permitting big fish to squeeze in but not to escape. Chunks of rotting squid, octopus, horseflesh or kangaroo meat are placed inside to attract them. Cages are dropped at intervals over known feeding grounds, attached to ropes with buoys and marker flags at the other end. After a few hours they are winched up and suspended over the deck. A latching rod is pulled out and one side opens, spilling out the catch.

Trapping is simple when practised by experts. One cage can yield many boxes of fish for the market. But if a boat's propeller should accidentally cut a line, expensive equipment as well as the catch is lost. Sometimes the markers are dragged under water by strong currents, and fishermen waste hours searching for them. And when they are visible, they can lead amateur anglers to grounds which the professionals would prefer to keep to themselves.

Sugar cane, heavily planted on the north coast, must be burnt before harvesting

The beauty and tranquillity of the Myall Lakes on the central coast encourage diverse leisure activities

Northern shores of Broken Bay

Less than two kilometres of water separate Sydney's northern extremities from the opposite shore of Broken Bay, yet the two are over 100 km apart by road. Despite the distance, a growing number of city commuters have settled in the towns between Gosford and Umina. A tide of brick and fibro is gradually engulfing the flat western shores of Brisbane Water, which reaches almost 8 km from Broken Bay to Gosford. Numerous bays and creeks lead off it, and most of the area is excellent for boating and fishing in spite of occasional sandy shoals and muddy shallows which make some of the shoreline unattractive. Ettalong, Blackwall Point, Woy Woy and Koolewong have public launching ramps. The boating channel from Brisbane Water into Broken Bay hugs the eastern shore of the entrance because most of the rest is blocked by sand bars. They cause lines of breaking waves hundreds of metres offshore, in what a sea-level observer would assume to be deep water.

The entrance to Broken Bay is 4 km wide, exposing the coastline inside the heads to the full force of ocean swells. At Umina, only the southern end of the beach escapes the full effects of southerly and easterly winds or seas. It is a busy part of the beach for most of the year, especially because a huge caravan park occupies most of this sheltered corner. Towering above the caravan park is the tree-clad bulk of Mount Ettalong, and the main road winds steeply past its summit and several excellent lookouts. A turn-off onto a dirt road at the water tank that dominates the top of the mountain leads to ample parking. Those who can resist the compulsion to park their cars exactly at the farthest lookout are rewarded with a pleasant ramble among the ridge-top trees, and excellent views that can be mentally pieced together into an almost 360° panorama. Dominating the foreground to the south-east is Lion Island, a nature reserve. Although it has plenty of lizards, there are none of the snakes that are

rumoured to abound. However the rumour has helped to keep at bay those who would disturb the nesting colonies of little penguins, wedge-tailed shearwaters and sooty shearwaters. Special permission and a scientific purpose are needed before a landing can be made.

Pearl Beach, surrounded on three sides by steep hills which are part of Brisbane Water National Park, is popular with Sydneysiders looking for a weekend retreat. But there is little to attract tourists, apart from curiosity. The beach slopes steeply into deep water, so waves break with alarming force almost at the water's edge—a dangerous situation for children and inexperienced swimmers. Picnickers can relax at the centre of the beach, where scrub-covered dunes afford some privacy. Beyond the Pearl Beach turn-off, and a bushland picnic spot near Warrah lookout, the road continues for only a couple of kilometres before it ends at Patonga. This is a cheerful, if slightly scruffy, little seaside

Large areas of natural bushland have been preserved in Bouddi and Brisbane Water National Parks

village, its dirt streets lined with a mixture of old fibro shacks and a sprinkling of more recent and substantial houses. The beach is wide and backed by low, grass-covered dunes that all but obscure the waterfront houses. No more than tiny waves reach the shoreline unless a giant swell is pushing into Broken Bay, but few people swim from the unpatrolled beach because the bay has a bad reputation for sharks. The best swimming is in the broad tidal creek, reputed to be safe as a result of a sand bar that partially blocks its mouth. Extensive sandbanks, exposed at low tide, provide an ideal playground for youngsters while their parents can hire a dinghy and drift up and down the creek's deep channel in pursuit of crabs, flathead and other fish that breed and feed in the extensive mangroves beyond the town. The jetty at the eastern end of the main beach is also a popular spot for anglers. A bushwalk along the eastern shore of Patonga Creek penetrates into the heart of the rugged southern section of Brisbane Water National Park, and determined hikers will eventually emerge on the main road north of Woy Woy. The park has brilliant displays of wildflowers between July and October and waratahs are particularly prolific. Park headquarters are at Girrakool, off the Pacific Highway west of the Woy Woy turn-off.

ETTALONG-UMINA south of Pacific Highway 95 km from Sydney (turn off 3 km west of Gosford).
TRANSPORT: train Sydney-Woy Woy; bus Woy Woy-Ettalong-Umina-Pearl Beach-Patonga daily.
SURF CLUB PATROL: Umina October-Easter, weekends and public holidays 09.00-17.00.

PEARL BEACH 6 km south of Ettalong.
TRANSPORT: as for Ettalong.

PATONGA (pop. 256) 11 km south of Ettalong.
TRANSPORT: as for Ettalong, or train Sydney-Hawkesbury River (Brooklyn) and ferry Brooklyn-Patonga daily; ferry Palm Beach-Patonga daily in school holidays.

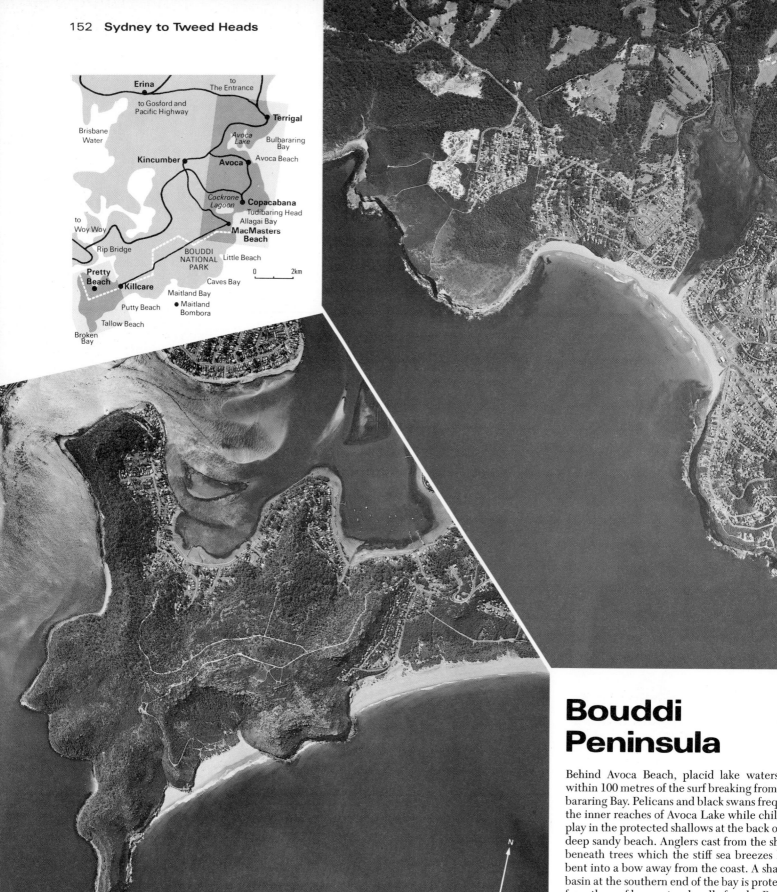

National park campsites back deep wedges of sand at Tallow (left) and Putty Beaches

Bouddi Peninsula

Behind Avoca Beach, placid lake waters lap within 100 metres of the surf breaking from Bulbararing Bay. Pelicans and black swans frequent the inner reaches of Avoca Lake while children play in the protected shallows at the back of the deep sandy beach. Anglers cast from the shores beneath trees which the stiff sea breezes have bent into a bow away from the coast. A shallow basin at the southern end of the bay is protected from the surf by a natural wall of rocks. Beyond them, board-riders chase the rolling waves inside the headlands. South of Avoca, Captain Cook Memorial Park runs to rugged Tudibaring Head, which overlooks the sweeping surf beaches of

Allagai Bay. Behind them is Cockrone Lagoon, a shallow body of water which, like Avoca Lake, occasionally breaks out to sea after heavy rains. MacMasters Beach and Copacabana are linked by a short walk across the lagoon sand bar—but by car the two settlements are separated by a 10 km drive looping inland through Kincumber.

A scenic road from MacMasters Beach to Killcare follows the ridges of a small coastal range running towards the southern end of Bouddi Peninsula. It overlooks the moors, rounded rocky cliffs and deep rainforest gullies of Bouddi National Park. The park has five points of car access, and walking tracks link many of its campsites, picnic grounds, lookouts and beaches. Above Little Beach and Tallow Beach, campers and day visitors leave their vehicles at a clifftop car park and walk down short, clearly marked trails to bush camping areas. Both sites are close to creeks with fresh water suitable for washing

and cooking. The camping area at Putty Beach can be reached directly by car but numbers are limited. Permits for any of the camps may be obtained at the ranger station just inside the Maitland Bay entrance to the park. A marine extension to the park, from Maitland Bay and Caves Bay to the Maitland Bombora, is open to snorkellers and scuba divers on condition that no fish or other marine specimens are taken. There are generous stretches of rock ledges and surf beaches for anglers in the rest of the park.

Bays at the entrance to Brisbane Water are popular with boating enthusiasts. Public wharves are dotted around the shores and Pretty Beach has a launching ramp for small boats. Marked channels lead south from the bay's muddy shallows to Broken Bay, Pitt Water and the wide estuary of the Hawkesbury River, or north under the high Rip bridge into the upper reaches of Brisbane Water towards Gosford.

Surfing beaches and boating lagoons from MacMasters Beach to Terrigal have attracted intensive development, centred on Avoca

AVOCA BEACH east of F3 Freeway and Pacific Highway 101 km from Sydney, 17 km east of Gosford (turn off for Gosford).
TRANSPORT: train Sydney-Gosford and bus Gosford-Avoca Beach daily.
SURF CLUB PATROLS: Avoca, North Avoca, Copacabana, MacMasters and Killcare October-Easter, weekends and public holidays 09.00-17.00.

AVOCA BEACH												
	Jan	Feb	Mar	Apr	May	Jun	Jul	Aug	Sep	Oct	Nov	Dec
Rainfall mm	112	120	142	117	128	151	83	102	77	89	80	90
Rain Days	10	10	11	10	10	11	9	9	9	10	9	9
Sunshine hrs	Summer 7 +			Autumn 6 +			Winter 6 +			Spring 6 +		

Residential development surrounds horseshoe-shaped Terrigal Lagoon, north of Broken Head

Terrigal to Forresters Beach

Below a commanding lookout on rugged Broken Head, busy beachfront development crowds Terrigal Haven. A boat club and wide concrete launching ramp are tucked between the promontory and a short stretch of sheltered beach backed by a large car park, camping grounds and playing fields. To the west a pool has been built on a rocky outcrop at the southern end of the patrolled surfing beach, which curves around the bay past Terrigal Lagoon. A towering row of Norfolk Island pines separates the beach from the town's lively shopping streets. Sometimes after heavy rains both Terrigal and Wamberal Lagoons break out to sea through the surfing beaches running beside the two towns. Normally their shallows are suitable for children, and canoes and paddle boats are for hire at Terrigal.

North of the Wamberal Lagoon entrance, the built-up beachfront gives way to rolling dunes which have been planted with binding grasses and fenced to protect them from the relentless assaults of wind, waves and people. Along Forresters Beach, housing restricts public access to the dunes and the sea. In a stretch of more than 1 km there are only two wooden stairways between private properties. The steps stop short of the bottom of the dunes, but regular use by swimmers and sunbathers has worn sideways paths, making a gentle slope to the firm beach sand. The southern end of Forresters is sheltered from the surf by a half-submerged reef, extending parallel to the beach well beyond the low-water mark. A rough, unsealed road leads to a clifftop lookout

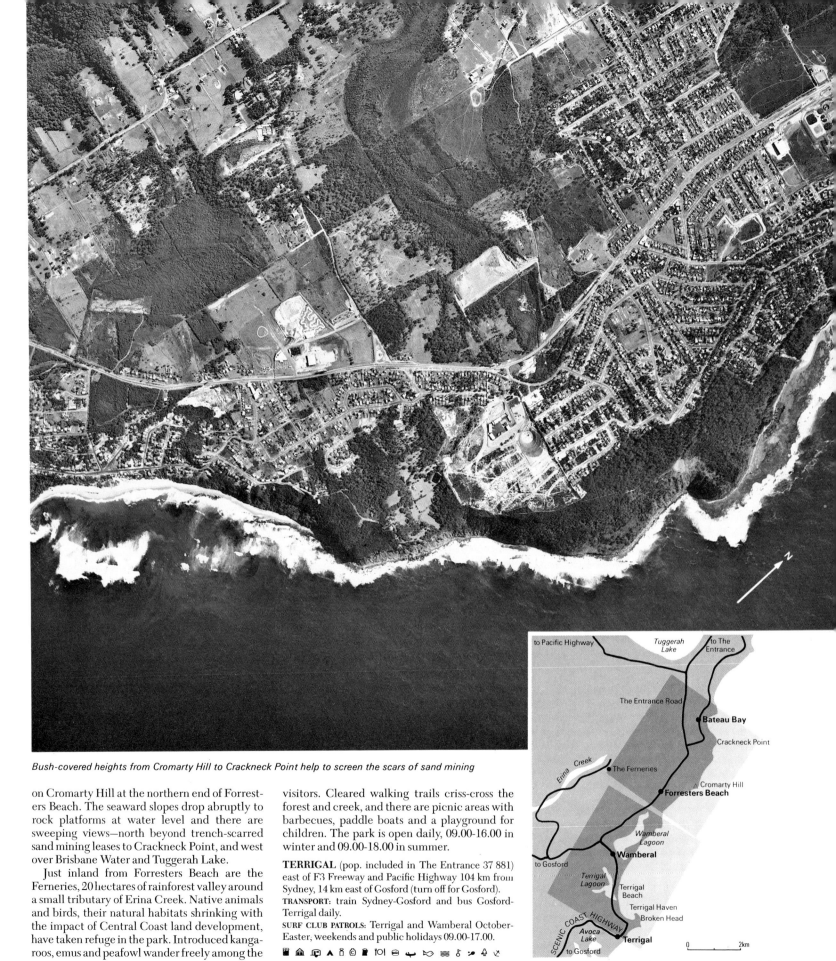

Bush-covered heights from Cromarty Hill to Crackneck Point help to screen the scars of sand mining

on Cromarty Hill at the northern end of Forresters Beach. The seaward slopes drop abruptly to rock platforms at water level and there are sweeping views—north beyond trench-scarred sand mining leases to Crackneck Point, and west over Brisbane Water and Tuggerah Lake.

Just inland from Forresters Beach are the Ferneries, 20 hectares of rainforest valley around a small tributary of Erina Creek. Native animals and birds, their natural habitats shrinking with the impact of Central Coast land development, have taken refuge in the park. Introduced kangaroos, emus and peafowl wander freely among the

visitors. Cleared walking trails criss-cross the forest and creek, and there are picnic areas with barbecues, paddle boats and a playground for children. The park is open daily, 09.00-16.00 in winter and 09.00-18.00 in summer.

TERRIGAL (pop. included in The Entrance 37 881) east of F3 Freeway and Pacific Highway 104 km from Sydney, 14 km east of Gosford (turn off for Gosford).
TRANSPORT: train Sydney-Gosford and bus Gosford-Terrigal daily.
SURF CLUB PATROLS: Terrigal and Wamberal October-Easter, weekends and public holidays 09.00-17.00.

The Entrance and Tuggerah Lake

Settlements around the southern shores of Tuggerah Lake, once small rural centres with a summertime influx of holidaymakers, have grown and merged into a continuous suburban sprawl. Along with tourists, the towns now accommodate a large resident population of retired people, commuters to the nearby cities and employees of the new industrial estates growing along the lake's western shores. The eastern shores remain the province of resort development with a concentration of hotels, motels and caravan parks taking advantage of the proximity of lake and ocean. Rocky promontories enclose patrolled surfing beaches between The Entrance and the picnic areas, barbecues and holiday cottages of sheltered Bateau Bay. Shelly Beach is flanked north and south by caravan and camping grounds, and buffered from housing development by reserves and golf links abutting the beach dunes. Sheltered swimming is found in the rock pools at the southern end of The Entrance surf beach and in the shallows around the lake entrance itself. At low tide the opening becomes a slow, shallow stream popular with children. But the ebb tide should be avoided: there is a fast run-out through the narrow channel. Tuggerah Beach stretches 8 km beyond the patrolled surf at Entrance North, backed by dunes extensively scarred and stripped by sand mining.

Wide weed patches and reedy shallows around Tuggerah Lake provide a natural fish nursery which attracts large numbers of amateur anglers as well as more than 70 professional

fishermen who earn their living from the lake. In summer months visitors can also catch a meal by dragging the lake for the prawns that emerge from their daytime resting places in the mud and swarm over the lake bottom at night. The most popular spot for prawning is along the easily accessible shores at Long Jetty. Waterfowl are prolific on the lake: shags and gulls are ever-present, and cormorants and curlews compete with human bait-hunters for worms and shellfish. Pelicans crowd the shores of Terilbah Island, just inside the lake entrance, and flock daily at 15.30 to be fed fish scraps at the little reserve on Marine

Parade, opposite the post office. Tuggerah Lake is fed by a number of small creeks with little flow of water and is encumbered by sand bars and shallows. Outside the developed areas the lake shores are fringed with marshes and swampy scrub, but five boat ramps and numerous jetties provide access for fishermen and sailors of shallow-draught boats. The lake entrance is occasionally dredged and under favourable conditions boats can make out to sea on high tides.

THE ENTRANCE (pop. 37 881) east of F3 Freeway and Pacific Highway 108 km from Sydney, 24 km north of Gosford (turn off for Gosford northbound or at Tuggerah southbound).

TRANSPORT: train Sydney-Wyong and bus Wyong-The Entrance daily.

SURF CLUB PATROLS: Toowoon Bay, The Entrance and Entrance North October-Easter, weekends and public holidays 09.00-17.00.

Densely settled shores are broken by the narrow outlet channel of Tuggerah Lake; heavy surf runs at Shelly Beach (left) and Tuggerah Beach, which at low tide can be reached on foot from The Entrance.

Toukley and Budgewoi

Within earshot of a pounding Tasman surf, Toukley and Budgewoi turn their backs on the sea. Instead they face each other across the smooth, shallow waters of Budgewoi Lake. The two towns form rival centres for sprawling housing development and holiday boating activity around the lake and its neighbours, Tuggerah and Munmorah. In contrast, ocean shores and the dunes sweeping north are largely deserted. Only around Norah Head and at Lakes Beach, on the narrow neck of land between the towns, does

the seashore compete with the pull of the lakes. At Cabbage Tree Harbour, a natural rock pool provides paddling water for children beside a quiet, sheltered bay where snorkellers and anglers can launch their boats to fish the scattered offshore reefs. A small curve of beach lines the bay below high, sandy cliffs overgrown with grasses and backed by the holiday cottages and camping grounds of Noraville. Norah Head lighthouse attracts visitors to share the sweeping views from its 46-metre-high platform. Per-

mission to go up can be obtained from the Department of Transport in Sydney. South of the headland, other rocky promontories enclose small surfing beaches. Soldiers Beach is the centre of board-riding activity and the site of a surf club surrounded by undeveloped dunes.

Canton Beach, on Tuggerah Lake directly south of Toukley, got its name because Chinese fishermen migrated there in the 1860s to cure prawns and fish for markets on the goldfields and in their homeland. Children now swim in the

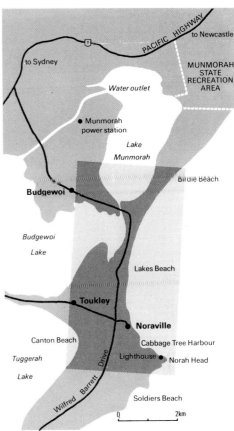

Boating and fishing opportunities on two spacious lakes leave the ocean beaches virtually deserted

shallows and play on the swings and slides of the shady lake shore. South of Canton is one of only two remaining stands of red gum, *Eucalyptus camaldulensis*, on the eastern seaboard. The trees were saved from destruction by sand mining after protests in the 1960s and 70s. The forest is now a protected reserve, with walking trails and picnic spots reached from two marked access points off Wilfred Barrett Drive.

Birdie Beach, stretching north of the surf club at Lakes Beach, was mined between 1963 and 1979. Undulating dunes were flattened and the thick coastal scrub was stripped and only sparsely replaced by sand-binding grasses. With access from Budgewoi limited to a loose, sandy track, the beach offers seclusion—but no surf patrols. A big offshore reef, running parallel with the beach, provides shelter from rough weather for surf anglers who in calm conditions can row out or cast from its firm footing.

At Lake Munmorah, fish are attracted by rich feeding around the warm-water outflow of the Munmorah power station, but in turn attract so many anglers that the area is now all but fished out. Handline fishing is popular at the Budgewoi camping grounds, from a wooden footbridge over the creek leading to Budgewoi Lake. The bridge connects the camping and caravan park with a small, shady reserve suitable for picnics and swimming.

Munmorah State Recreation Area, on the coast north-east of the lake, has picnic areas and camping grounds in heath-covered valleys on the beach front. Teatree, the camp on Birdie Beach, attracts board-riders and surf anglers, but is the only site without lavatories or a water supply. Fire trails and walking tracks connect the beaches with headland lookouts and a popular rock fishing spot at Wybung Head.

TOUKLEY-BUDGEWOI east of Pacific Highway 126 km from Sydney (turn off at Gorokan northbound, Doyalson southbound).
TRANSPORT: train Sydney-Wyong daily; bus Wyong-Toukley-Budgewoi daily.
SURF CLUB PATROLS: Soldiers Beach and Lakes Beach October-Easter, weekends and public holidays 09.00-17.00.

NORAH HEAD												
	Jan	Feb	Mar	Apr	May	Jun	Jul	Aug	Sep	Oct	Nov	Dec
Maximum C°	25	25	24	23	20	18	18	18	20	22	22	25
Minimum C°	19	20	18	16	12	10	9	10	12	14	16	18
Rainfall mm	165	129	124	52	84	72	42	72	96	85	139	104
Humidity %	76	83	67	55	55	50	62	68	57	62	69	73
Rain Days	14	16	14	10	9	13	11	9	5	12	16	10
Sunshine hrs	Summer 7 +		Autumn 6 +			Winter 6 +			Spring 7 +			

North of the entrance at Swansea, settlement forsakes the surfing coast of Nine Mile Beach and clusters on Lake Macquarie's shores

Lake Macquarie

Industrial and residential development, creeping south from Newcastle since the early 1960s, has expanded what used to be scattered holiday settlements around the shores of Lake Macquarie. The fuel firing the growth is coal, scooped from open-cut lakeside mines to supply three nearby power stations. Even the ocean shore bears the marks of the coal industry. At Catherine Hill Bay, the southern end of the beach is dominated by the long wooden jetty of the Wallarah Colliery. Coal from Crangan Bay, 5 km inland, is brought here to be washed and stored. Small freighters loaded in the shallow harbour take the coal to Newcastle or Sydney for transshipment to larger vessels bound for distant markets. A bowling club and hotel among the small settlement's weatherboard bungalows overlook a sheltered crescent beach backed by undeveloped grassy dunes. Just north of the Crangan Bay mine, Nords Wharf has wooden-fenced swimming baths off a grassy, shaded shore and Cams Wharf offers a sandy beach with boats for hire and a line of red buoys enclosing a swimming area to protect bathers from power boats and water-skiers.

Mawsons Breakwater, 3 km north of Catherine Hill Bay, extends 500 metres out to the natural outcrop of Spoon Rocks. The breakwater was constructed in 1969 as the jetty for a proposed new mining operation, but never used. The long wall now attracts fishermen and beach walkers. Lookouts in the park above the breakwater give a clear view of disused coal cuts and gravel pits from Quarry Beach to Point Morisset, and the rolling surf of Caves Beach stretching towards the rocky foreshores of Swansea Heads. Across the channels of the Lake Macquarie entrance the popular surfing spot of Blacksmiths Beach lies at the southern end of Nine Mile Beach. To the

Map labels:
- Toronto
- to Newcastle
- Rathmines
- Belmont
- Nine Mile Beach
- Wangi Wangi
- PACIFIC HIGHWAY
- Blacksmiths Beach
- Lake Macquarie
- Swansea
- Swansea Heads
- Silverwater
- Caves Beach
- Crangan Bay
- Mawsons Breakwater
- Quarry Beach
- Gwandalan
- Nords Wharf
- Catherine Hill Bay
- Wallarah Colliery
- to Sydney
- 0   2km

north the beach is a desolate stretch backed by a wide expanse of dunes, stripped by sand mining and separated from the lakeside boating centre of Belmont by shallow lagoons and swamp areas.

High, timbered hills around Lake Macquarie are indented by small bays and inlets with areas suitable for fishing and cruising. Boating enthusiasts find jetties and constructed launching ramps in abundance, along with numerous boat-hire companies, swimming enclosures and parks where they can pull ashore for a picnic. A double-decker ferry makes two-hour cruises of the northern part of the lake, leaving from Belmont or Toronto on Wednesdays and Sundays except during July. The former residence of the painter Sir William Dobell is preserved as a memorial at Wangi Wangi, opposite Swansea.

Many of his paintings, and photographs illustrating his life and work, are on display 14.00-16.00 on Sundays and public holidays.

SWANSEA-CAVES BEACH on Pacific Highway 152 km from Sydney.

TRANSPORT: train Sydney-Wyong and bus Wyong-Swansea daily.

SURF CLUB PATROLS: Blacksmiths, Caves Beach and Catherine Hill Bay October-Easter, Saturday 13.00-17.00, Sunday and public holidays 08.30-17.00.

YOUTH HOSTEL: 5.6 km from township, open year-round.

BELMONT on Pacific Highway 159 km from Sydney.
TRANSPORT: bus Swansea-Belmont most days.

Newcastle beaches

To most outsiders Newcastle means coal, steel and a concentration of heavy, dirty industry. Motorists travelling through are led on inland bypass routes offering little to induce them to pause. They hurry on to the vineyards of the Hunter Valley, or to resort beaches far to the north or south. Yet Newcastle is exceptionally favoured by its coastline. Few cities in the world, and no others in Australia, have first-class ocean beaches so close to their hearts. From the downtown shops and offices of Hunter Street to the reliable surf of Newcastle Beach is less than five minutes' walk. Nobbys Beach, formed by the southern breakwater of Australia's second-busiest port, is little farther. Other good bathing spots, strung between Bar Beach and Merewether, are easily accessible from the city centre. All are patronised throughout the week in summer. Bar Beach is floodlit, and big ocean pools at Merewether and Newcastle Beach also remain open at night.

The Hunter River mouth was known in Sydney as Coal Harbour as early as 1801. A shipment of coal that year to India was Australia's first commercial export—traded for barrels of rum. The town was founded in 1804, not primarily to tap the district's resources but because Sydney authorities wanted an inescapable penal settlement for convicts who re-offended. Until 1824 prisoners were put to hard labour under brutal discipline on Coal Island, which was renamed Nobbys Head when the breakwater was completed in 1846. Newcastle's seafaring heritage is well depicted in the Maritime Museum, open 12.00-16.00 from Tuesday to Sunday at Fort Scratchley, just south of Nobbys. Exhibits include shipbuilders' half-scale models and a rare 19th-century lifeboat which figured in many celebrated rescues. The fort, built in 1843 and relinquished by the army in 1972, is distinguished among Australian defence posts for having engaged in action against an enemy. Its guns returned the fire of a Japanese submarine which shelled the fort in June 1942.

A splendid coastal drive starts immediately south of Newcastle Beach, at King Edward Park. The park's expansive, shaded lawns and sunken flower gardens make it a popular picnic spot, and the road above commands good views of the coast and the array of shipping waiting for harbour berths. The drive gives access to the southern beaches as far as Merewether before swinging inland to meet the Pacific Highway at the head of Murdering Gully. It was known as Murmuring Gully until the 1890s, when a ship

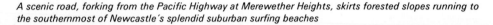

A scenic road, forking from the Pacific Highway at Merewether Heights, skirts forested slopes running to the southernmost of Newcastle's splendid suburban surfing beaches

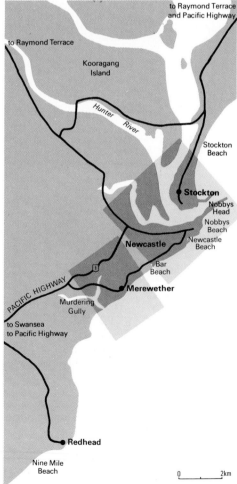

deserter confessed to killing a man there. No corpse could be found, so he was deported without further penalty. Years later schoolboys discovered the victim's skeleton. To the south at Redhead, the swell on a good day pushes up a 5-metre surf to the foot of the lifesaving clubhouse. Behind is a sheer sandstone cliff, red and ochre at the top below moss-green shrubbery. A small rock outcrop breaks the beach and provides a base for the club's shark-spotting tower. On summer weekends, crowds pack the beach for more than 1 km south of the headland. Beyond, lonely Nine Mile Beach forms a straight white stretch to the Lake Macquarie entrance and Swansea.

NEWCASTLE (pop. 258 965) on Pacific Highway 177 km from Sydney.

TRANSPORT: train Sydney-Newcastle daily.

SURF CLUB PATROLS: Stockton, Nobbys, Newcastle, Dixon Park and Merewether Beaches October-Easter, Saturday 13.00-17.00, Sunday and public holidays 09.00-17.00.

REDHEAD east of Pacific Highway 167 km from Sydney, 16 km south of Newcastle.

TRANSPORT: bus Newcastle-Redhead daily.

SURF CLUB PATROL: October-Easter, weekends and public holidays 09.00-17.00.

Nobbys and Newcastle Beaches, hard by the city centre and railway station, and Stockton Beach to the north shield the Hunter River mouth

NOBBYS HEAD												
	Jan	Feb	Mar	Apr	May	Jun	Jul	Aug	Sep	Oct	Nov	Dec
Maximum C°	24	24	24	23	20	18	17	18	19	21	23	24
Minimum C°	19	19	18	16	12	10	8	9	11	14	16	18
Rainfall mm	93	103	120	117	114	112	103	80	77	74	66	86
Humidity %	72	74	69	62	58	62	55	55	57	62	66	72
Rain Days	11	11	12	12	12	12	11	10	10	11	10	10
Sunshine hrs	Summer 7 +			Autumn 6 +			Winter 6 +			Spring 7 +		

Anna Bay

Rocky inlets around Birubi Point, fringing Anna Bay village, make ideal training grounds for snorkelling and scuba diving—so much so that a diving school brings its pupils 12 km from Nelson Bay in Port Stephens. On a summer afternoon there may be as many as 50 youngsters investigating the mysteries of the submarine world. The water is crystal-clear and the rocks are abundant, providing resting places up to 100 metres from the shore. A road just west of the village drops to the beginning of Stockton Beach. Its dunes and broad, flat sands, reaching for nearly 30 km along Newcastle Bight, are inaccessible except on foot or by four-wheel-drive. East of Birubi Point is Fishermans Bay, a tiny inlet protected by a reef

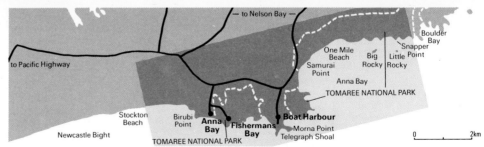

300 metres offshore. Boat Harbour, tucked between Telegraph Shoal and Morna Point, is another haven for young snorkellers, as well as learner yachtsmen. A grassy picnic park, shaded by banksias, backs a flat, sandy beach.

Past blunt, hilly Morna Point, eucalypts fringe

the south of One Mile Beach to Samurai Point, a brown sandstone intrusion. Beyond it lie naked sandhills, and people just as naked—the northern end of One Mile Beach, inaccessible by car, is designated for nude bathing. Two nearshore islands, Big and Little Rocky, mark the eastern

Fishing settlements fringe the rugged promontory between Stockton Beach and Anna Bay

end of Anna Bay. Opposite Little Rocky is a natural pool, enclosed except for a 10-metre sea entrance. Green water rises and falls gently and invitingly. It would make an ideal swimming hole—but once in, there is no easy way out. Boulder Bay, north around Snapper Point, reeks with the odours of a sewage outfall and attracts only the keenest walkers and rock fishermen.

ANNA BAY-BOAT HARBOUR (pop. 796) east of Pacific Highway 237 km from Sydney (turn off at Raymond Terrace).

TRANSPORT: train Sydney-Newcastle and bus Newcastle-Anna Bay-Boat Harbour daily.

🏠 📷 ⛺ 🛏 🚻 🎣 ⚓ ⛵

The ocean giant that broke its back

HALF of a massive, modern steel ship towers over the sands of lonely Stockton Beach, 20 km south of Anna Bay. This was the stern section of the 53 000-tonne Norwegian bulk carrier *Sygna*, wrecked early on 26 May 1974. Winds gusting to 165 km/h wreaked havoc throughout the Sydney-Newcastle region that night. The *Sygna*, waiting outside Newcastle harbour for a coal loading berth, dragged its anchor. Even under full power the unladen, high-riding ship would not steer, and it ploughed into the beach 8 km north of the port.

The bow came to rest on flat sand but the heavy stern, carrying the engines and superstructure, protruded into deep water. As soon as the storm subsided, the stern slumped and the ship broke in half. Crewmen were lifted off unharmed, and the wreck was put up for sale as scrap. A Japanese salvage company—agreeing on double pay for waterfront union members who helped—succeeded in dragging the empty bow section from the beach.

Salvaging the flooded stern was a more difficult job, requiring the aid of tugs. But tug companies, anticipating a double-pay demand from their crews and anxious not to set such a precedent, would not charter to the Japanese. Time and again the stern was winched out to sea, only to be scuttled to secure it when no tugs came. Each time its joints were further damaged, so that finally it was unsalvageable. Stripped of saleable fittings, the *Sygna's* stern can be seen by walkers or four-wheel-drive motorists from either end of the beach or from Fullerton Cove, on the Stockton-Williamstown route.

A hawser holds the wreck to the beach to stop it from endangering shipping in deeper waters

Port Stephens south

Stubby, workmanlike fishing boats crowd the wharf at Nelson Bay, the main town on Port Stephens. In summer the commercial fleet mingles with power launches owned by the residents of multi-storey bayside houses, screened from visitors by towering eucalypts. Cruises of the port, jetboat runs and water-skiing are available near the wharf. The grassy backshore and beach are jammed with family groups. North at Little Nelson Bay, traffic around the concrete boat ramp on a summer morning is like that at a city intersection, impatient and incessant. To the west, past the main shopping area, Dutchmans Bay offers picnic spots on white sand shaded by casuarinas and eucalypts. Beyond Bagnalls Beach, a silent shoreline is shielded by bush. On past the oyster leases of Salamander Bay, however, the holiday hubbub resumes at a string of caravan parks and playgrounds along Wanda Beach and Soldiers Point.

To the east, in the last scoop of the port shore before Tomaree Head, Shoal Bay's gentle waves and spotless, grainy sand are thronged throughout the summer with family groups. Rainbow-sailed catamarans accelerate away from the beach as if under power, threading between snorkellers, windsurfers and children in canoes or on rubber rafts. The headland, 158 metres at its summit, dominates the scene. But visitors cannot go up without NSW Health Commission approval because it is in the grounds of a holiday lodge for psychiatric patients. Zenith Beach, south around Tomaree Head, is often exposed to wind, and its rougher seas are favoured mainly by swimmers in their late teens and early 20s. At the south end of the beach, rocks rise vertically to high bushland. Farther on, Box Beach is accessible by a fenced sand track from a dirt road. Surf anglers make good catches, sometimes including groper, from the rocks at either end of the beach.

Fingal Beach is another magnet for young families, generally less affluent and flamboyant than the boat-owning groups at the inner bays of Port Stephens. From the south end, the spit to Point Stephens appears as an unbroken stretch of sand. In fact it is partly submerged at all but the lowest tides, and the headland appears on most maps as an island. Fast tidal currents sweep across the spit, making it extremely dangerous to attempt to reach the point. The lighthouse, built in 1862, has been automatically operated since 1973 so it is not open to visitors.

Sweeping curves of sand at Shoal Bay and Fingal Bay offer a choice of quiet water or ocean surf

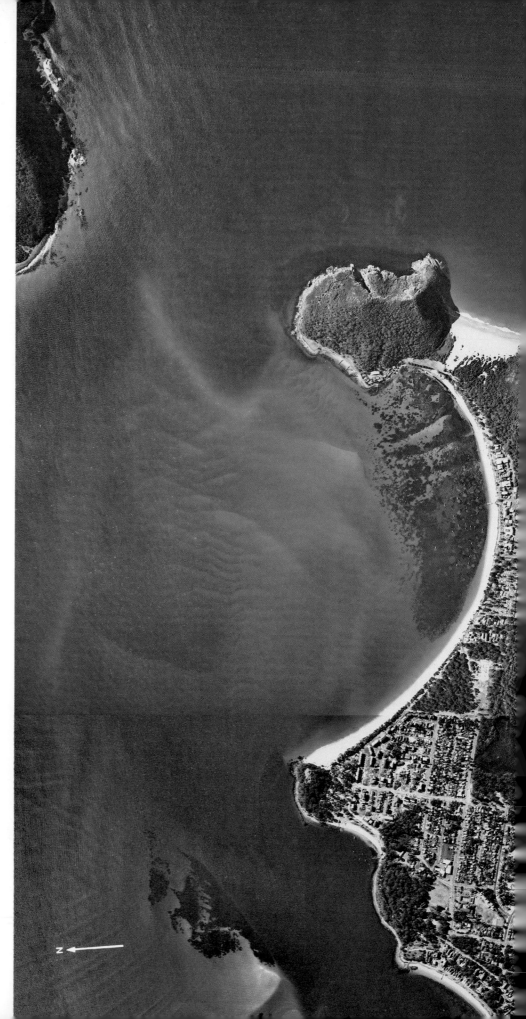

NELSON BAY (pop. 7930) east of Pacific Highway 245 km from Sydney (turn off at Raymond Terrace).
TRANSPORT: train Sydney-Newcastle and bus Newcastle-Nelson Bay daily.
SURF CLUB PATROL: Fingal October-Easter, Saturday 13.00-17.00, Sunday and public holidays 09.00-17.00.

	NELSON BAY											
	Jan	Feb	Mar	Apr	May	Jun	Jul	Aug	Sep	Oct	Nov	Dec
Maximum C°	27	27	26	24	20	18	18	19	20	23	25	26
Minimum C°	19	19	17	15	12	10	8	9	10	14	15	17
Rainfall mm	102	106	119	119	147	155	143	106	92	78	69	96
Humidity %	70	70	67	61	64	63	51	53	62	59	64	66
Rain Days	12	11	12	12	13	13	12	11	11	11	10	11
Sunshine hrs	Summer 7 +			Autumn 7 +			Winter 6 +			Spring 7 +		

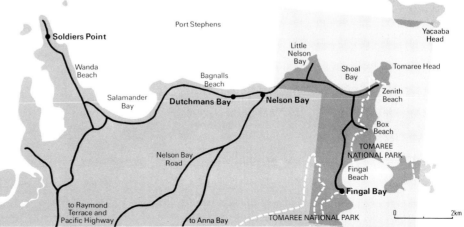

Port Stephens north

Twin towns of Hawks Nest and Tea Gardens line opposite shores of the Myall River's lower reaches

The concrete arc of the Singing Bridge, leaping the Myall River just inside its mouth, links the towns of Tea Gardens and Hawks Nest. But it divides their residents. Some hear a pure contralto voice when a strong south-west wind vibrates the handrails, others a tuneless screech. Their debate is good-humoured—unlike the bitter argument raised in the early 1970s when yachtsmen learned that the bridge, replacing a

50-year-old ferry service, would bar tall-masted craft from the river and the Myall Lakes. Other boat enthusiasts fare better. Cabin cruisers crowd the moorings and private jetties at Tea Gardens, on the river bend enfolding Witts Island. Hired power boats, canoes and catamarans are snapped up by visitors jamming the tidy green town during school holidays. For non-sailors, the 98-seat motor cruiser *Tamboi Queen*

makes tours of varying duration around Port Stephens or upriver to the lakes.

Tea Gardens came into prominence in the mid-19th century as a port for red cedar cut on the Myall Lakes shores. Paddlewheel barges brought the timber downriver for transfer to sailing ships bound for Newcastle or Sydney. The town's name derives from an unsuccessful attempt to grow tea in the 1850s, when the Australian Agricultural Company imported Chinese labourers to work its land leases.

Oyster leases fringe the mangroves west of the Myall mouth towards Pindimar Bay. Fishermen make good catches and children find sheltered swimming to the east, in clear water inside Paddy Marrs Bar. But it is salty here: to be entirely safe from sharks, youngsters should be directed north of the bridge. Behind the dunes of Jimmys Beach, reached through Hawks Nest, goannas bask in scrub and scuttle across the fenced access tracks. Speedboats tow waterskiers across the deep, protected waters of Port Stephens while toddlers explore the shallows.

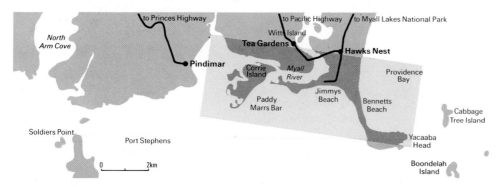

To the east, inside the peninsula ending in Yacaaba Head, anglers cast their lines.

On the ocean side of the peninsula, Bennetts Beach starts its great, clear sweep, 15 km north-east to Dark Point. Cabbage Tree Island and the Broughton Islands, facing the beach from Providence Bay, are noted game fishing grounds. The beach itself, patrolled at the Hawks Nest end, is a safe, pleasant shore for family groups. Yacaaba Head can be reached on foot across the spit from Jimmys Beach or Bennetts Beach. Where rocks begin on the ocean side of the headland, a track leads to the 217-metre summit. It is a steep climb, rewarded by exceptional views of the complex harbour and its surroundings.

TEA GARDENS (pop. 601) east of Pacific Highway 249 km from Sydney (turn off 14 km east of Karuah).
TRANSPORT: train Sydney-Newcastle daily; bus Newcastle-Tea Gardens-Hawks Nest most days.

HAWKS NEST (pop. 1071) 2 km east of Tea Gardens.
TRANSPORT: as for Tea Gardens.
SURF CLUB PATROL: South Bennetts Beach October-Easter, Saturday 13.00-17.00, Sunday and public holidays 09.00-17.00.

Cities that never took shape

AROUND wooded bays to the west of Tea Gardens two drawing-board cities have waited a lifetime to be built. Their faded plans represent the blighted hopes of land speculators—repeatedly raised and dashed since Port Stephens was proposed in 1911 as the site of a naval base. The federal government resumed land on the south side of the bay for that purpose in 1916 and held it until the 1960s, giving encouragement for a succession of schemes for urban development on the opposite shore. In the 1970s the 'city' site of about 80 hectares was bought by an investing company and it was passed to a Sydney group in 1981. Residential-sized blocks have been sold but at present the land is zoned non-urban, and the developers are hoping that a zoning change will eventually permit home building.

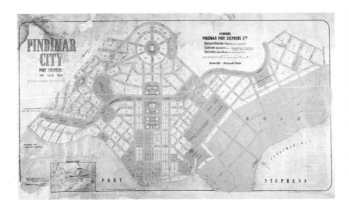

This ambitious plan for Pindimar City was drawn up by a Sydney man, W. Scott Griffiths, around 1918. The scheme included a cathedral, linked by a boulevard to no less than 13 government and civic buildings, and even an airport. Equally grandiose schemes were made for a city at North Arm Cove. One plan was submitted by the American architect, Walter Burley Griffin, who designed Canberra.

Myall Lakes and Seal Rocks

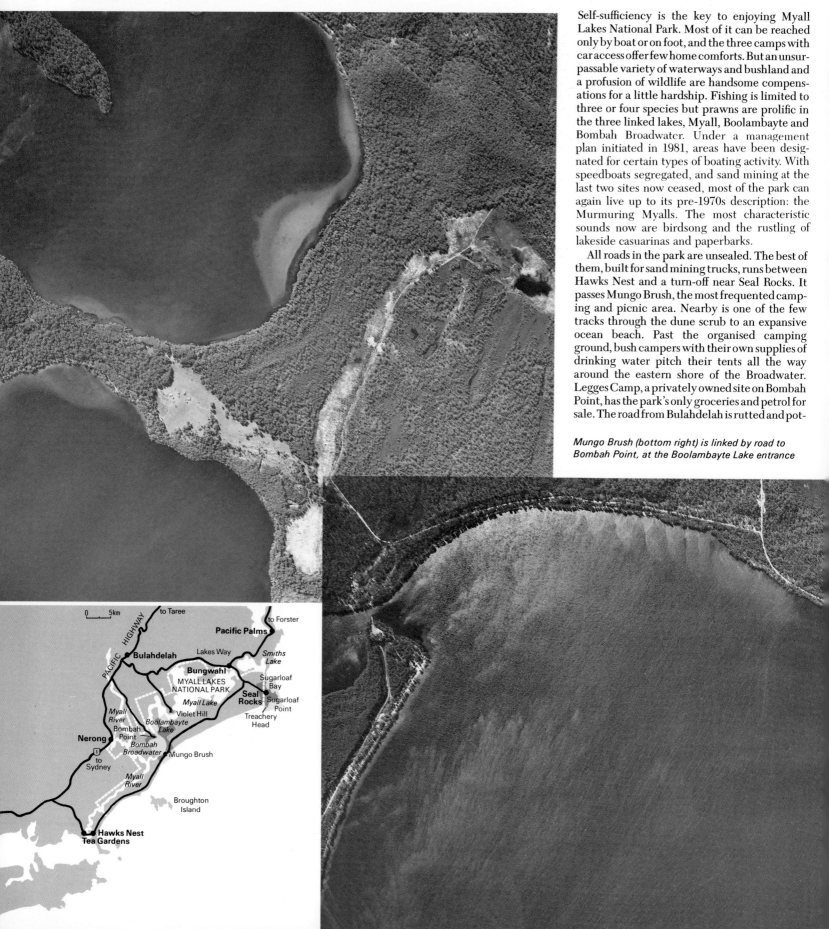

Self-sufficiency is the key to enjoying Myall Lakes National Park. Most of it can be reached only by boat or on foot, and the three camps with car access offer few home comforts. But an unsurpassable variety of waterways and bushland and a profusion of wildlife are handsome compensations for a little hardship. Fishing is limited to three or four species but prawns are prolific in the three linked lakes, Myall, Boolambayte and Bombah Broadwater. Under a management plan initiated in 1981, areas have been designated for certain types of boating activity. With speedboats segregated, and sand mining at the last two sites now ceased, most of the park can again live up to its pre-1970s description: the Murmuring Myalls. The most characteristic sounds now are birdsong and the rustling of lakeside casuarinas and paperbarks.

All roads in the park are unsealed. The best of them, built for sand mining trucks, runs between Hawks Nest and a turn-off near Seal Rocks. It passes Mungo Brush, the most frequented camping and picnic area. Nearby is one of the few tracks through the dune scrub to an expansive ocean beach. Past the organised camping ground, bush campers with their own supplies of drinking water pitch their tents all the way around the eastern shore of the Broadwater. Legges Camp, a privately owned site on Bombah Point, has the park's only groceries and petrol for sale. The road from Bulahdelah is rutted and pot-

Mungo Brush (bottom right) is linked by road to Bombah Point, at the Boolambayte Lake entrance

Seal Rocks township, beside the quiet waters of Sugarloaf Bay, is backed by high hills and the exposed sands of Lighthouse Beach

holed for the last 12 km, so motorists find it easier to approach from Mungo Brush, using a cable-punt ferry service across the Bombah Point narrows. The third organised camping ground, at Violet Hill, has an even worse access road that may not be negotiable after heavy rain. But its broad, grassy slopes and shaded lakeside bays make it attractive to campers seeking a quieter spot for their holiday.

All three camping grounds have boat ramps. Private craft may also be launched outside the park—at Tea Gardens or Hawks Nest on the lower Myall outlet, at Nerong or Bulahdelah on the Pacific Highway, and at Bungwahl, to the east on the Lakes Way. Houseboats are based at Bulahdelah, and smaller cruising craft can be hired at Tea Gardens. Legges Camp has canoes with space to stow camping gear and food.

On the approach to Seal Rocks, east of the national park, newcomers are treated to a succession of charming scenes. A hilly, dusty forest road winds down to a sudden vista of beaches and headlands north to Pacific Palms. Sugarloaf Bay has the genuine look of an old-fashioned fishing village. Simple cottages perch on the hillside, while boats, nets and fishing traps clutter Boat Beach. The road climbs again to the Sugarloaf Point lighthouse, dating from 1875 and open to visitors 10.00-12.00 and 13.00-15.00 on Tuesdays and Thursdays. Down an easy track from the lighthouse gates there is a view of a vast rock chasm where foam spurts from a blowhole if the ocean swell is heavy. The Seal Rocks, from which the settlement took its name, are 2-3 km offshore, south of the lighthouse. Fur seals sometimes rest there in winter sunshine. Lighthouse Beach, stretching west to Treachery Head, offers solitude but is exposed to heavy seas, and the sand track access is not recommended.

SEAL ROCKS east of Pacific Highway 304 km from Sydney (take Lakes Way 4 km north of Bulahdelah, turn off at Bungwahl).
TRANSPORT: trains Sydney-Newcastle daily; bus Newcastle-Bungwahl most days, none beyond Bungwahl, 11 km away.

BOMBAH POINT east of Pacific Highway 275km from Sydney (turn off for Tea Gardens and take Mungo Brush Road to ferry, or turn off at Bulahdelah).
TRANSPORT: as for Seal Rocks; none beyond Hawks Nest or Bungwahl.

SUGARLOAF POINT												
	Jan	Feb	Mar	Apr	May	Jun	Jul	Aug	Sep	Oct	Nov	Dec
Rainfall mm	107	107	139	134	152	144	135	95	85	78	78	95
Rain Days	9	9	11	10	11	11	9	9	8	9	9	8
Sunshine hrs	Summer 7 +		Autumn 7 +			Winter 6 +			Spring 7 +			

Playgrounds for every taste

MARITIME pleasures of matchless variety mark Port Stephens as the Central Coast's most rewarding spot for active holidays. Waterways of the harbour and the Myall Lakes system offer 1400 square kilometres for sheltered sailing and motorcruising. A string of ocean beaches lures surfers, while quiet bays abound for less accomplished swimmers.

Fisherman are in heaven—their choices almost too wide if their time is limited. They can fish the harbour from boats or the shores, surf-cast, or try freshwater angling along the many rivers that feed the port's inner reaches. Shoal Bay is the base of the Newcastle and Port Stephens Game Fishing Club. Marlin, yellowfin tuna and kingfish are caught not far out from the twin headlands of Tomaree and Yacaaba. Game fishing contests, hosted by the club late every February, are claimed to attract more participants than any other such competition in the world.

Spearfishing is tightly restricted, but scuba divers and snorkellers enjoy an underwater world of surprising diversity. Along with reefs and caves there are dozens of shipwrecks dotted in and around the port, some of them accessible. Soft and hard corals grow profusely in clear waters, among fascinating sponge gardens. On some diving cruises, huge fish have become tame enough to feed by hand.

Prawning is a favourite pastime from October to April, on nights when the moon is not too bright and the tide is ebbing. Big commercial catches are made with drag nets, operated by two people. Amateurs may use them too, but the equipment has to be registered. Simplest to use, particularly for children, is a small scoop net fixed to a hoop. It can be carried about while wading in sandy shallows, spotting runs of prawns with a torch.

As a change from the delights of the waterways, bush walks can be taken in almost any direction from the port. Myall Lakes National Park, to the north, has been complemented by the recent declaration of Tomaree National Park. Its areas, broken in a few places, embrace most of the surfing beaches and cover coastal bushland reaching from Tomaree Head south to Fishermans Bay.

Spring wildflowers deck the steep heights of Tomaree National Park

Families favour the gentle waters of Shoal Bay

High tide washes volcanic rocks at Zenith Beach, just south of Tomaree Head

Away from it all on the Bombah Broadwater, in Myall Lakes National Park

Pelicans abound on the lakes

Smiths Lake and Pacific Palms

But for boat ramp pointers, visitors to Smiths Lake might despair of finding their way to the waterfront. Roads wind over the hilly, forested promontory in a bewildering maze, until the last turning reveals a lakeside store and jetty. On the point an attractive picnic ground is shaded by tall gums and bordered—if the lake is low—by a broad spread of clean white sand. Water levels are a sensitive issue here. Campers and sunbathers like the lake low. Boat enthusiasts enjoy more scope when it is high. If it rises too far after prolonged rains and threatens to swamp shoreline properties, a channel is bulldozed through

Smiths Lake approaching its highest level; usually the circular hole breaking Little Island is dry

the eastern sand barrier and into the Tasman Sea. But if the cut has to be made late in the year, just before the peak summer season, prawns leave the lake and holidaymakers are denied one of the area's chief pastimes.

Unsealed tracks lead from the Sandbar caravan park across a large expanse of replanted dunes, bared by rutile mining in the early 1970s, to the long bar enclosing the lake. The northern track—a private route for which a small toll is charged—leads to Cellito Beach, which is sheltered by Bald Head and not as subject to dangerous rips as the surf is farther south.

At the north-west corner of the lake, Sugar Creek Road branches off from the Lakes Way into Wallingat State Forest. A signposted scenic

drive leads west to campsites, picnic grounds and a boat launching ramp on the Wallingat River. The hilly route then curves east past a tree reserve with a picnic area and an easy nature walk through dense groves of cabbage palms and over several creek crossings. The road to Whoota Whoota Hill is a diversion off the main scenic route and leads to a lookout commanding views over Wallis Lake and south to Port Stephens.

Pacific Palms, originally a lakeside township on Charlotte Bay, has given its name to a grouping of settlements north of Smiths Lake. All have easy boat access to Wallis Lake, which reaches all the way to Tuncurry, as well as a choice of sheltered ocean beaches. Elizabeth Beach is attractively backed by dunes, grassy picnic

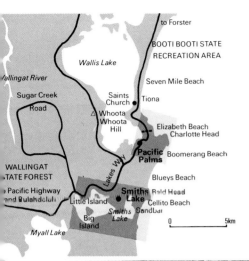

Pacific Palms has sheltered bathing to the north at Elizabeth and Shelly Beaches, and surf to the south

grounds and a profuse growth of palms among eucalypts and ferns. Tiny Shelly Beach, farther east, is accessible only by a sand track. South of Charlotte Head, Boomerang and Blueys Beaches have much more generous expanses of sand but rips are frequent, and the dunes are fenced and backed by housing. Boomerang Point's windy heights attract hang-gliding enthusiasts.

North of Pacific Palms, the Lakes Way carries travellers into the rugged southern section of the Booti Booti State Recreation Area. Wallis Lake is easily accessible, or adventurous bushwalkers can strike out east to a steep and rocky coast. Farther on, the northern section of the recreation area runs along lonely Seven Mile Beach, reaching almost to Forster. At Tiona, between the two reserve areas, there are organised camp-ing and caravan sites and the remarkable open-air 'Green Cathedral'—formally named Saints Church. Shaded in a grove of palms, it has pews and choir stalls of palm logs, and a stone altar at the lake's edge. Travellers are welcome to pause in a setting of unusual tranquillity.

SMITHS LAKE east of Pacific Highway on Lakes Way 302 km from Sydney.
TRANSPORT: train Sydney-Newcastle daily; bus Newcastle-Smiths Lake-Pacific Palms most days.

🏠 🏤 ▲ 🚻 ⚓ ∾ ⚐

PACIFIC PALMS on Lakes Way 307 km from Sydney, 7 km from Smiths Lake.
TRANSPORT: as for Smiths Lake.

🏠 🏤 ▲ ⛽ ♀ 🍴 🚻 ∾ ⚓

Sydney to Tweed Heads 175

Forster and Tuncurry

Forster's smart shopping arcades and its little cluster of waterfront apartment buildings, up to eight storeys high, suggest an embryo Surfers Paradise. But commercial development does not yet intrude too brashly on Forster or on Tuncurry, its sister town across the inlet to Wallis Lake. Together they form a well-appointed but relaxed centre for ocean and inland waterway recreation. The two towns have been linked by their 630-metre bridge only since 1959. A ferry, and before that punts and rowing boats, used to take passengers and vehicles between the settlements. North Forster was so cut off that in the 1870s its residents started clamouring for their own civic amenities. They took up the old Aboriginal name for the district, Tuncurry, and had it adopted officially in 1889 when they gained a separate post office.

Wallis Lake is noted for prawns, oysters, crabs and an abundance of fish. Its entrance breakwaters and its many sandbanks and islands are popular fishing spots, and there are numerous ramps and jetties. Boat sheds on both sides of the lake sell fish directly from the trawlers of the local fleet and have motorboats, canoes, half-cabin cruisers and catamarans for hire. From Fisherman's Wharf, near the shopping centre in Forster, the launch *Bardoo* makes day cruises through a maze of islands in the northern part of Wallis Lake and south to Pacific Palms. The town bridge has a 6-metre boat clearance over channels near each end. Sailors making out to sea, however, should check with the Forster pilot station or with boatshed proprietors. The bar is stabilised by the breakwaters, but can be dangerous in heavy weather.

Water-skiing is most popular in Pipers Creek and on the Wallamba River, which is navigable for small craft as far as Nabiac. The Wallingat River can be explored deep into Wallingat State Forest, where there are picnic spots and campsites on the eastern shores. Islands in the northern part of Wallis Lake are sandy and mostly covered by low-lying scrub. Some are surrounded by mangroves and mud, others by clean, sandy beaches where boats can be run on to the shores for picnics, swimming and fishing. Channels are marked between most of the islands, but beyond the tidal limit at the Step and the Cut, markings end and a sharp lookout should be kept for shallows. Beaches in the area include the long, deserted stretch of Nine Mile Beach, reaching beyond Tuncurry Beach, as well as a patrol-

Breakwaters stabilising the entrance to Wallis Lake have trapped sand to give Forster and Tuncurry competing town beaches, with grassy backshores that accommodate hundreds of caravans

led surf beach and an ocean pool at Forster, and a beach protected by a shark net inside the entrance at Tuncurry.

The 233-metre summit of Cape Hawke is a steep, strenuous walk of about 400 metres from the end of Minor Road, which turns off the Lakes Way at Forster Keys. There are sheltered tables at the summit lookout with magnificent views south along the sweeping crescent of Seven Mile Beach to the knotted green hills around Pacific Palms, and north to Crowdy Head, 40 km away.

FORSTER-TUNCURRY (pop. 9260) east of Pacific Highway on Lakes Way 325 km from Sydney.
TRANSPORT: train Sydney-Taree daily with connecting bus (8 hrs); flights Sydney-Forster daily.
SURF CLUB PATROL: Forster Beach October-Easter, Saturday 12.30-16.30, Sunday and public holidays 09.30-16.30.

	FORSTER											
	Jan	Feb	Mar	Apr	May	Jun	Jul	Aug	Sep	Oct	Nov	Dec
Rainfall mm	112	119	144	135	115	121	93	79	69	77	73	101
Rain Days	8	9	10	8	8	8	8	7	7	9	7	7
Sunshine hrs	Summer 7 +			Autumn 7 +			Winter 6 +			Spring 7 +		

to Pacific Highway and Taree
Nine Mile Beach

Tuncurry Beach

Wallamba River

Tuncurry

Forster
Fisherman's Wharf

The Cut

Lakes Way

Wallis Island

Pipers Creek

Minor Road

The Step

Forster Keys

Cape Hawke

Wallis Lake

Coomba

Green Point

BOOTI BOOTI STATE
RECREATION AREA

0   2km

to Pacific Highway and Bulahdelah   Seven Mile Beach

Cape Hawke's summit, reached by walking trails, commands the NSW central coast's most extensive views

Hallidays Point and Old Bar

Dark, glistening rocks rise from a boisterous sea to form the base of the high promontory overlooking Hallidays Point township. Locals sometimes apply its name, Black Head, to the whole district. On its flat top, bowlers play within earshot of crashing waves and sightseers can take in a 360° panorama—east over the Tasman, south along Nine Mile Beach, west past the town over farms and swamp to Kiwarrak State Forest, and north to the Manning River.

The sheltered southern part of Black Head Beach is lined with palms and grassy slopes which stretch for almost 1 km past a tree-studded caravan park to Red Head. The patrolled beach has a concrete pool, flooding at high tide, built into the rocks at one end. In front of the Halliday's Point shops a small park with shaded tables and a stone barbecue overlooks a creek which is crossed by a wooden bridge leading directly on to the beach sand.

Seas around Black Head have a reputation for being rough, but they support a small commercial fishing fleet. There is a concrete ramp near

South of Black Head and Hallidays Point township, Nine Mile Beach stretches virtually untouched

the lifesavers' clubhouse, where boats up to 5 metres long can be lowered by tractor or four-wheel-drive and launched into Black Head Bay. A new settlement of lavish homes and resort buildings is growing behind the dunes of Diamond Beach. Tracks lead on to Saltwater Beach, or inland through Kiwarrak State Forest to join up with the Lakes Way.

At Old Bar, the hard brown sand after a storm is dotted with stones smaller than a fist—red, orange, grey, yellow and some jet black. As the surf pushes up the beach, they rattle like falling tenpins. A mat of grass holds the back of the beach together as the ocean undercuts it, making half-metre cliffs where the edge of the plateau cracks and falls. Offshore reefs create good rolling surf from the township north to the 'old bar' itself—a sand barrier that confines the outlet of the Manning River's south channel. A gravel road runs 2 km from the township, between the caravan park and a small airstrip, to Mudbishops Flat. There a reserve and shady picnic grounds overlook the river loop of Oyster Arm. Sandbanks exposed at low tide can be pumped for fishing bait. The rich silt soil of Cabbage Tree Island supports dairying, but there is no bridge: farmers

must bring their produce out by boat. The main channel of the Manning River is navigable north of the island, and boats can be launched at a concrete ramp near the road bridge at Bohnock, or travel down from the numerous ramps at Taree. The lower section of the channel has constantly changing shoals and should be negotiated with caution. The outlet to the Tasman Sea at Farquhar is not navigable.

HALLIDAYS POINT east of Pacific Highway 322 km north of Sydney (turn off 5 km north of Nabiac).
TRANSPORT: train Sydney-Taree daily (6½ hrs) with connecting bus some days; flights Sydney-Forster daily; bus from Forster some days.
SURF CLUB PATROL: October-Easter, Sunday and public holidays 10.00-16.00, Saturdays during school holidays only 11.00-14.00.

OLD BAR (pop. 970) east of Pacific Highway 341 km from Sydney (turn off at Purfleet).
TRANSPORT: train Sydney-Taree (6½ hrs); bus Taree-Old Bar weekdays; flights Sydney-Taree daily.
SURF CLUB PATROL: October-Easter, weekends and public holidays 10.00-16.00.

The south channel of the Manning River, north of Old Bar, splits around Cabbage Tree Island

Map labels:
to Taree
to Manning Point
Oxley Island
Manning River South Channel
Cabbage Tree Island
Bohnock
Oyster Arm
Mudbishops Flat
Farquhar Inlet
Old Bar
PACIFIC HIGHWAY
KIWARRAK STATE FOREST
to Newcastle
Lakes Way
Saltwater Beach
Diamond Beach
Red Head
Black Head Beach
Black Head
Hallidays Point
to Tuncurry
0   2km
Nine Mile Beach

How tea-trees came by their name

DUNES and waste ground near Hallidays Point are studded with 'tea-tree' scrub. It is no coincidence that the clean, clear waters of Frogalla Swamp, to the west, and of the creek at the south end of Black Head Beach, are stained a dark brown—like tea.

Many trees and plants contain tannin, the colouring agent of tea. Some shrubs also have oils in their leaves similar to those which give Indian or Chinese teas their flavour and aroma. *Leptospermum* species, discovered in New Zealand but also widespread in Australia, make a tolerable substitute for tea. Explorers and early settlers made use of them, and of some *Melaleuca* species. All acquired the nickname of tea-tree.

The spelling 'ti-tree' is a mistake. It arose from confusion with the Polynesian *ti*, which originally referred to a Pacific Islands lily, *Cordyline terminalis*, and was later applied to the common cabbage-tree, *Cordyline australis*.

Leptospermum laevigatum, a coastal tea-tree

Manning River and Crowdy Head

The unruly Manning River has been defying attempts to master it for more than a century. In the mid-1800s, when red cedar timber and maize from upriver became important, ships could not negotiate the shifting entrance channels without a local pilot, and Harrington village was established to serve the pilot station. In 1894 a determined and expensive effort was made to stabilise a channel by building a 4 km training wall along the northern shore of the inlet. Rock was quarried at Crowdy Head and brought to Harrington on a specially built 6 km railway. Sand dredged from the entrance, year after year, was dumped over the wall, creating a long back-channel island. In the 1920s, two angled spur walls were added. But still the unpredictable, flood-prone Manning built up a dangerous bar. An obelisk on Pilot Hill records the wrecking of

four ships on the bar and two on the training wall—the latest in 1941. Now the entrance is officially listed as not navigable from the sea. Small boats launched inside, however, find good cruising all the way up to Taree and Wingham.

From Manning Point a network of roads and tracks spreads over Mitchells Island. They allow long, quiet walks past rich dairy pastures, through a small state forest or along 10 km of sandy ocean beach. The beach provides fine fishing and is popular with swimmers and sunbathers, but board-riders find the surf too irregular. Boats for hire at Manning Point can be pulled up at many spots on Mitchells, or on other islands in the river delta, to picnic or to barbecue a morning's catch of fish. At the northern end of the township, a shady picnic reserve has short tracks leading through to the ocean beach.

The long training wall at Harrington is popular with anglers—especially at the gantry, a wooden bridge in the wall about 500 metres south of where it meets the road. Ramps near the centre of town and west of the inlet island give access for upriver boating. Just north-east of Harrington a safe, shallow lagoon is enclosed by a park-like camping ground, a thick belt of coastal bush and high, rolling sand dunes which separate it from the wide ocean beach running to Crowdy Head.

Crowdy Head's man-made harbour, completed in the 1960s, is the base for a co-operative commercial fishing fleet and little other space is available. Conditions outside can become very rough, especially on shallow banks to the north. There is good surf fishing along the beach of Crowdy Bay, and from the cliffs of the headland. Mermaid Reef, 12 km north and 5 km offshore,

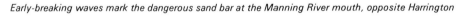
Early-breaking waves mark the dangerous sand bar at the Manning River mouth, opposite Harrington

is well known for its runs of snapper. Board-riders are drawn to the surf on South Beach—also known as Back Beach—while calmer water for swimming is found on Crowdy Beach in front of the lawns of the lifesaving clubhouse. Crowdy Bay National Park runs north-east to Diamond Head. Its picnic ground and overnight campsites are at the headland, and more easily approached from the north.

MANNING POINT east of Pacific Highway 356 km from Sydney (turn off at Purfleet to Bohnock, Oxley Island and Mitchells Island).
TRANSPORT: train Sydney-Taree daily (6½ hrs); bus Taree-Manning Point weekdays; flights Sydney-Taree daily.

HARRINGTON (pop. 1183) east of Pacific Highway 380 km from Sydney (turn off at Coopernook).
TRANSPORT: train Sydney-Taree daily (6½ hrs); bus Taree-Harrington weekdays; flights Sydney-Taree daily.

CROWDY HEAD east of Pacific Highway 387 km from Sydney, 7 km from Harrington.
TRANSPORT: none beyond Harrington.
SURF CLUB PATROL: October-Easter, Saturday 10.00-14.00, Sunday 09.00-16.00.

HARRINGTON												
	Jan	Feb	Mar	Apr	May	Jun	Jul	Aug	Sep	Oct	Nov	Dec
Maximum C°	27	27	26	25	21	19	18	19	21	23	25	26
Minimum C°	18	18	17	14	10	9	7	8	9	13	14	17
Rainfall mm	125	151	149	144	121	131	98	89	78	86	90	111
Humidity %	66	68	63	60	57	62	52	52	60	66	62	66
Rain Days	13	13	15	13	12	11	10	11	10	12	11	12
Sunshine hrs	Summer 7 +			Autumn 7 +			Winter 6 +			Spring 7 +		

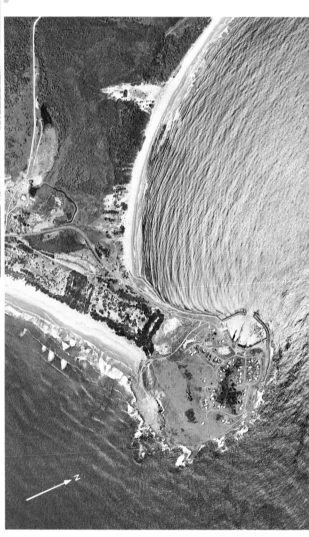
Swells striking south of Crowdy Head or bending around it bring a variety of waves to suit all surfers, from novices to expert board-riders

Camden Haven to Lake Cathie

North Brother's massive, forested mound rises 487 metres over a cluster of settlements around Camden Haven Inlet. It commands sweeping views of inland lakes and rivers and of long ocean beaches to the east. A firm road winds through the thick woods of Camden Haven State Forest to picnic tables and barbecues at the top of the mountain. Watson Taylors Lake and Queens Lake are spacious, but boating is restricted to shallow-draught craft. Deep, well-marked channels run to both lakes from ramps along the inlet, and the river is navigable as far as Kendall. Henry Kendall Forest Park has shaded picnic grounds and barbecues at the entrance to Queens Lake. The park, like the town inland, was named in honour of the famous poet, who lived in the district from 1875 to 1881.

To the east past North Haven, there is good surfing near the river mouth at Grants Beach. A hooked breakwater on the opposite side of the inlet gives more sheltered swimming. It is reached by a wide but unsealed road past Gogleys Lagoon. The lagoon entrance, at Dunbogan, has deep water and a gravel ramp below a small reserve with picnic tables, barbecues, lavatories, fish-cleaning tables and a swimming enclosure. The lagoon is shallow and heavily farmed for oysters but remains popular for fishing from small boats. Rough tracks lead through bush east of the lagoon to Perpendicular Point or to Hamey Lookout on the cliffs of Camden Head, where there are low ledges for rock fishing. Beach fishing is popular along the whole stretch of Dunbogan Beach from Camden Head to Diamond Head, at the north end of Crowdy Bay National Park. Overnight camping facilities are available at Diamond Head, but supplies of drinking water are unreliable.

Bonny Hills, sheltered by Grants Head, is a quiet resort giving access to the long sweep of Rainbow Beach. At its southern end, near the lifesaving clubhouse, the beach is backed by a large park with a playground and barbecues. A concrete ramp suitable for light craft leads into a channel offering some protection from the surf. Launching is limited to high tides and calm weather, however.

Lake Cathie—pronounced 'cat-eye' by the locals—is a shallow, mangrove-lined waterway which depends on spring tides breaking through the entrance bar to fill it. Prawns swarm in favourable seasons and fishing can be rewarding, although only shallow-draught boats are suitable. Paddle boats are for hire near the bridge, and shady picnic areas with barbecues and playgrounds surround the lake from the bridge to the entrance south of Lighthouse Beach. The inlet is often closed, and boat access to the sea is impossible even when it is open. Board-riders follow the surf along the entire stretch of coast from Camden Haven to Port Macquarie. Lighthouse Beach and Middle Rock are two particularly popular surfing spots near Lake Cathie.

Dunbogan Beach runs to a narrow spit at Camden Head; behind is Gogleys Lagoon

LAURIETON-NORTH HAVEN (pop. 3161) east of Pacific Highway 401 km from Sydney (turn off at Kew northbound, south of Hastings River southbound).

TRANSPORT: train Sydney-Kendall daily; none beyond Kendall, 10 km away.

SURF CLUB PATROL: Grants Beach October-Easter, Saturday 13.00-16.00, Sunday and public holidays 10.00-16.00.

🛢 🏠 ⌸ ▲ ⛺ ☺ ✶ 🚉 ♟ |O| ⊟ 🛶 ⋈ ≋ ⚓ ⚲

LAKE CATHIE (pop. 941) east of Pacific Highway 418 km from Sydney, 13 km north of Camden Haven.

TRANSPORT: coach Sydney-Port Macquarie daily (7½ hrs); bus to Lake Cathie weekly; flights Sydney-Port Macquarie most days.

🏠 ⌸ ▲ ⛺ ♟ ⊟ 🛶 ⋈ ⚓ ⚲

LAURIETON												
	Jan	Feb	Mar	Apr	May	Jun	Jul	Aug	Sep	Oct	Nov	Dec
Rainfall mm	150	186	184	164	132	139	101	98	84	102	107	124
Rain Days	9	10	11	9	8	7	7	7	7	8	8	9
Sunshine hrs	Summer 7 +			Autumn 7 +			Winter 6 +			Spring 7 +		

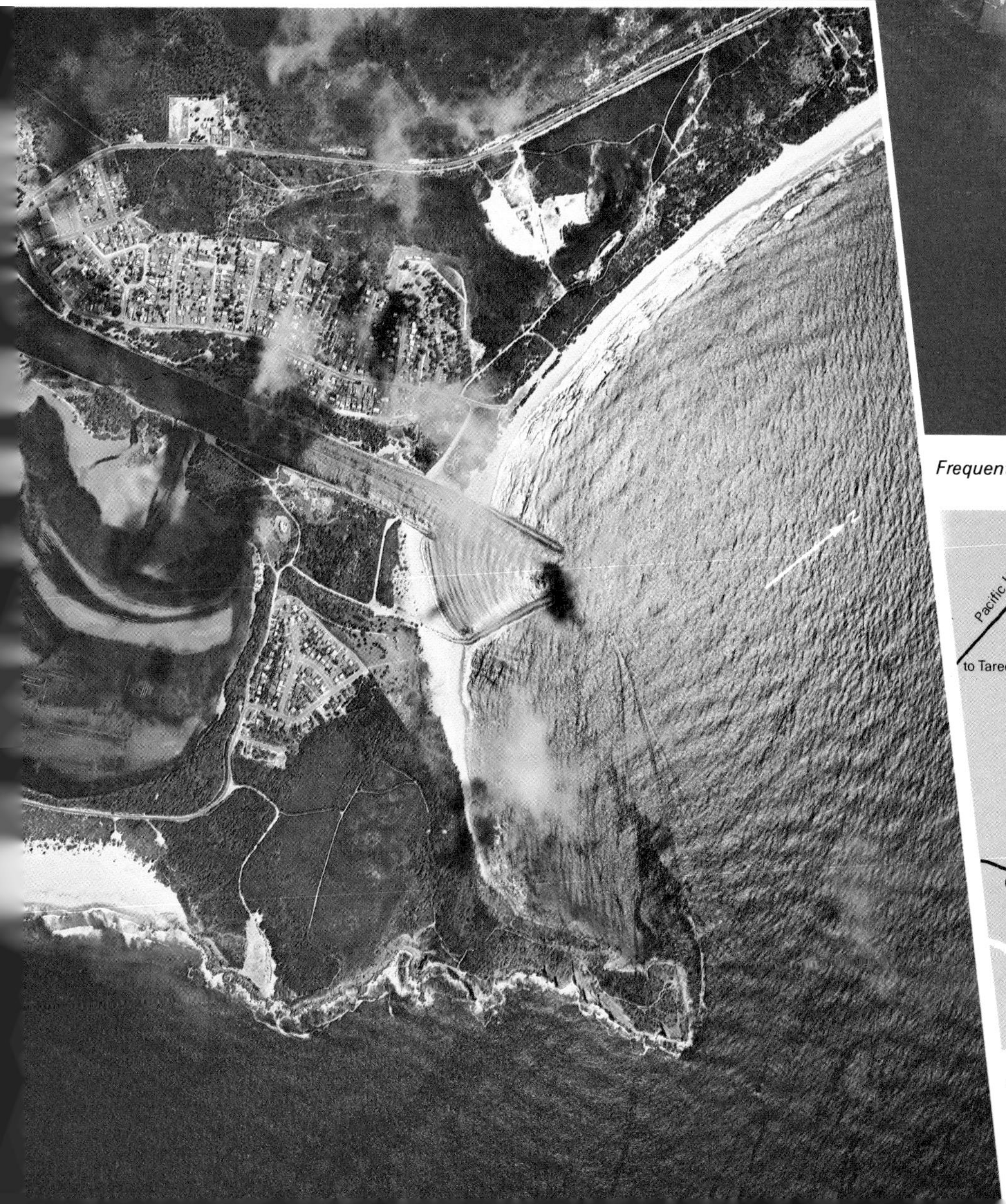

Frequent closure of Lake Cathie links beaches on either side

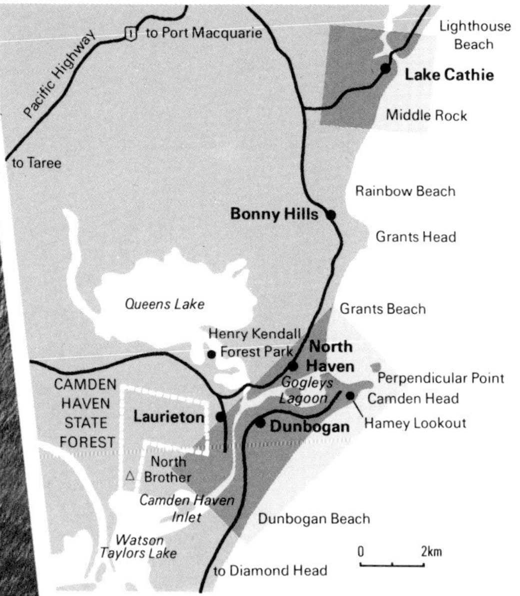

Sydney to Tweed Heads 183

Port Macquarie

Poplars and banksias beside Kooloonbung Creek, in the heart of Port Macquarie, shade the blackened gravestones of its first generation of residents—convicts and officers who arrived to establish a penal settlement in 1821, and free settlers who flocked to the timber-rich farming and fishing district after 1840. Late in the 19th century the wealthier citizens of Sydney and Newcastle recognised its leisure attractions. Port Macquarie became Australia's first resort town. A century later, superbly equipped, it is still expanding. Ocean bathing beaches are strung south of the Hastings River mouth. Town Beach has sheltered swimming for children at the southern end. Picnic areas with tables and barbecues adjoin Oxley Beach, Shelly Beach and the highly popular Flynns Beach. Flynns and Lighthouse Beaches are noted for good surf. In addition to weekend lifesaving club patrols, they are patrolled daily by lifeguards during the summer school holidays. From Settlement Point, north of a new town marina development, a three-minute ferry trip takes cars or pedestrians across the Hastings to riverbank picnic grounds and less frequented beaches. With the exception of Big Bay and Kooloonbung Creek, all the waterways are easily navigable by small craft and offer good fishing. Offshore fishing is also rewarding, but the entrance bar is tricky and should not be crossed without local advice. Surf casting and rock fishing spots abound.

The Hastings Museum in Clarence Street has collected an impressive display of relics from

convict and pioneer days. It is open 09.30-12.30 and 14.00-17.00 Monday to Saturday, and 14.00-17.00 on Sundays. St Thomas' Church, open daily on Hay Street, was designed by Australia's first architect, Francis Greenway, who was transported from England for forgery but is pictured on $10 banknotes. He won a pardon by his contribution to public works in Sydney. The church was built by convicts between 1824 and 1828. Its box pews and interior panelling were made from the district's prized red cedar.

PORT MACQUARIE (pop. 19581) east of Pacific Highway 425 km from Sydney (turn off at Oxley Highway northbound or Hastings River Drive southbound). TRANSPORT: coach Sydney-Port Macquarie daily (7½ hrs); trains Sydney-Wauchope daily (8½ hrs) with connecting buses most days; flights Sydney-Port Macquarie most days.
SURF CLUB PATROLS: October-Easter, Lighthouse Beach Saturday 10.00-16.00, Sunday and public holidays 09.00-16.00; Flynns Beach Saturday 13.00-16.00, Sunday and public holidays 09.00-16.00.

PORT MACQUARIE												
	Jan	Feb	Mar	Apr	May	Jun	Jul	Aug	Sep	Oct	Nov	Dec
Maximum C°	25	26	25	23	20	18	18	19	20	22	23	24
Minimum C°	18	19	17	14	11	9	7	8	10	13	15	17
Rainfall mm	160	180	173	168	145	132	103	92	89	97	95	129
Humidity %	79	77	75	71	67	68	62	65	68	75	77	78
Rain Days	12	13	15	13	12	10	10	9	9	11	10	11
Sunshine hrs	Summer 7 +			Autumn 7 +			Winter 6 +			Spring 7 +		

Modern shops and an extensive caravan park overlook the Hastings River mouth; a chain of sheltered pocket beaches and bush reserves reaches to the south

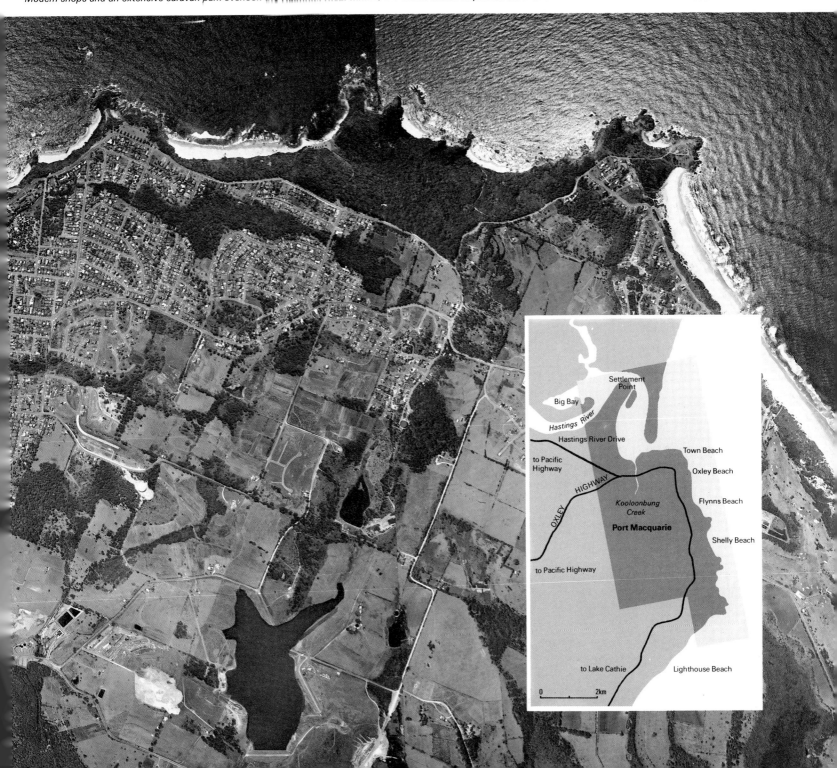

Crescent Head and Hat Head

With a strong southerly swell pushing past Crescent Head, slow waves bending left around Little Nobby give expert surfers a ride of up to 300 metres to Killick Beach, and plenty of time to perform competitive routines. In the 1960s, when longer boards were in vogue, these waves gave the area a world-class reputation. Today's champions look for short-board speed on steeper, faster waves. But Crescent Head remains popular for the reliability of its surf and for the ease with which it can be entered. A path down to the

Little Nobby, the northern tip of Crescent Head, is a launching spot for board rides to Killick Beach

rocks of Little Nobby allows strong swimmers to launch themselves into deep water, instead of having to paddle out.

From a lookout on the headland, the full sweep of surf beaches north to Hat Head and south to Port Macquarie can be seen. Immediately south of Little Nobby is the dark, rocky bay called Pebbly Beach. Its black stones spread back to a nine-hole golf course with a well-appointed clubhouse where visitors are welcome. A wide concrete boat ramp provides access to Killick Creek just short of the beach, and a footbridge crosses it 100 metres upstream. The creek affords calm, sheltered water for children, but parents should

be alert to strong tidal currents running either way. The creek mouth itself should be avoided. Anglers do well from the banks, and there are shady trees, picnic tables and barbecues at the town end of the bridge.

An interesting road, unsealed and rough in some parts, runs between Crescent Head and the Settlement Point ferry at Port Macquarie. The 28 km route skirts long stretches of untouched coast with wide sandy beaches, rocky headlands and many pleasant picnic spots. Point Plomer, 14 km south of Crescent Head, has a camping ground and holiday cabins.

At Hat Head, a large camping reserve with

Hat Head township, confined between Korogoro Creek and the dunes of a sheltered surf beach, is embraced by national park bushland

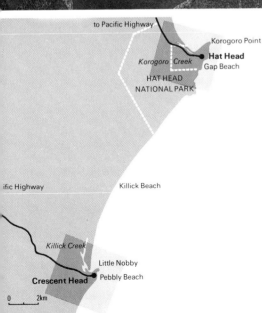

shady trees, picnic tables and barbecues occupies a spit of land formed where Korogoro Creek curves below the headland and joins the sea. A footbridge leads to trails for Gap Beach and the 164-metre-high summit. Fishermen can follow the rocky shoreline around to Korogoro Point, noted for Spanish mackerel. At the mouth of Korogoro Creek a boat ramp leads into shallow water but the entrance bar is difficult. Hat Head's professional fishermen launch over the beach. The creek provides sandy beaches for children and there is good fishing, especially from the road bridge upstream.

South of Hat Head, a thickly forested hill has a lookout giving a view 20 km north to the Smoky Cape lighthouse. The coastal strip is occupied by Hat Head National Park, rich in bird life and wildflowers. Permits are not required for camping areas just south of Hat Head and at Smoky Cape. They have pit lavatories, but fresh water supplies are unreliable. Old forest trails nearby lead to secluded sandy beaches.

CRESCENT HEAD (pop. 944) east of Pacific Highway 485 km from Sydney (turn off at South Kempsey).
TRANSPORT: train Sydney-Kempsey daily (8½ hrs); bus Kempsey-Crescent Head weekdays; flights Sydney-Kempsey daily.
SURF CLUB PATROL: Killick Beach October-Easter, Saturday 10.00-13.00, Sunday and public holidays 10.00-16.00.

HAT HEAD (pop. 330) east of Pacific Highway 496 km from Sydney (turn off at Kempsey for South West Rocks, then at Kinchela).
TRANSPORT: train Sydney-Kempsey daily (8½ hrs); bus Kempsey-Hat Head weekdays; flights Sydney-Kempsey daily.
SURF CLUB PATROL: October-Easter, Saturday 08.00-12.00, Sunday and public holidays 10.00-16.00.

South West Rocks

South West Rocks township has expanded south and east of Horseshoe Bay—well clear of the flood-prone lower reaches of the Macleay River

Tiny Horseshoe Bay, where today's carefree holiday town of South West Rocks had its beginnings, was the scene of one of the ugliest episodes of the penal colony era. In 1816 its gleaming rocks claimed the brig *Trial*, which had been seized by convicts in Sydney Harbour. The escapers salvaged materials from the wreck to make a small boat, and left the crew and passengers to their fate. A rescue party found no survivors. But 15 years later a woman thought to be the captain's wife was recovered from Aborigines with whom she had been living. She was insane, and died soon after. Convicts came again to Trial Bay—named after the wreck—in 1880. A prison was built on Laggers Point to house men brought to work on a breakwater. That would have made the bay a major port, but Macleay River floods destroyed it in 1902, when it had

reached a length of 300 metres. The prison was closed in 1903, re-opened for German internees in 1915, and closed finally in 1918. Its granite ruins have been partly restored, and include a museum open 09.00-17.00 daily. On the beach below, as part of the Arakoon State Recreation Area, there are picnic grounds and a campsite with showers and lavatories, but no power or hot water. Other shady picnic grounds overlook the wide, sandy beach of Little Bay, south of Laggers Point, but the beach is not patrolled and the surf can be dangerous.

A caravan park occupies the western end of Front Beach—a sheltered swimming place—and a boat ramp on the opposite side of Horseshoe Bay lets small craft into the shallow waters of South West Rocks Creek. At New Entrance Reserve on the Macleay River, bait and tackle are

available. Boats can be hired near a jetty and concrete boat ramp leading into the canal which has stabilised the mouth of the river. The bar can be dangerous and should be crossed only on the last of the flood tide. A maze of mangrove swamps, islands, sand bars, creeks and changing channels make up the Macleay's delta. It is navigable at high tide as far north as Grassy Head, where the river originally entered the sea, 10 km north of its new entrance. Fishing is said to be good in the creeks and channels. Upstream, the river is navigable by shallow-draught boats to the Belgrave Falls, 5 km beyond Kempsey.

To the south-east at Smoky Cape, a lighthouse stands 140 metres above sea level, giving excellent views of the coastline and the densely forested Smoky Cape Range. The tower is open 10.00-11.45 and 13.00-14.45 on Tuesdays and

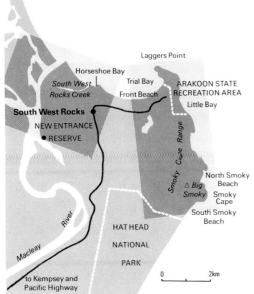

Thursdays and there is a picnic area with tables, barbecues and fresh water in the grounds. A track from the lighthouse lookout winds a few hundred metres down to North Smoky Beach, where there are rocky platforms for fishing and a waterfall dropping to the beach from the gullies of Big Smoky, towering 309 metres behind the beach. Signs on the lighthouse road mark a short walking track through jungle vines to a camping area on South Smoky Beach, in the northern section of Hat Head National Park. Permits are not required for camping but water supplies should be carried. Swamps and lagoons along the 20 km coastal strip are breeding grounds for a wide variety of waterfowl including black swans, egrets, spoonbills, herons and several species of duck. In spring and early summer the low, scrubby heathland has magnificent displays of wildflowers.

SOUTH WEST ROCKS (pop. 1314) east of Pacific Highway 497 km from Sydney (turn off at Clybucca).
TRANSPORT: train Sydney-Kempsey daily (8½ hrs); bus Kempsey-South West Rocks weekdays; flights Sydney-Kempsey daily.
SURF CLUB PATROL: Front Beach September-April, Saturday 09.30-12.30, Sunday 10.00-16.00.

🏕 🏛 🏞 ⚲ 🅿 ⊙ ✻ 🍴 ♨ |◯| ⊟ 🛶 ⇝ ≋ ⚓ 🔱 ⚓ ⚲

	SMOKY CAPE											
	Jan	Feb	Mar	Apr	May	Jun	Jul	Aug	Sep	Oct	Nov	Dec
Maximum C°	27	27	26	24	21	19	19	20	22	23	24	26
Minimum C°	19	20	18	17	14	12	11	12	13	15	17	18
Rainfall mm	151	166	192	164	115	138	82	111	56	104	93	120
Humidity %	68	70	71	64	71	69	46	58	71	75	73	73
Rain Days	14	14	16	13	10	10	8	9	9	11	10	12
Sunshine hrs	Summer 6 +			Autumn 7 +			Winter 7 +			Spring 7 +		

South of the old Trial Bay prison on Laggers Point, tracks skirt the heights of Smoky Cape Range to reach secluded beaches on each side of the cape; South Smoky Beach has national park campsites

Grassy Head and Scotts Head

Where a blind arm of the Macleay River now seeps into marshes behind Grassy Head, a pilot station used to stand. The Macleay had its main entrance channel here, open to ships for more than 60 years until 1893. Then floods created a new opening, well to the south near South West Rocks. Extensive training walls established the southern entrance as the permanent shipping channel. Grassy Head was forgotten, its river mouth silted up, until holidaymakers discovered the appeal of its ample beaches and dunes. The rocky ledges of the headland are popular with fishermen and walkers, who can climb to a summit lookout. There is a day visitors' area with picnic tables, barbecues and lavatories in the tree-shaded caravan park behind the dunes of the surf beach, north of the headland. Beside the caravan park is the Yarrahapinni Ecology Centre, a rainforest reserve belonging to a church group. A walk taking about an hour may be made with permission from the manager's office. The hill immediately behind the headland gives a clear view of the three mounds of South West Rocks. A track up passes the gravestone of a youthful pioneer who died in 1857.

At Scotts Head, rocky promontories enclose sheltered beaches between good fishing ledges. The headland also protects the little bay to the north of the township, where there is sheltered swimming a short distance from good surfing waves farther along Forster Beach. Shaded picnic grounds in the camping reserve near the headland can be used by day visitors. Behind the surf clubhouse at the southern end of Forster Beach, a short track leads through thickly matted bitou bush to Little Beach. Warrell Creek winds past the township and north along the coast to join the Nambucca River just inside its mouth. There is a launching ramp into the creek near the weir north of town, but the creek is shallow. A concrete ramp for ocean boating crosses the sand in front of the surf club.

An interesting alternative route to Scotts Head is through Way Way State Forest, leaving the Pacific Highway at Rosewood Road, just north of Warrell Creek township. Opposite the Pines picnic area along the way, a marked 20-minute walking trail loops through rainforest heavily overgrown with vines, orchids, ferns, mosses and strangler figs. More than 70 tree species have been found here, and many are labelled for visitors. A short side road south climbs to a lookout on Mount Yarrahapinni (495 metres), rewarding the traveller with views from Crescent Head to Coffs Harbour.

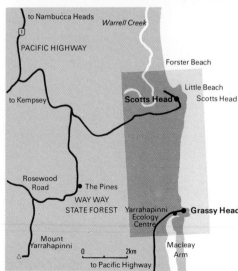

Bush has regenerated around the base of Grassy Head (right), where until 1893 the Macleay River had its outlet; on hillsides north towards Scotts Head, farmers mix dairying with banana growing

GRASSY HEAD east of Pacific Highway 508 km from Sydney (turn off 13 km north of Clybucca).
TRANSPORT: train Sydney-Eungai Rail daily (9 hrs); none beyond Eungai Rail, 13 km away.
NEAREST SERVICES: Stuarts Point.

SCOTTS HEAD (pop. 516) east of Pacific Highway 524 km from Sydney (turn off 4 km south of Macksville).
TRANSPORT: none beyond Macksville, 13 km away; train Sydney-Macksville daily (9 hrs).
SURF CLUB PATROL: October-Easter, Saturday 12.00-16.00, Sunday and public holidays 09.30-16.00.

Gardener's nightmare

BITOU BUSH, flowering a brilliant yellow on a creeping mat of cool green foliage, brightens many a sandy coastal slope where nothing else will grow. Travellers may be tempted to take some home to try as ground cover. If they do they will regret it—given a chance to consolidate, this timid-looking plant changes its character and becomes a dense, fast-spreading shrub that can take over a garden, overshading and killing anything else.

Bitou, *Chrysanthemoides monilifera*, is also known as boneseed, Higgins' curse or South African star bush. In its Cape Province homeland it co-exists innocently with other native South African vegetation. But since its introduction as an ornamental plant in Melbourne in the 1850s, it has become an aggressor, seizing territory from Australian species or preventing them from returning to bared land. Repeated uprooting is the only way to kill it.

Appealing as a creeper, bitou bush can exceed 2 metres in height and develop a trunk that takes an axe to cut

Nambucca Heads

Sawdust from millions of metres of timber has been spilt beside Nambucca Heads' inner harbour, where picnickers at Gordon Park now strew their crumbs. Late last century, life on the lower Nambucca revolved around milling on this site. The first loggers, cedar-getters in the 1840s, found the bar at the river mouth too dangerous for boats. They had to use bullocks to haul their logs overland to the Macleay River. But Sydney's hunger for timber soon justified the construction of a northern breakwater. With a reliable entrance the settlement and its mill were firmly established by the 1870s, and farming prospered

inland on ground cleared by the axemen. Today Nambucca timber is trucked to Coffs Harbour, and the river entrance is little used except by fishermen. It lies between a long sandspit to the south and the high hills of Nambucca North Head, where lookout points command panoramic views of the coast. There is a deep channel, hard against the entrance training wall, which can be used in calm conditions—but local advice should be sought before making out to sea. The channels inside the entrance are changeable and cluttered with islands and extensive shoal areas. Boats can be launched for fishing upriver from

several good ramps on the north bank. There is a sea-going ramp in front of the lifesaving clubhouse at sheltered Shelly Beach, with fish-cleaning tables nearby.

The long sweep of Forster Beach usually has excellent surf, but its rips can be dangerous and it is off the beaten track. Visitors without a boat to cross the Nambucca can reach the beach via Macksville, using a self-operated ferry across Warrell Creek. They take the Gumma road along the southern banks of the Nambucca for 4 km, then turn east down a gravel road to a camping ground with showers, lavatories and barbecues.

A flat-bottomed dinghy is chained to a cable running across the creek and ropes are used to pull the boat. A pleasant five-minute walk through bush and high, wide dunes on the eastern side of the creek brings travellers to the long, secluded beach. Just as secluded and little spoiled, north past Deep Creek, is Valla Beach. It has sheltered swimming as well as good surf.

NAMBUCCA HEADS (pop. 4053) on Pacific Highway 530 km from Sydney.
TRANSPORT: train Sydney-Nambucca Heads daily (9½ hrs).
SURF CLUB PATROL: Shelly Beach October-Easter, Saturday 10.00-14.00, Sunday and public holidays 09.00-16.00.

NAMBUCCA HEADS												
	Jan	Feb	Mar	Apr	May	Jun	Jul	Aug	Sep	Oct	Nov	Dec
Rainfall mm	153	178	193	153	111	109	74	75	64	89	91	111
Rain Days	10	11	12	10	8	7	5	6	6	8	8	10
Sunshine hrs	Summer 7+			Autumn 7+			Winter 7+			Spring 7+		

Deep Creek (right), south of Valla Beach, trickles into the surf over a little-used shore

Sprawling growth at Nambucca Heads (below) keeps rigidly to the river's northern bank; Forster Beach is deserted in spite of its promise of challenging surf

A remnant of nature's bounty

TRAVELLERS crossing the Bellinger River, between Urunga and Coffs Harbour, miss a treat if they cannot take the time to turn inland. What they will find is worth half a day of anyone's life. The valley drive, climbing to the broken edges of the New England plateau, is exhilarating in itself. The goal is a rare wilderness of rock precipices, waterfalls and superb virgin sub-tropical rainforest.

Dorrigo National Park was named not in memory of vanished Aborigines, but for a Spanish general who fought against Napoleon. He was idolised by a pioneer settler, who called the once-vast forests on the lip of the escarpment the Don Dorrigo Scrub. Timber-getters raided these forests wherever they could, for their prized cabinet woods. Otherwise they were despised as an obstacle to agriculture, to be burned and cleared as soon as possible. Now, the remaining 7900 hectares of the Dorrigo forest form a major element of the world's subtropical rainforest and the area has been nominated for the World Heritage List.

The park consists mainly of a craggy amphitheatre cut by countless gullies, each gushing year-round with streams that feed the northern arm of the Bellinger River. In falls and cascades the waters descend more than 700 metres to the coastal plain. The range of altitude enriches the staggering variety of plants and wildlife preserved here. Dominant among scores of tree species are sassafras, red cedar, coachwood, yellow carabeen and the giant stinging tree. Orchids, ferns and lichens grow luxuriantly in constant moisture, and mosses and fungi carpet the dark forest floor. Bowerbirds, lyrebirds and brush turkeys are among more than 100 species of birds seen in the park. It also supports many marsupials, including gliders and native 'cats'.

Even the unadventurous can enjoy some of Dorrigo's best sights on easy walks from the Glade picnic ground, close to the main road. The Wonga Walk and Mudginbil Trail, together forming a spectacular 7 km circuit, pass some magnificent waterfalls, fine tree specimens, and several lookouts that give remarkable views down the river valley.

Spray and mist sustain exuberant rainforest growth at Casuarina Falls

Tree ferns thrive in open areas

Frogs revel in constant moisture

Dorrigo's heights command remarkable views of the Bellinger Valley and the broad, fertile plain fringing the Tasman Sea

Walkers pass under Crystal Shower Falls

The New England Escarpment rises steeply behind Coffs Harbour

Urunga to Sawtell

Urunga and the beach resort of Mylestom are only 4 km apart by boat up the Bellinger River; motorists, however, have to make a long inland detour

Twisting waterways all but surround Urunga, preventing road access to the nearby Bellinger River. But from the caravan park on the eastern side of town, a rickety plank footbridge crosses the mangrove flats of Urunga Lagoon to a rock training wall on the south bank. From there a walk of a few hundred metres leads to the river mouth and a driftwood-littered beach running 2 km south to Hungry Head. It is not patrolled at this end, and frequented more by surf anglers than by swimmers. The town's bathing area and surf patrol are at Hungry Head, accessible by road. A popular swimming spot, south of the wall cutting the Bellinger from the lagoon, was converted into an unusual aquatic centre, the Sea Lido, at the end of 1981. A survey of tourists showed that they were not interested in yet another chlorinated freshwater pool. The salt-water playground includes a sand entrance to a horseshoe-shaped concrete walkway, springboards and an eight-lane conventional pool across the centre.

The Bellinger and Kalang Rivers, joining beside the town, carve out Newry Island to the south-west and Urunga Island to the north. Seaward boating is dangerous over the entrance

bar, but both rivers are navigable for fishing and cruising upstream in shallow-draught boats. The Bellinger can also be followed by a road branching west off the Pacific Highway 4 km north of town. The route passes through Bellingen and Thora before climbing to a high plateau in Dorrigo National Park.

Mylestom, wedged between ocean beach dunes and a wide bend of the Bellinger, is less than 4 km up North Beach from Urunga, but 18 km by road. When a stiff sea breeze is blowing, waves running past the town towards the Dorrigo hills make it look as if the river is defying gravity. Surf roars on North Beach—deep, clean and 7 km long. At the end of a track from the township's riverside picnic ground is a giant dune which locals say covers the foundations of a line of pre-1940 holiday shacks. Neglected during World War II, they were pushed into the river by the moving sand. Other houses farther south are said to have been buried by dunes, now stabilised by the roots of bitou bush. From the beach north of Mylestom, walkers find a maze of old forestry trails through the thick woods of Pine Creek State Forest.

At Sawtell, twin creeks beside high headlands

deny the town direct road access to extensive surfing beaches on each side—Boambee running north to Coffs Harbour, and Bonville and Bundagen to the south. But Sawtell has its own generous beach, backed by parks, between the headlands. Keen surfers looking for more room can reach Boambee by the rail bridge north from town, and there is sheltered swimming just inside the mouth of Bonville Creek. Both creeks are shallow and permit little boating, but there are good fishing spots on the banks. Surf casting is easy from Sawtell Beach or the rock ledges of either headland. The beach has a concrete boat ramp just north of Bonville Head, but at all but the highest tides it leads mockingly to a barrier of rocks. Local experts use it and find a narrow channel out to sea, but visitors are advised to launch from Coffs Harbour. Lookouts on each headland command attractive views of the town and beaches, and of the creeks winding back into forested hills to the west. Sawtell has extensive facilities for holidaymakers, but remains a quiet and slow-paced place. For more elaborate commercial amusements, the town's tourist association unselfishly lists those of Coffs Harbour, 14 km away by car or bus.

URUNGA (pop. 2045) on Pacific Highway 550 km from Sydney.
TRANSPORT: train Sydney-Urunga daily (9½ hrs).
SURF CLUB PATROL: Hungry Head October-March, Saturday 10.00-14.00, Sunday and public holidays 09.00-16.30.

MYLESTOM (pop. 388) east of Pacific Highway 565 km from Sydney (turn off at Repton).
TRANSPORT: train Sydney-Raleigh daily (9½ hrs); none beyond Raleigh, 7 km away.
SURF CLUB PATROL: October-Easter, weekends and public holidays 09.00-16.00.

SAWTELL (pop. 5963) east of Pacific Highway 577 km from Sydney (turn off at Boambee).
TRANSPORT: train Sydney-Sawtell daily (10 hrs).
SURF CLUB PATROL: October-Easter, Saturday 10.00-14.00, Sunday and public holidays 09.30-16.00.

URUNGA											
	Jan	Feb	Mar	Apr	May	Jun	Jul	Aug	Sep	Oct	Nov	Dec
Rainfall mm	158	185	190	166	120	119	80	70	62	86	102	129
Rain Days	11	12	12	9	8	7	6	6	6	9	8	9
Sunshine hrs	Summer 7+			Autumn 7+			Winter 7+			Spring 7+		

Sawtell and its popular surfing beach are confined between lofty headlands backed by creeks

Coffs Harbour

Coffs Harbour's nearshore islets are the breeding grounds of thousands of shearwaters—called muttonbirds by meat-starved pioneers who acquired a taste for their flesh. Each spring the birds return from winter quarters in the northern or western Pacific to nest. A favourite place is Muttonbird Island, even though the harbour walls link it to a busy town. Visitors can walk across, but must not disturb the birds: the island is a nature reserve. Chicks start hatching in late January—more than 1000 to the hectare in a good season. Most are wedge-tailed shearwaters, although other species mingle with them. By April the fledglings are ready to migrate, and another long journey begins.

Extensive breakwaters and landfills have made Coffs Harbour a reliable port since late last century. But until the 1970s it was subject to heavy swells and storm surges which menaced small craft. Now they have excellent protection from additional inner-harbour walls, and a wide concrete ramp is capable of launching several boats at a time. Fishing off nearby reefs and around the rugged Solitary Islands is noted for its variety. The port was founded on the timber industry and took its name from John Korff, an 1840s farmer who supplied food to cedar-getters. When a township was established in the 1860s, his name was mis-spelt. A later settler, Hermann Rieck, introduced commercial banana varieties from Fiji and had a plantation in production near Sapphire Gardens before 1900. Since then Coffs Harbour has become the centre for Australia's leading banana-producing region—called 'the Banana Republic' in tourist literature after a mock secession in 1979. Scenic drives pass plantations covering the hillsides north of town, and some of them give tours explaining their work.

Coffs Harbour is a busy tourist centre with a wide range of facilities and amusements including a marine park and wildlife sanctuary. As well there are the natural attractions of patrolled surf beaches and sheltered swimming in the harbour and the creek running through town. The Big Banana, 3 km north on the Pacific Highway, is a blatant advertisement for the restaurant and shops inside. In spite of its vulgarity, or perhaps because of it, it is a memorable sight.

Headlands and islands north of a spacious boat haven give Coffs Harbour a varied shoreline and beaches to suit all tastes; Park Beach is the most popular with families

The great banana cover-up

BANANA plantations in New South Wales and southern Queensland are dotted not with the gold of ripening fruit but with the gaudy colours—usually blue—of polythene plastic. Each bunch is hooded with a section of tubing to prevent skin blemishes and to ward off cold during winter and spring, so that development takes place evenly.

Bunch covers play no part in ripening. The fruit must be harvested hard and green, or it suffers in transport. Major city markets ripen bananas by exposing them to ethylene gas. By precise control of temperature they can time the process to suit retail demand, bringing out batches of bananas for sale in anything from three to eight days, and at different stages of ripeness to meet the varying tastes and purposes of shop customers.

Blue-bagged bananas near Coffs Harbour

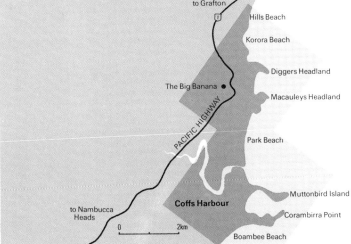

to Grafton

Hills Beach

Korora Beach

Diggers Headland

The Big Banana ●

Macauleys Headland

PACIFIC HIGHWAY

Park Beach

to Nambucca
Heads

Coffs Harbour

Muttonbird Island

Corambirra Point

0   2km

Boambee Beach

COFFS HARBOUR (pop. 16 018) on Pacific Highway
578 km from Sydney, 427 km from Brisbane.
TRANSPORT: train Sydney-Coffs Harbour daily (10 hrs);
coach Brisbane-Coffs Harbour daily (7 hrs); flights from
Sydney and Brisbane daily.
SURF CLUB PATROL: Park Beach October-Easter, Saturday 10.00-14.00, Sunday and public holidays 09.00-
16.00; mobile patrols at other beaches.

	COFFS HARBOUR											
	Jan	Feb	Mar	Apr	May	Jun	Jul	Aug	Sep	Oct	Nov	Dec
Maximum C°	27	27	26	24	21	19	19	20	22	23	25	26
Minimum C°	19	19	18	15	11	9	7	8	11	14	16	18
Rainfall mm	215	251	250	191	134	126	65	105	68	105	100	149
Humidity %	69	69	73	62	64	62	58	57	61	72	70	77
Rain Days	20	18	15	10	10	11	8	7	8	14	13	13
Sunshine hrs	Summer 7 +			Autumn 7 +			Winter 7 +			Spring 7 +		

Sapphire Gardens to Emerald Beach

Hillsides covered with banana trees rise to the west of the highway running north from Coffs Harbour. The coast is lined with wide, sandy surf beaches, and camping grounds and picnic sites cluster around small, quiet holiday towns. South of Sapphire Gardens, the route passes a corner of Bruxner Park Flora Reserve, which has a short nature trail and a 2 km walking track winding through subtropical rainforest. Wild orchids and ferns trail down from the branches of the tall trees, their crowns joined in a tangle of vines.

Banana cropping tracks follow hillside contours in the rich plantation area behind Sapphire Gardens

Early settlers cleared forest like this by half-cutting the trees of a large area, then felling a key tree. The clinging creepers overhead would bring down the whole section in a domino effect. Scenic drives in Orara East State Forest, which surrounds Bruxner Park, lead to lookouts at Mt Coramba and Sealy Park, with sweeping views over a patchwork of forest and banana plantations. An unsealed road branches east off the Pacific Highway 2 km north of Mid Sapphire Beach to a parking area behind the sand dunes. A walking track leads north to Green Bluff, a grassy headland at the entrance to Moonee Creek. There are good beach and rock fishing

around the headland, excellent surfing waves to the south, and sheltered areas to the north and in the shallows of the creek. A caravan park close to the creek mouth has casual picnic facilities and a long jetty into the creek for fishing. At low tide visitors can walk across the creek bed to the long stretch of Moonee Beach and the nature reserve which lies behind it. Kumbaingeri Land, a privately owned wildlife sanctuary open daily 3 km north of Moonee Beach, has more than 500 animals and birds. Walking tracks and horse-riding trails criss-cross the heavily wooded banks of Moonee Creek.

At Emerald Beach, twin headlands command

sweeping views and provide shelter for little Shelly Beach, tucked between them. The surf past the southern headland, Look at Me Now, is popular with board-riders. On the northern side, behind Dammerals Head, a narrow concrete boat ramp crosses the end of Emerald Beach. It finishes short of the water except at high tide. Behind it a thick mat of buffalo grass covers a picnic ground which has barbecues and tables. Farther north, the rocky promontory of Diggers Point makes a good base for anglers.

Moonee Creek winds through a nature reserve separating the townships of Moonee Beach and Emerald Beach. Rips are frequent along the deserted beach between

SAPPHIRE GARDENS-MID SAPPHIRE BEACH on Pacific Highway 586 km from Sydney, 419 km from Brisbane.

TRANSPORT: see Coffs Harbour, previous page; bus Coffs Harbour-Sapphire Gardens-Moonee Beach-Emerald Beach-Woolgoolga daily.

MOONEE BEACH east of Pacific Highway 5 km north of Mid Sapphire Beach.

TRANSPORT: as for Sapphire Gardens.

EMERALD BEACH east of Pacific Highway 10 km north of Mid Sapphire Beach.

TRANSPORT: as for Sapphire Gardens.

Woolgoolga to Red Rock

Woolgoolga's imposing headland, which once provided shelter for boats loading hardwoods from the surrounding forests, now protects a ramp used by amateur fishermen, and a safe swimming beach. The headland also has impressive views along the coast and out to the rugged Solitary Islands. Board-riders chase the rolling waves which break off the headland point and fishermen cast into the turbulent surf from its rocky ledges. Bare Bluff, Mullaway, Ocean View and Arrawarra, the smaller headlands around Woolgoolga, provide similar shelter for the beaches and picnic areas of small settlements which have grown around them, all attracting

Woolgoolga sprawls from the Pacific Highway to the high headland that shelters a fine surfing beach and gives anglers a generous spread of rock ledges

their following of anglers. Offshore fishing concentrates on the reefs along Woolgoolga Beach and among the Solitary Islands. Lake and creek fishing is found in several small waterways which open to the sea intermittently. Hearns Lake, south of Woolgoolga, opens briefly once or twice a year, flooding with revitalising water which brings fish—mainly flathead—and prawns. The lake is shallow and provides safe canoeing and swimming for children. From the caravan park on the lake shore a short walking track leads to the gentle surf of the ocean beach and a spit of sand exposed at low tide connects the beach with Flat Top Rock. Its grassy plateau is reached by an easy climb, and the low ledges of the landward side are pitted with rock pools.

On the hill overlooking Woolgoolga stands the Guru Nanak Sikh Temple, unmistakably white

and onion-domed. Visitors are welcome to see the ornate decorations inside at weekends, or daily during school holidays—but they are asked to remove their shoes and cover their heads.

An alternative route between Woolgoolga and Coffs Harbour is along the winding and hilly roads of the Wedding Bells State Forest drive. The route passes through stands of various timber and along Gentle Annie Road, following the track used last century by bullock teams pulling carts over the Coast Range between Woolgoolga and Bucca Creek.

North of Mullaway Head, breakers wash past a jagged brown rock platform to a flat, straight beach. Behind it, banksias are bent to the west by the constant sea breeze. Ocean View Headland looks south over Mullaway Beach and north to the narrow peninsula of Arrawarra. Beyond is

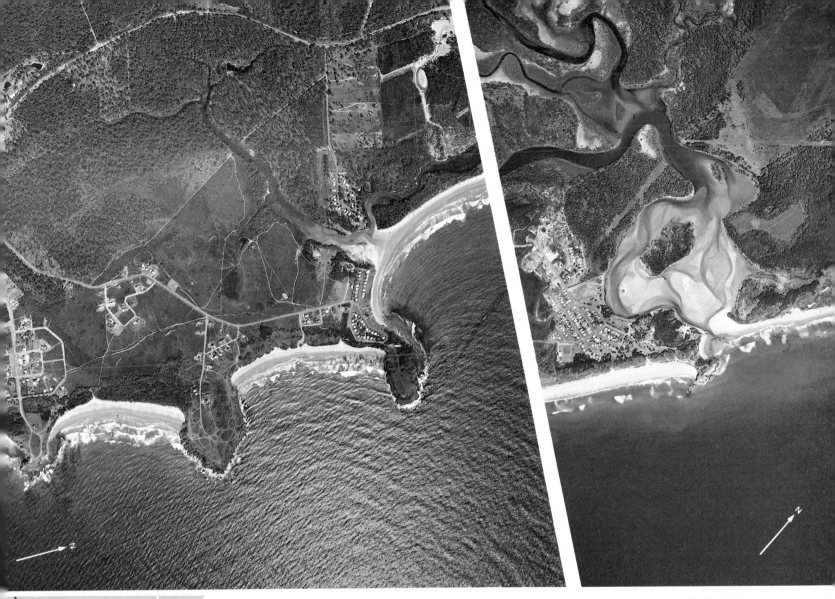

Headlands from Mullaway (left) to Arrawarra embrace attractive but little-used beaches; Red Rock (right) faces across the sluggish Corindi River to the wilderness of Yuraygir National Park

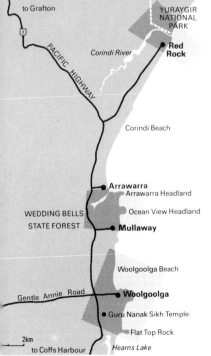

the 8 km stretch of Corindi Beach, backed at the Arrawarra end by a thickly grassed plateau. At Red Rock, the last settlement before the southern section of Yuraygir National Park takes over the coast, a short walk to the headland through the shaded caravan park and picnic grounds reveals a striking outcrop of shining red jasper washed by the waves at the entrance to the Corindi River. At low tide the sprawling estuary can be crossed on foot. Sheltered swimming is found in the estuary shallows and near a picnic area at the river mouth. The long ocean beach is subject to rips.

WOOLGOOLGA (pop. 2079) on Pacific Highway 600 km from Sydney, 405 km from Brisbane.
TRANSPORT: train Sydney-Coffs Harbour daily (10 hrs); coach Brisbane-Coffs Harbour daily (7 hrs); flights Sydney-Coffs Harbour, Brisbane-Coffs Harbour daily; bus Coffs Harbour-Woolgoolga daily.
SURF CLUB PATROL: October-Easter, Saturday 13.00-16.30, Sunday and public holidays 09.00-16.30.

MULLAWAY east of Pacific Highway 5 km north of Woolgoolga.
TRANSPORT: none beyond Woolgoolga.

ARRAWARRA east of Pacific Highway 8 km north of Woolgoolga.
TRANSPORT: none beyond Woolgoolga.

RED ROCK north of Pacific Highway 16 km north of Woolgoolga.
TRANSPORT: none beyond Woolgoolga.

	WOOLGOOLGA											
	Jan	Feb	Mar	Apr	May	Jun	Jul	Aug	Sep	Oct	Nov	Dec
Maximum C°	27	27	26	25	22	20	19	20	23	24	26	26
Minimum C°	18	19	18	16	13	11	9	10	12	14	15	17
Rainfall mm	217	212	246	235	125	149	74	118	56	91	100	145
Humidity %	75	73	71	65	60	68	61	69	62	71	62	80
Rain Days	11	11	15	12	8	9	5	8	6	10	10	12
Sunshine hrs	Summer 7 +			Autumn 7 +			Winter 7 +			Spring 7 +		

Station Creek, where a campsite is hemmed by bush and dunes, has its outlet between a broad surfing beach and a sheltered bay

Wooli and Yuraygir National Park

A careful course must be steered to find the Station Creek camping ground in the southern section of Yuraygir National Park. The approach from the Pacific Highway is intersected by a maze of forestry tracks and not all are marked. The best turn-off is 16 km north of Woolgoolga, along the Barcoongere Forest Way until park signposts are reached. The camping ground near marshy Station Creek is surrounded by dense forest and sand dunes, but is only a short walk from the sheltered bay of Pebbly Beach and long stretches of surf beach. The park is rich in wildlife and at dusk kangaroos come to graze in a grass clearing near the creek while the trees fill with

screeching lorikeets. Freshwater, 2 km north, is another popular spot to pitch a tent. Tannin from tea-trees discolours the creek water, but it is drinkable. Walking trails lead through the park and along the beaches to the Corindi River and to the Wooli Wooli River in the north. There hikers must swim across if they have not arranged for a boat to pick them up.

Below high sand cliffs on the southernmost banks of the Wooli Wooli, a narrow, flat strip of land reaches north to the township of Wooli. From here a small fleet of fishing boats works the waters around North Solitary Island, 12 km offshore. There are boat ramps near the Fisher-

men's Co-operative, and at a kiosk around the bend from the river mouth visitors can hire rowing boats and canoes for fishing or cruising to sandy banks among the mangrove patches and oyster leases.

Yuraygir National Park, named for the Aborigine tribe who occupied this coast, is an incorporation of the former Red Rock and Angourie parks, together with additional lands dedicated in 1980. Its initial area, in three sections, is 13 000 hectares covering 40 km of coastline. A further 14 000 hectares, linking the three sections, are designated for future acquisition.

The central section of the park is approached

Brooms Head, butting against the ocean swell with a wide shield of rocks, is favoured by surf fishermen

from the Pacific Highway by Wooli Road, with turn-offs leading to beach settlements at Diggers Camp and Minnie Water. Northern section access is from Maclean, south-east along Brooms Head Road.

The isolated little community at Brooms Head has provided generously for its stream of holiday visitors. Some of the township's best land, grassed and shaded, has been given up for a camping reserve which lies directly behind the beach and stretches almost the length of the settlement, from the bridge over Cakora Lagoon to a caravan park on the headland hill. Steep, jagged rocks running out from the headland create a small, sandy-bottomed lagoon which fills at high tide and is popular with children. Calm water extends along the beach below the camping reserve, but rolling surf forms beyond the headland's shelter.

Wooli occupies a narrow spit with access to both a long ocean beach and to quiet river waters that are popular for cruising and fishing

WOOLI (pop. 453) east of Pacific Highway 683 km from Sydney, 394 km from Brisbane (turn off 12 km south of Grafton).
TRANSPORT: train Sydney-Grafton (11½ hrs) and Brisbane-Grafton (4½ hrs) daily; coach Brisbane-Grafton daily (6 hrs); Grafton-Wooli bus weekly in school holidays.

BROOMS HEAD east of Pacific Highway 722 km from Sydney, 327 km from Brisbane (turn off at Maclean).
TRANSPORT: Grafton services as for Wooli; bus Grafton-Maclean most days; none beyond Maclean, 22 km away.

Yamba and Angourie

An island-hopping road from Maclean gives a taste of the extensive system of waterways waiting to be explored around the fishing town and popular holiday resort of Yamba. Its maze of creeks and channels in the Clarence River delta is confusing at first, but signposting is good. And Yamba makes no secret of its best fishing spots: billboard maps show where to catch various species from the ocean beaches, in the Clarence or in Wooloweyah Lagoon. A sheltered backwater just inside the Clarence entrance is the base for a commercial fishing fleet and provides moorings for visiting craft. There is a public wharf, and a concrete boat ramp leads into deep water with parking space nearby. Dredging, begun in 1982, has improved the boat harbour.

Three town beaches shelter north of Yamba Point—known locally as Lovers' Point. Pippi Beach to the south is flat and open, and subject to rips. Yamba Beach has a rock pool, and other calm water for children can be found off the sandy northern shore of Hickey Island, just inside the river mouth. Keen board-riders make for the narrow, rock-enclosed bay just north of Angourie Point. Its waves are rated among the best on the east coast. Behind a massive rock wall, within a stone's throw of the surf, are two deep freshwater rock pools. Blue Pool, the bigger of the two, has a 5-metre wall on one side which makes a natural diving tower. The pool, about 20 metres deep, was a quarry for the breakwaters at the river mouth. Tree-lined banks, here and to the south at Green Pool, make pleasant picnic spots.

From Angourie village a 12 km walking trail strikes out along the bays and rocky bluffs of the northern section of Yuraygir National Park, to camping grounds at Red Cliff and Lake Arragan. The trail skirts the crescent bay of Shelley Beach, with its unserviced bush camping site and big rock platform for fishermen. At low tide, walkers can reach three caves gouged out of cliffs on the southern point of Shelley Beach Headland.

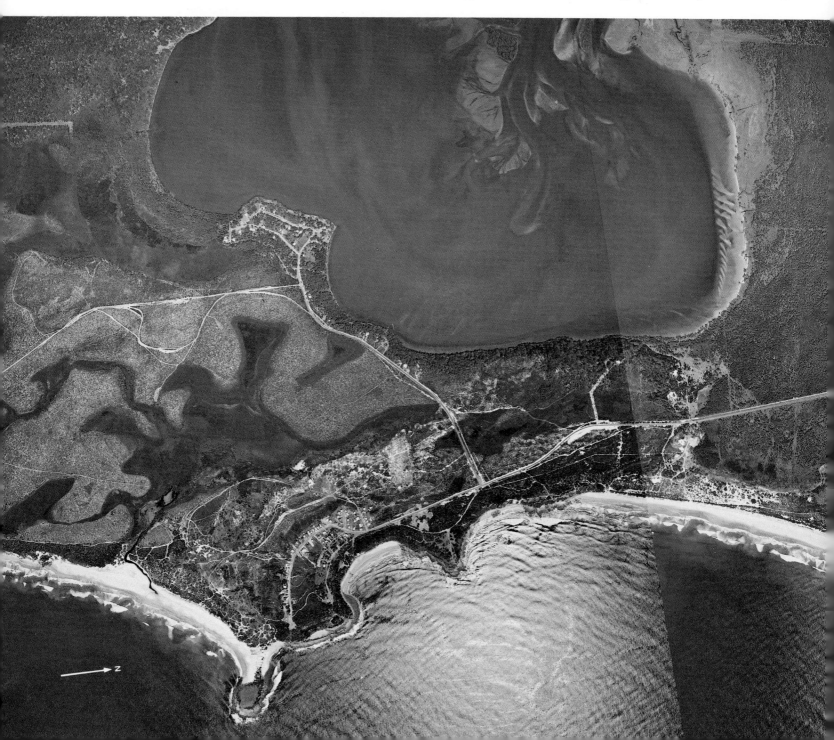

YAMBA (pop. 2528) east of Pacific Highway 597 km from Sydney, 312 km from Brisbane (turn off at Clarence River).

TRANSPORT: train Sydney-Grafton (11½ hrs) and Brisbane-Grafton (4½ hrs) daily; coach Brisbane-Grafton daily (6 hrs); flights Sydney or Brisbane to Grafton daily; bus Grafton-Yamba most days.

SURF CLUB PATROL: October-Easter, Saturday 10.00-14.00, Sunday and public holidays 09.00-17.00.

🔋 🏨 ⛽ ⛺ ▲ ⓘ ☺ ✦ ⛴ ☕ 🍽 🚌 ⛵ 🏄 ⚓ ≈ ⚓ 🎣 ⚓ ⚓ ✗

YAMBA												
	Jan	Feb	Mar	Apr	May	Jun	Jul	Aug	Sep	Oct	Nov	Dec
Maximum C°	26	26	26	24	22	20	19	20	21	23	24	25
Minimum C°	20	20	19	17	13	11	9	10	12	15	17	19
Rainfall mm	146	155	179	155	149	128	110	83	63	78	85	116
Humidity %	75	75	75	71	65	64	59	60	64	71	72	76
Rain Days	12	13	15	13	12	10	9	8	9	9	9	10
Sunshine hrs	Summer 6 +			Autumn 7 +			Winter 7 +			Spring 7 +		

Long training walls and breakwaters stabilise the deep mouth of the Clarence River, between Yamba and Iluka; small boats are moored close to town in the backwater that is formed by Hickey Island

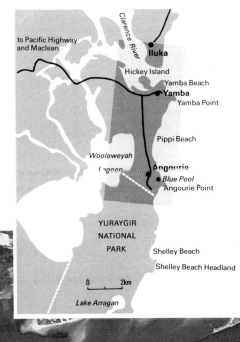

Iluka and Clarence River

Iluka is not as well known to travellers as Yamba, its sister town across the heads of the Clarence River. It offers a more tranquil alternative, especially for boating and fishing enthusiasts. While Yamba crowds the slopes overlooking its part of the coast, Iluka is buffered from the sea by a wide belt of dunes and forest. Its surf and breakwater beaches seem remote from the busy fishing harbour, just 1 km away in the Clarence estuary. The river delta is a jumble of islands sep-

Iluka's fishing harbour lies inside a Clarence River training wall; freighters continue far upstream

arated by navigable channels and creeks for motor-cruising and fishing, and broad expanses for sailing and water-skiing. Oyster leases are a widespread hazard, but sailors are compensated by an invitation to eat as many as they like from public beds when the oysters reach maturity between November and January. The only restriction is that they must be eaten on the spot.

Upstream the Clarence winds more than 70 km to Grafton, past Maclean and many small riverside settlements. Inland, sugar-cane plant-ations give way to open banks flanked by dairy pastures. At Grafton a double-deck road and rail

bridge limits mast height to less than 8 metres, but small power boats can carry on 48 km farther to Copmanhurst. Freighters used to ply regularly to Grafton, and bulk sugar carriers of up to 3000 tonnes still load at Goodwood Island, upstream from Iluka. The island, screened from the Iluka road by forest, is densely planted with cane. A wharf at the western end is lined throughout the year by anglers. Roads criss-crossing the canefields of many of the delta islands lead to secluded sandy riverbanks, and often to old jet-ties where barges once took on cargoes of cane. Most of the jetties have fallen into disrepair and

can be dangerous, but they remain popular spots to dangle a line or tie a boat up for a picnic.

Opposite the golf course just north of Iluka, a gravel road leads into a rainforest reserve. Near the junction there is a short nature trail. The road continues to the dunes behind Iluka Bluff, thickly knotted with bitou bush, and a wide rock platform giving easy access for anglers.

ILUKA (pop. 1359) east of Pacific Highway 734 km from Sydney, 305 km from Brisbane (turn off at Mororo).
TRANSPORT: Grafton services as for Yamba (previous page); coach Grafton-Maclean most days; none beyond Maclean, 34 km away

Evans Head and Bundjalung

Evans Head, a prosperous prawning port and popular holiday town flanked by national parks, still has noisy reminders of its World War II role as an air force training base. RAAF jets make regular runs from Amberley, near Brisbane, for target practice on the bombing range extending 8 km south-west. Townsfolk are accustomed to the distant thunder of explosions and the eerie sight of firetrails flaring in the sky during night exercises. But the local air base, north of town, has been abandoned. Its barracks and all but one of its hangars were removed, leaving desolate streets and hectares of tarmac now used only by amateur pilots and a small air charter company.

Emphasis is on the Evans River estuary and its boat harbour, crowded with brightly coloured prawn trawlers. East of the road bridge a wide concrete ramp leads into a deep channel to the river's breakwater entrance. On the banks below the town centre and a tree-studded camping reserve, a wooden jetty reaches over the shallows into the river. Boats and canoes can be hired close by, and charter parties can be arranged for

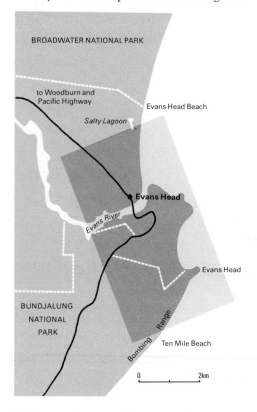

offshore fishing. Evans Head Beach is a popular surfing spot with grassed picnic grounds surrounding the lifesaving clubhouse. Sheltered, shallow bathing areas are found in the river inside the northern breakwater wall, adjoining the ocean beach, and along the caravan park's river frontage. Board-riders have a secluded alternative beach south of Evans Head.

Ten Mile Beach, farther south, is flanked by the coastal reserve of Bundjalung National Park. There is a well-developed camping ground at Black Rocks, where dark outcrops of rock jut from the beach and form cliffs in the dunes. Lavatories, barbecues and firewood are provided, but campers must take their own water. Nearby Jerusalem Creek is suitable for swimming, fishing, and boating along a wide stretch of shallow, reed-lined water which flows parallel with the coast for more than 4 km. Access to both spots is by Gap Road, from 5 km south of Woodburn.

The Evans River section of Bundjalung National Park was formerly an Aboriginal reserve for the Bundjalung people of the district. A great kurrajong tree on the riverbank, just

below an ancient campsite, intrigues botanists. Kurrajongs usually grow on high inland slopes, not estuarine flats. The seed of the Evans River specimen was probably carried from west of the Great Dividing Range accidentally, among intertribal trading goods.

North from Evans Head, the heathland scrub and swamps of Broadwater National Park line both sides of the road. Spring wildflowers transform the heath into a mosaic of colour, while a keen and patient observer will find the park rich in wildlife. A 1 km walking trail branches off the road 3 km north of town to the wetlands of Salty Lagoon. There are picnic facilities at a lookout nearby, but no drinking water. Surfing and fishing are good off a 7 km stretch of ocean beach, backed by outcrops of dark rock. At Broadwater, on the Richmond River, visitors can tour the sugar mill in daylight hours throughout the cane-crushing season, normally June to December. A koala reserve has been developed at Rileys Hill, about 3 km south of the township. Nearby is a dry dock where trawlers too big for the Ballina slipway can be painted or repaired.

Bomb craters (bottom right) speckle scrubland behind Ten Mile Beach, south of Evans Head; part of Bundjalung National Park is an air force range

EVANS HEAD (pop. 1802) east of Pacific Highway 764 km from Sydney, 261 km from Brisbane (turn off at Woodburn).
TRANSPORT: see Ballina, next page, for main services; bus Ballina-Evans Head weekdays.
SURF CLUB PATROL: October-Easter, Saturday 10.00-14.00, Sunday and public holidays 09.00-16.30.

Ballina and Richmond River

Two of Ballina's most popular swimming spots, Lighthouse Beach and Shaws Bay, are the product of human handiwork. Before breakwater walls were built in the 1880s to stabilise the Richmond River, the entrance sprawled over wide sand bars and a narrow shipping channel lay against Ballina Head. The completed breakwater trapped sand south of the headland, creating a new ocean beach and enclosing a deep tidal lagoon. Fed by water seeping through a rock training wall, the lagoon provides sheltered and shark-free swimming with a shallow area for non-swimmers and children.

Clean, sandy beaches are found just west of Shaws Bay, by Missingham Bridge, and Shelly Beach has a rock pool. Lighthouse Beach is Ballina's patrolled surfing area, but waves for board-riding can also be found to the north, off the sealed road to Lennox Head. The long, isolated surf beach south of the river entrance can be reached through South Ballina, by a vehicular ferry crossing the Richmond River to Brynes Point on the southern banks.

Launching ramps, a modern trawler harbour and a boat harbour for pleasure craft are sited along the north bank of the Richmond River, close to the centre of town, together with boat-building yards where most of the Ballina trawlers are constructed. Public oyster beds are located at several spots on the Ballina waterfront and farther up the Richmond. Oysters may be opened and eaten on the site, but not taken away.

Fish are abundant throughout the year, off shore and in the river and its tributary creeks. Land-based anglers use the surf beaches and breakwaters as well as the river jetties.

BALLINA (pop. 9735) on Pacific Highway 789 km from Sydney, 216 km from Brisbane.
TRANSPORT: train Sydney-Lismore (14½ hrs) and Brisbane-Lismore (2 hrs) daily; bus Lismore-Ballina daily; coach Sydney-Ballina daily (12 hrs); coach Brisbane-Ballina daily (3½ hrs); flights Sydney and Brisbane to Lismore daily.
SURF CLUB PATROL: Lighthouse Beach October-April, Saturday 10.00-14.00, Sunday and public holidays 09.00-17.00.

BALLINA												
	Jan	Feb	Mar	Apr	May	Jun	Jul	Aug	Sep	Oct	Nov	Dec
Rainfall mm	189	203	214	177	195	162	136	105	73	94	103	136
Rain Days	12	13	15	12	12	10	8	8	8	9	9	10
Sunshine hrs	Summer 6 +			Autumn 7 +			Winter 7 +			Spring 8 +		

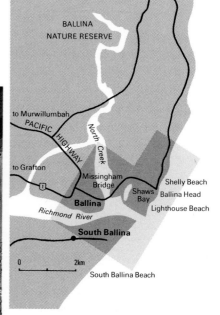

North Creek, spanned by Missingham Bridge, separates the riverside town of Ballina from the resort of Shaws Bay

The southern end of Seven Mile Beach has been scoured to a meagre strip opposite Lennox Head township

Map labels: to Byron Bay · PACIFIC HIGHWAY · 1 · Seven Mile Beach · Lake Ainsworth · **Lennox Head** · BALLINA NATURE RESERVE · Boulder Beach · Shag Rock · to Ballina · North Creek · 0 · 2km

Lennox Head

Lennox Head, at the southern end of Seven Mile Beach, is well acquainted with the power of the sea in its constant assault on the coastline. Cyclonic winds have taken a heavy toll, whipping up seas which have severely eroded the beach, washed away seaside roads, destroyed tennis courts and threatened houses. The lifesaving clubhouse is built on a concrete sled so that it can be towed out of reach of storm surges. A protective fence designed to trap wind-blown sand is buried below a new line of dunes. Such problems are merely part of a short-term cycle of beach fluctuations, in which sand washed offshore during storms is slowly returned during calm periods. But a long-term, more damaging shoreline recession has been taking place for the past 6000 years from Lennox Head to the Queensland Gold Coast. The rate of recession varies greatly—it is negligible in some places, and nearly 2 metres a year in others.

Reefs of smooth black rock have been un-covered by the loss of beach sand near the town. Anglers can wade out over them to cast lines in knee-deep water 60 metres from the shore. South of Lennox Head, near Shag Rock, is a fishing spot known locally as the Spike. Fisherman rope themselves to a metal pole driven into the rocks, as a safeguard against surprise waves that used to sweep men to their deaths. Both fishing spots are also popular with board-riders. The inshore reefs produce excellent windsurfing waves, and those rolling around Lennox Head on to the reef are reckoned by surfers to be among the biggest in warm water around Australia. However the take-off point under the cliff face has acquired a bad reputation for sharks: a leading professional surfer, Mark Richards, reportedly will not enter these waters. At the Spike, surfers push off from a sand bar exposed at low tide to chase the waves breaking into Boulder Beach, a rock-strewn bay to the south which can be reached only by a track down the steep cliff face.

Sheltered swimming is found in gaps in the inshore reef close to the town beach and in Lake Ainsworth, a freshwater lagoon behind the dunes north of town. The lake is ringed by grassy areas, picnic grounds, a caravan park and a youth camp. It is heavily used in summer and can become polluted by the end of the season.

LENNOX HEAD (pop. 843) east of Pacific Highway 800 km from Sydney, 211 km from Brisbane (turn off at Ballina northbound, 13 km south of Bangalow southbound).
TRANSPORT: main services as for Ballina, bus Ballina-Lennox Head daily.
SURF CLUB PATROL: October-Easter, Saturday 10.30-15.00, Sunday and public holidays 09.00-17.00.

Byron Bay and Suffolk Park

Cape Byron's steep cliffs are the first on the Australian coast to catch the rays of the rising sun. This is the easternmost point of the continent, where the coastline 'turns the corner' and the influence of prevailing winds and ocean currents changes from temperate to subtropical. Marine life abounds, thriving on the nourishment that is found in a boundary region. And the cape, jutting out where massive ocean movements clash, offers a constant challenge to surfers. Board-riders go to Byron Bay in the near-certainty of good waves, regardless of wind direction, because the

headland has beaches facing east, north and even west. Wategos and the Pass, at Palm Valley, are renowned for their long-running breakers—sometimes more than 250 metres—when a southeasterly swell bends round the cape. Suffolk Park and the beaches farther south at Broken Head are less remarkable but have consistent surf. Suffolk Park also attracts visitors with its Everglades Aquatic Gardens, a 20-hectare park full of bird life and with canals containing 80 varieties of water lilies. The garden buildings are modelled on oriental pagodas and depict the Willow Pat-

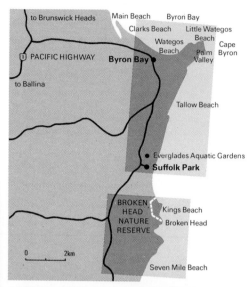

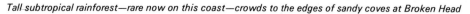
Tall subtropical rainforest—rare now on this coast—crowds to the edges of sandy coves at Broken Head

tern legend of forbidden love between a mandarin's daughter and a poor man, both of them executed but reincarnated as doves.

Clarks Beach shelters west of the headland, and Main Beach, the patrolled swimming area, skirts the town's northern shore. Just behind, near the surf clubhouse, is an Olympic-size freshwater pool. Little Reef, 1 km north-east, and Julian Rocks, 3 km north of the cape, are popular fishing and diving grounds. Cape Byron lighthouse perches on the cliffs 113 metres above sea level, commanding extraordinary views. The grounds are open every day. Visitors may go up the tower on Tuesdays and Thursdays, 10.00-11.30 or 13.00-14.30, in limited numbers. To be sure of getting in, applications should be made in advance to the surface operations division of the Department of Transport in Sydney. A walking trail from the lighthouse leads along the cliff edge and down a steep track to Little Wategos

Beach. Hang-gliders are often seen swooping around the cliffs: the cape is a contest venue.

Early settlers knew the country between Byron Bay and Lismore as 'the Big Scrub'. It was Australia's largest area of tall subtropical rainforest, covering 75 000 hectares. Now its remnants total no more than 300 hectares. One of them is the Broken Head nature reserve, of 40 hectares. A gravel road branching off 400 metres before the headland camping site leads along a ridge above the reserve to the northern section of Seven Mile Beach. From a car park along the ridge road, a walking track curls down a steep gully and emerges at the sandy cove of Kings Beach, which can also be reached by a track around the northern point of the headland. At low tide it is possible to continue south along the rocky shore past other sandy coves to Seven Mile Beach, with spots for rock fishing below a thick curtain of rainforest.

BYRON BAY (pop. 3183) east of Pacific Highway 828 km from Sydney, 188 km from Brisbane (turn off at Bangalow northbound, 13 km south of Brunswick Heads southbound).
TRANSPORT: train Sydney-Byron Bay daily (15½ hrs); bus Brisbane-Byron Bay weekdays (3½ hrs).
SURF CLUB PATROL: October-Easter, Saturday 09.00-15.00, Sunday and public holidays 09.00-16.30.
YOUTH HOSTEL: open year-round.

SUFFOLK PARK (pop. 239) 2 km south of Byron Bay.
TRANSPORT: bus Byron Bay-Suffolk Park weekdays.

CAPE BYRON												
	Jan	Feb	Mar	Apr	May	Jun	Jul	Aug	Sep	Oct	Nov	Dec
Rainfall mm	184	212	196	148	161	150	96	107	65	108	101	139
Humidity %	73	74	72	70	65	66	61	61	63	69	72	74
Rain Days	18	21	17	14	16	16	11	10	11	12	13	11
Sunshine hrs	Summer 6 +			Autumn 7 +			Winter 7 +			Spring 8 +		

Renowned surfing beaches sweep towards Cape Byron, mainland Australia's most easterly point

Brunswick Heads

Construction of breakwaters and a fishing fleet harbour in the late 1950s has breathed new life into a town which had stagnated since the turn of the century. When Byron Bay was chosen as the north coast railhead in 1894, trade was drawn away from Brunswick Heads. Its courthouse, hotel, school and store were dismantled and carted off to Mullumbimby. Sixty years later, however, Brunswick Heads came back into favour when gales ripped through the Byron Bay fishing fleet, destroying 26 boats and severely

damaging the jetty. It was decided to stabilise the Brunswick River entrance and build a more sheltered harbour upstream. Today the Brunswick Heads boat harbour is the base for a fleet of colourful prawning trawlers. The fishermen's co-operative sells prawns and fish direct to the public, along with oysters from commercial leases in the river. A boat ramp near the harbour leads into a deep channel to the entrance through a complex system of training walls. The river entrance is narrow and the bar can be

tricky, so visiting boatmen should seek local advice. The two creeks feeding into the Brunswick River near its mouth wind away into shallow, mangrove-lined swampy areas, but the river is navigable at high water to Mullumbimby and is suited for cruising, canoeing and fishing.

The breakwater construction that revived Brunswick Heads had an unexpected price—the sacrifice of the small seaside settlement of Sheltering Palms. Sand which would normally have been deposited along the shore north of the en-

trance was held back by the breakwaters. By 1977 the beach at Sheltering Palms was so depleted that the settlement, in danger of being engulfed by the sea, was abandoned. Meanwhile South Beach, on the other side of the breakwaters, has accumulated a broad sweep of sand where residents and holidaymakers enjoy ample space for sunbathing and patrolled surfing. Other beaches created by training walls in the creeks and estuary provide good swimming for young children, with picnic grounds nearby. North at New Brighton, the shore erosion problem is strikingly indicated by a row of beachfront telephone poles—originally on the landward side of a road behind the beach. Residents have attempted to conserve their surf beach by building protective works including fences and a groyne. West of Marshalls Creek, which winds between New Brighton and Brunswick Heads, is the extensive new real estate development of Ocean Shores—an imaginative name, since none of it reaches to the seaward side of the creek. Hectares of swampland were drained and consolidated for its recreational areas, which include a country club with an 18-hole golf course, a bowling green, a swimming pool and a restaurant. Club facilities are open to travellers. A boating marina is proposed.

A yellow double-decker bus on the riverfront at Brunswick Heads serves as an information centre, dispensing maps, brochures and advice on the town and surrounding areas. Among the trips recommended is the Nightcap forest drive through Whian Whian State Forest. The route passes the Minyon Falls, tumbling 120 metres into a gorge of palm trees, and the Nightcap walking track, the pioneers' link between Murwillumbah and Lismore. Many other walking trails pierce the fern-matted rainforest. The scenic drive ends at a picnic area beside the Rocky Creek Dam.

BRUNSWICK HEADS (pop. 1877) on Pacific Highway 836 km from Sydney, 169 km from Brisbane.
TRANSPORT: train Sydney-Mullumbimby daily (16 hrs); bus Mullumbimby-Brunswick Heads weekdays; coach Brisbane-Brunswick Heads daily (3 hrs).
SURF CLUB PATROL: October-Easter, Saturday 10.00-14.00, Sunday and public holidays 09.00-16.30.

🎒 🏠 📷 ⛺ ♨ ☺ ✈ ⛽ ⚑ 🍴 🍽 ⚓ 🐟 🎿 🏊 🔱 ⚓

NEW BRIGHTON 5 km north of Brunswick Heads.
TRANSPORT: none beyond Brunswick Heads.

🎒 🏠 🍽 🐟 🏊 ♨ ⚓

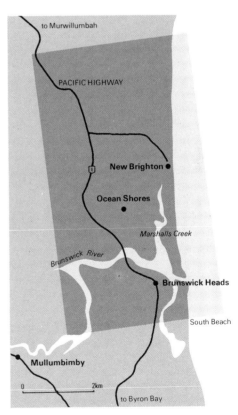

Brunswick Heads, tightly confined on the south bank of the Brunswick River, has been outgrown by the Ocean Shores development; canals farther north were dug for another scheme, since deferred

Tweed Coast

Travellers leaving the Pacific Highway at Mooball or Chinderah find a short-cut skirting 20 km of beaches separated by rocky headlands and narrow creek entrances. Surfing, swimming, fishing and peaceful, low-key development can be enjoyed at a string of small holiday towns, each with its camping ground and basic services. At Pottsville, a wide sand bar in the mouth of Mooball Creek limits access to the sea at low tide. At high tide, only very small boats can squeeze under the road bridge. From the road running south along the narrow spit between the creek and the dunes, tracks give access to a long surf beach. At Hastings Point, Cudgera Creek curls around a dune peninsula and dribbles to the ocean across a pebbly beach overlooked by sheltered wooden tables and stone barbecues in a headland park. A knot of rocks popular for fishing and skindiving lies 300 metres offshore.

The Cabarita Beach Park development, at Bogangar, is backed by Cudgen Lake, where a resort hotel caters for water sports. Catamarans and canoes can be hired and there is a public boat ramp on the lake's southern shores. The lake feeds into Cudgen Creek, which flows 10 km north to Kingscliff. Between Cudgen Headland and picnic grounds sloping towards the beach below Kingscliff, a concrete boat ramp dips into the creek, which is almost dry at low tide. A long, grassy park dotted with pines and stunted pandanus trees runs behind the dunes to North Kingscliff. The beach continues unbroken to Fingal Point past Womin Lagoon, which is suitable for canoeing, fishing and prawning.

Shallow, muddy bays cluttered with mangrove islands branch off the Tweed River north and south of Banora Point. Boat ramps below the caravan parks grouped around Barneys Point bridge lead to the wide waters of the lower Tweed. Shallow-draught craft can reach Murwillumbah, 23 km upstream, past canefields, dairy pastures and the Stotts Island nature reserve. River cruises from Tweed Heads stop off at a jetty on the island's western shores, allowing a short walk through rainforest and palm groves.

KINGSCLIFF east of Pacific Highway 895 km from Sydney, 116 km from Brisbane (turn off at Chinderah).
TRANSPORT: train Sydney-Byron Bay daily (15½ hrs); coach Byron Bay-Chinderah daily; coach Brisbane-Chinderah daily; bus Chinderah-Kingscliff daily.
SURF CLUB PATROL: October-Easter, Saturday 10.00-14.00, Sunday and public holidays 08.45-16.30.

🗑 🏠 📷 ▲ 🛢 🛐 🍴 🖥 🍴 🍽 ⛵ 🐚 ≋ 🐟 ⚓ 🎿

BOGANGAR (pop. 957) 8 km south of Kingscliff.
TRANSPORT: as for Kingscliff; bus Chinderah-Bogangar most days.
SURF CLUB PATROL: at Cabarita Beach October-Easter, weekends and public holidays 09.00-17.00.

🗑 🏠 📷 ▲ 🛢 🛐 🍴 🖥 🍴 ⛵ 🐚 ≋ 🐟 ⚓ 🎿

POTTSVILLE (pop. 673) 16 km south of Kingscliff.
TRANSPORT: as for Kingscliff; bus Chinderah-Pottsville most days.

🗑 📷 ▲ 🛢 🐚 ⚓ 🎿

The Tweed River (above) turns sharply inland between Banora Point and Chinderah, leaving a broad wedge of rich sugar-growing and crop-farming land towards Kingscliff and Cudgen Headland

Scrub-covered dunes and tiny creeks back the quiet beaches (below) that run each side of Hastings Point to the bigger townships of Bogangar and Pottsville

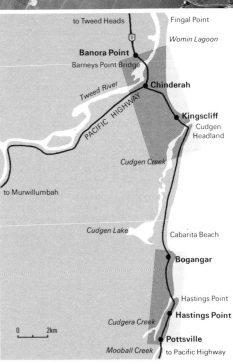

to Tweed Heads

Fingal Point

Womin Lagoon

Banora Point

Barneys Point Bridge

Tweed River

Chinderah

PACIFIC HIGHWAY

Kingscliff

Cudgen Headland

Cudgen Creek

to Murwillumbah

Cudgen Lake

Cabarita Beach

Bogangar

Hastings Point

Hastings Point

Cudgera Creek

Pottsville

to Pacific Highway

Mooball Creek

0   2km

Sydney to Tweed Heads 219

Subject index

Place index

All towns and geographical features mentioned in *Guide to the coast of New South Wales* are listed below. Page numbers in bold type indicate a major entry dealing with the place concerned

A B